**More praise from acros[s]
JobBank series:**

"One of the better publishers of employment almanacs is Adams Media Corporation ... publisher of *The Metropolitan New York JobBank* and similarly named directories of employers in Texas, Boston, Chicago, Northern and Southern California, and Washington DC. A good buy...."
-Wall Street Journal's
National Business Employment Weekly

"*JobBank* books are all devoted to specific job markets. This is helpful if you are thinking about working in cities like San Antonio, Washington, Boston, or states such as Tennessee or the Carolinas. You can use them for research, and a particularly useful feature is the inclusion of the type of positions that are commonly offered at the companies listed."
-Karen Ronald, Library Director
Wilton Library, Wilton, CT

"If you are looking for a job ... before you go to the newspapers and the help-wanted ads, listen to Bob Adams, publisher *of The Metropolitan New York JobBank.*"
-Tom Brokaw, NBC

"Since 1985 the Adams *JobBank Series* has proven to be the consummate tool for the efficient job search."
-Mel Rappleyea, Human Resources Director
Starbucks Coffee Company

"Having worked in the Career Services field for 10 years, I know the quality of Adams publications."
-Philip Meade, Director of Graduate Career Services
Baruch School of Business (New York NY)

"I read through the 'Basics of Job Winning' and 'Resumes' sections [in *The Dallas-Fort Worth JobBank*] and found them to be very informative, with some positive tips for the job searcher. I believe the strategies outlined will bring success to any determined candidate."
-Camilla Norder, Professional Recruiter
Presbyterian Hospital of Dallas

"The ultimate in a superior series of job hunt directories."
-Cornell University Career Center's
Where to Start

"Help on the job hunt … Anyone who is job-hunting in the New York area can find a lot of useful ideas in a new paperback called *The Metropolitan New York JobBank*…."

-Angela Taylor, *New York Times*

"A timely book for Chicago job hunters follows books from the same publisher that were well received in New York and Boston … [*The Chicago JobBank* is] a fine tool for job hunters…."

-**Clarence Peterson, *Chicago Tribune***

"Because our listing is seen by people across the nation, it generates lots for resumes for us. We encourage unsolicited resumes. We'll always be listed [in *The Chicago JobBank*] as long as I'm in this career."

-Tom Fitzpatrick, Director of Human Resources
Merchandise Mart Properties, Inc.

"Job hunting is never fun, but this book can ease the ordeal …*[The Los Angeles JobBank*] will help allay fears, build confidence, and avoid wheel-spinning."

-Robert W. Ross, *Los Angeles Times*

"*The Seattle JobBank* is an essential resource for job hunters."

-Gil Lopez, Staffing Team Manager
Battelle Pacific Northwest Laboratories

"*The Phoenix JobBank* is a first-class publication. The information provided is useful and current."

-Lyndon Denton
Director of Human Resources and Materials Management
Apache Nitrogen Products, Inc.

"*The Florida JobBank* is an invaluable job-search reference tool. It provides the most up-to-date information and contact names available for companies in Florida. I should know – it worked for me!"

-Rhonda Cody, Human Resources Consultant
Aetna Life and Casualty

"I read through the 'Basics of Job Winning' and 'Resumes' sections [in *The Dallas-Fort Worth JobBank*] and found them to be very informative, with some positive tips for the job searcher. I believe the strategies outlined will bring success to any determined candidate."

-Camilla Norder, Professional Recruiter
Presbyterian Hospital of Dallas

"Through *The Dallas-Fort Worth JobBank,* we've been able to attract high-quality candidates for several positions."

-Rob Bertino, Southern States Sales Manager
CompuServe

What makes the JobBank series the nation's premier line of employment guides?

With vital employment information on thousands of employers across the nation, the JobBank series is the most comprehensive and authoritative set of career directories available today.

Each book in the series provides information on **dozens of different industries** in a given city or area, with the primary employer listings providing contact information, telephone and fax numbers, e-mail addresses, Websites, a summary of the firm's business, internships, and in many cases descriptions of the firm's typical professional job categories.

All of the reference information in the JobBank series is as up-to-date and accurate as possible. Every year, the entire database is thoroughly researched and verified by mail and by telephone. Adams Media Corporation publishes **more local employment guides more often** than any other publisher of career directories.

The JobBank series offers **20 regional titles**, from Boston to San Francisco. All of the information is organized geographically, because most people look for jobs in specific areas of the country.

A condensed, but thorough, review of the entire job search process is presented in the chapter **The Basics of Job Winning**, a feature that has received many compliments from career counselors. In addition, each JobBank directory includes a section on **resumes and cover letters** the *New York Times* has acclaimed as "excellent."

The JobBank series gives job hunters the most comprehensive, timely, and accurate career information, organized and indexed to facilitate your job search. An entire career reference library, JobBank books are designed to help you find optimal employment in any market.

Top career publications from Adams Media Corporation

The JobBank Series:
each JobBank book is $17.95

The Atlanta JobBank, 15th Ed.
The Austin/San Antonio JobBank, 4th Ed.
The Boston JobBank, 19th Ed.
The Carolina JobBank, 7th Ed.
The Chicago JobBank, 18th Ed.
The Colorado JobBank, 13th Ed.
The Connecticut JobBank, 3rd Ed.
The Dallas-Fort Worth JobBank, 14th Ed.
The Florida JobBank, 15th Ed.
The Houston JobBank, 12th Ed.
The Los Angeles JobBank, 17th Ed.
The New Jersey JobBank, 3rd Ed.
The Metropolitan New York JobBank, 18th Ed.
The Ohio JobBank, 11th Ed.
The Greater Philadelphia JobBank, 14th Ed.
The Phoenix JobBank, 9th Ed.
The San Francisco Bay Area JobBank, 17th Ed.
The Seattle JobBank, 13th Ed.
The Virginia JobBank, 4th Ed.
The Metropolitan Washington DC JobBank, 16th Ed.

The National JobBank, 2005
    (Covers the entire U.S.: $475.00 hc)

Other Career Titles:
The Adams Cover Letter Almanac ($12.95)
The Adams Executive Recruiters Almanac, 2nd Ed. ($17.95)
The Adams Job Interview Almanac ($12.95)
The Adams Jobs Almanac, 8th Ed. ($16.95)
The Adams Resume Almanac ($12.95)

Business Etiquette in Brief ($7.95)
Career Tests ($12.95)
Closing Techniques, 3rd Ed. ($9.95)
Cold Calling Techniques, 5th Ed. ($9.95)
College Grad Job Hunter, 5th Ed. ($14.95)
The Complete Resume & Job Search Book for College Students, 2nd Ed. ($12.95)
Cover Letters That Knock 'em Dead, 6th Ed. ($12.95)
The Everything Alternative Careers Book ($14.95)
The Everything Cover Letter Book ($12.95)
The Everything Get-A-Job Book ($12.95)
The Everything Hot Careers Book ($12.95)
The Everything Job Interview Book ($14.95)
The Everything Leadership Book ($12.95)
The Everything Online Business Book ($12.95)
The Everything Online Job Search Book ($12.95)
The Everything Resume Book ($14.95)
The Everything Selling Book ($14.95)
Knock 'em Dead, 2005 ($14.95)
Knock 'em Dead Business Presentations ($12.95)
Market Yourself and Your Career, 2nd Ed. ($12.95)
The New Professional Image ($12.95)
The 150 Most Profitable Home Businesses for Women ($9.95)
The Resume Handbook, 4th Ed. ($9.95)
Resumes That Knock 'em Dead, 6th Ed. ($12.95)
The Road to CEO ($10.95)
The 250 Job Interview Questions You'll Most Likely Be Asked ($9.95)
Your Executive Image ($10.95)

4th Edition
THE Austin/ San Antonio
JobBank

adams
media

Published by Adams Media, an F+W Publications Company
57 Littlefield Street, Avon, MA 02322 U.S.A.
www.adamsmedia.com

ISBN: 1-59337-221-3
ISSN: 1098-9749
Manufactured in Canada

This book is available on standing order and at quantity discounts for bulk purchases. For information, call 800/872-5627 (in Massachusetts, 508/427-7100) or e-mail: jobbank@adamsmedia.com

TABLE OF CONTENTS

SECTION ONE: INTRODUCTION

How to Use This Book/12
An introduction to the most effective way to use The Austin/San Antonio JobBank.

SECTION TWO: THE JOB SEARCH

The Basics of Job Winning/16
A review of the elements of a successful job search campaign. Includes advice on developing effective strategies, time planning, and preparing for interviews. Special sections address situations faced by jobseekers who are currently employed, those who have lost a job, and graduates conducting their first job search.

Resumes and Cover Letters/30
Advice on creating strong resumes and cover letters with examples.

SECTION THREE: PRIMARY EMPLOYERS

The Employers/49
The Austin/San Antonio JobBank *is organized according to industry. Many listings include the address and phone number of each major firm listed, along with a description of the company's basic product lines and services, and, in many cases, a contact name and other relevant hiring information.*

Accounting and Management Consulting/51
Advertising, Marketing, and Public Relations/52
*   *Direct Mail Marketers, Market Researchers*
Aerospace/54
*   *Aerospace Products and Services*
*   *Aircraft Equipment and Parts*
Apparel, Fashion, and Textiles/56
*   *Broadwoven Fabric Mills, Knitting Mills, and Yarn and Thread Mills*
*   *Curtains and Draperies*
*   *Footwear*
*   *Nonwoven Fabrics*
*   *Textile Goods and Finishing*
Architecture, Construction, and Engineering/58
*   *Architectural and Engineering Services*
*   *Civil and Mechanical Engineering Firms*
*   *Construction Products, Manufacturers, and Wholesalers*
*   *General Contractors/Specialized Trade Contractor*
Arts, Entertainment, Sports, and Recreation/61
*   *Botanical and Zoological Gardens*
*   *Entertainment Groups*
*   *Motion Picture and Video Tape Production and Distribution*
*   *Museums and Art Galleries*
*   *Physical Fitness Facilities*
*   *Professional Sports Clubs; Sporting and Recreational Camps*
*   *Public Golf Courses and Racing and Track Operations*
*   *Theatrical Producers and Services*
Automotive/63
*   *Automotive Repair Shops*

- *Automotive Stampings*
- *Industrial Vehicles and Moving Equipment*
- *Motor Vehicles and Equipment*
- *Travel Trailers and Campers*

Banking, Savings and Loans, and Other Depository Institutions/64
- *Banks*
- *Bank Holding Companies and Associations*
- *Lending Firms/Financial Services Institutions*

Biotechnology, Pharmaceuticals, and Scientific R&D/68
- *Clinical Labs*
- *Lab Equipment Manufacturers*
- *Pharmaceutical Manufacturers and Distributors*

Business Services and Non-Scientific Research/70
- *Adjustment and Collection Services*
- *Cleaning, Maintenance, and Pest Control Services*
- *Credit Reporting Services*
- *Detective, Guard, and Armored Car Services/Security Systems Services*
- *Miscellaneous Equipment Rental and Leasing*
- *Secretarial and Court Reporting Services*

Charities and Social Services/73
- *Social and Human Service Agencies*
- *Job Training and Vocational Rehabilitation Services*
- *Nonprofit Organizations*

Chemicals, Rubber, and Plastics/75
- *Adhesives, Detergents, Inks, Paints, Soaps, Varnishes*
- *Agricultural Chemicals and Fertilizers*
- *Carbon and Graphite Products*
- *Chemical Engineering Firms*
- *Industrial Gases*

Communications: Telecommunications and Broadcasting/77
- *Cable/Pay Television Services*
- *Communications Equipment*
- *Radio and Television Broadcasting Stations*
- *Telephone, Telegraph, and Other Message Communications*

Computer Hardware, Software, and Services/79
- *Computer Components and Hardware Manufacturers*
- *Consultants and Computer Training Companies*
- *Internet and Online Service Providers*
- *Networking and Systems Services*
- *Repair Services/Rental and Leasing*
- *Resellers, Wholesalers, and Distributors*
- *Software Developers/Programming Services*

Educational Services/85
- *Business/Secretarial/Data Processing Schools*
- *Colleges/Universities/Professional Schools*
- *Community Colleges/Technical Schools/Vocational Schools*
- *Elementary and Secondary Schools*
- *Preschool and Child Daycare Services*

Electronic/Industrial Electrical Equipment and Components/92
- *Electronic Machines and Systems*
- *Semiconductor Manufacturers*

Environmental and Waste Management Services/96
- *Environmental Engineering Firms*
- *Sanitary Services*

Fabricated Metal Products and Primary Metals/98
- *Aluminum and Copper Foundries*

- *Die-Castings*
- *Iron and Steel Foundries/Steel Works, Blast Furnaces, and Rolling Mills*

Financial Services/100

- *Consumer Financing and Credit Agencies*
- *Investment Specialists*
- *Mortgage Bankers and Loan Brokers*
- *Security and Commodity Brokers, Dealers, and Exchanges*

Food and Beverages/Agriculture/102

- *Crop Services and Farm Supplies*
- *Dairy Farms*
- *Food Manufacturers/Processors and Agricultural Producers*
- *Tobacco Products*

Government/106

- *Courts*
- *Executive, Legislative, and General Government*
- *Public Agencies (Firefighters, Military, Police)*
- *United States Postal Service*

Health Care Services, Equipment, and Products/110

- *Dental Labs and Equipment*
- *Home Health Care Agencies*
- *Hospitals and Medical Centers*
- *Medical Equipment Manufacturers and Wholesalers*
- *Offices and Clinics of Health Practitioners*
- *Residential Treatment Centers/Nursing Homes*
- *Veterinary Services*

Hotels and Restaurants/125
Insurance/128
Legal Services/130
Manufacturing: Miscellaneous Consumer/131

- *Art Supplies*
- *Batteries*
- *Cosmetics and Related Products*
- *Household Appliances and Audio/Video Equipment*
- *Jewelry, Silverware, and Plated Ware*
- *Miscellaneous Household Furniture and Fixtures*
- *Musical Instruments*
- *Tools*
- *Toys and Sporting Goods*

Manufacturing: Miscellaneous Industrial/132

- *Ball and Roller Bearings*
- *Commercial Furniture and Fixtures*
- *Fans, Blowers, and Purification Equipment*
- *Industrial Machinery and Equipment*
- *Motors and Generators/Compressors and Engine Parts*
- *Vending Machines*

Mining, Gas, Petroleum, Energy Related/135

- *Anthracite, Coal, and Ore Mining*
- *Mining Machinery and Equipment*
- *Oil and Gas Field Services*
- *Petroleum and Natural Gas*

Paper and Wood Products/139

- *Forest and Wood Products and Services*
- *Lumber and Wood Wholesale*
- *Millwork, Plywood, and Structural Members*
- *Paper and Wood Mills*

Printing and Publishing/140

- *Book, Newspaper, and Periodical Publishers*
- *Commercial Photographers*
- *Commercial Printing Services*
- *Graphic Designers*

Real Estate/143
- *Land Subdividers and Developers*
- *Real Estate Agents, Managers, and Operators*
- *Real Estate Investment Trusts*

Retail/145

Stone, Clay, Glass, and Concrete Products/148
- *Cement, Tile, Sand, and Gravel*
- *Crushed and Broken Stone*
- *Glass and Glass Products*
- *Mineral Products*

Transportation and Travel/150
- *Air, Railroad, and Water Transportation Services*
- *Courier Services*
- *Local and Interurban Passenger Transit*
- *Ship Building and Repair*
- *Transportation Equipment*
- *Travel Agencies*
- *Trucking*
- *Warehousing and Storage*

Utilities: Electric, Gas, and Water/152

Miscellaneous Wholesaling/154
- *Exporters and Importers*

SECTION FOUR: INDUSTRY ASSOCIATIONS

Associations by Industry/155

SECTION FIVE: INDEX

Index of Primary Employers/217

INTRODUCTION

HOW TO USE THIS BOOK

Right now, you hold in your hands one of the most effective job-hunting tools available anywhere. In *The Austin/San Antonio JobBank*, you will find valuable information to help you launch or continue a rewarding career. But before you open to the book's employer listings and start calling about current job openings, take a few minutes to learn how best to use the resources presented in *The Austin/San Antonio JobBank*.

The Austin/San Antonio JobBank will help you to stand out from other jobseekers. While many people looking for a new job rely solely on newspaper help-wanted ads, this book offers you a much more effective job-search method -- direct contact. The direct contact method has been proven twice as effective as scanning the help-wanted ads. Instead of waiting for employers to come looking for you, you'll be far more effective going to them. While many of your competitors will use trial and error methods in trying to set up interviews, you'll learn not only how to get interviews, but what to expect once you've got them.

In the next few pages, we'll take you through each section of the book so you'll be prepared to get a jump-start on your competition.

Basics of Job Winning

Preparation. Strategy. Time management. These are three of the most important elements of a successful job search. *Basics of Job Winning* helps you address these and all the other elements needed to find the right job.

One of your first priorities should be to define your personal career objectives. What qualities make a job desirable to you? Creativity? High pay? Prestige? Use *Basics of Job Winning* to weigh these questions. Then use the rest of the chapter to design a strategy to find a job that matches your criteria.

In *Basics of Job Winning,* you'll learn which job-hunting techniques work, and which don't. We've reviewed the pros and cons of mass mailings, help-wanted ads, and direct contact. We'll show you how to develop and approach contacts in your field; how to research a prospective employer; and how to use that information to get an interview and the job.

Also included in *Basics of Job Winning*: interview dress code and etiquette, the "do's and don'ts" of interviewing, sample interview questions, and more. We also deal with some of the unique problems faced by those jobseekers who are currently employed, those who have lost a job, and college students conducting their first job search.

Resumes and Cover Letters

The approach you take to writing your resume and cover letter can often mean the difference between getting an interview and never being noticed. In this section, we discuss different formats, as well as what to put on (and what to leave off) your resume. We review the benefits and drawbacks of professional resume writers, and the importance of a follow-up letter. Also included in this section are sample resumes and cover letters which you can use as models.

The Employer Listings

Employers are listed alphabetically by industry. When a company does business under a person's name, like "John Smith & Co.," the company is usually listed by the surname's spelling (in this case "S"). Exceptions occur when a company's name is widely recognized, like "JCPenney" or "Howard Johnson Motor Lodge." In those cases, the company's first name is the key ("J" and "H" respectively).

The Austin/San Antonio JobBank covers a very wide range of industries. Each company profile is assigned to one of the industry chapters listed below.

Accounting and Management Consulting
Advertising, Marketing, and Public
  Relations
Aerospace
Apparel, Fashion, and Textiles
Architecture, Construction, and Engineering
Arts, Entertainment, Sports, and Recreation
Automotive
Banking/Savings and Loans
Biotechnology, Pharmaceuticals, and
  Scientific R&D
Business Services and Non-Scientific
  Research
Charities and Social Services
Chemicals/Rubber and Plastics
Communications: Telecommunications and
  Broadcasting
Computer Hardware, Software, and
  Services
Educational Services
Electronic/Industrial Electrical Equipment
  and Components

Environmental and Waste Management
  Services
Fabricated/Primary Metals and Products
Financial Services
Food and Beverages/Agriculture
Government
Health Care: Services, Equipment, and
  Products
Hotels and Restaurants
Insurance
Legal Services
Manufacturing: Miscellaneous Consumer
Manufacturing: Miscellaneous Industrial
Mining/Gas/Petroleum/Energy Related
Paper and Wood Products
Printing and Publishing
Real Estate
Retail
Stone, Clay, Glass, and Concrete Products
Transportation/Travel
Utilities: Electric/Gas/Water
Miscellaneous Wholesaling

Many of the company listings offer detailed company profiles. In addition to company names, addresses, and phone numbers, these listings also include contact names or hiring departments, and descriptions of each company's products and/or services. Many of these listings also feature a variety of additional information including:

Positions advertised - A list of open positions the company was advertising at the time our research was conducted. Note: Keep in mind that *The Austin/San Antonio JobBank* is a directory of major employers in the area, not a directory of openings currently available. Positions listed in this book that were advertised at the time research was conducted may no longer be open. Many of the companies listed will be hiring, others will not. However, since most professional job openings are filled without the placement of help-wanted ads, contacting the employers in this book directly is still a more effective method than browsing the Sunday papers.

Special programs - Does the company offer training programs, internships, or apprenticeships? These programs can be important to first time jobseekers and college students looking for practical work experience. Many employer profiles will include information on these programs.

Parent company - If an employer is a subsidiary of a larger company, the name of that parent company will often be listed here. Use this information to supplement your company research before contacting the employer.

Number of employees - The number of workers a company employs.

Company listings may also include information on other U.S. locations and any stock exchanges the firm may be listed on.

A note on all employer listings that appear in *The Austin/San Antonio JobBank*: This book is intended as a starting point. It is not intended to replace any effort that you, the jobseeker, should devote to your job hunt. Keep in mind that while a great deal of effort has been put into collecting and verifying the company profiles provided in this book, addresses and contact names change regularly. Inevitably, some contact names listed herein have changed even before you read this. We recommend you contact a company before mailing your resume to ensure nothing has changed.

Industry Associations

This section includes a select list of professional and trade associations organized by industry. Many of these associations can provide employment advice and job-search help, offer magazines that cover the industry, and provide additional information or directories that may supplement the employer listings in this book.

Index of Primary Employers

The Austin/San Antonio JobBank index is listed alphabetically by company name.

THE JOB SEARCH

THE BASICS OF JOB WINNING: A CONDENSED REVIEW

This chapter is divided into four sections. The first section explains the fundamentals that every jobseeker should know, especially first-time jobseekers. The next three sections deal with special situations faced by specific types of jobseekers: those who are currently employed, those who have lost a job, and college students.

THE BASICS:
Things Everyone Needs to Know

Career Planning

The first step to finding your ideal job is to clearly define your objectives. This is better known as career planning (or life planning if you wish to emphasize the importance of combining the two). Career planning has become a field of study in and of itself.

If you are thinking of choosing or switching careers, we particularly emphasize two things. First, choose a career where you will enjoy most of the day-to-day tasks. This sounds obvious, but most of us have at some point found the idea of a glamour industry or prestigious job title attractive without thinking of the key consideration: Would we enjoy performing the *everyday* tasks the position entails?

The second key consideration is that you are not merely choosing a career, but also a lifestyle. Career counselors indicate that one of the most common problems people encounter in jobseeking is that they fail to consider how well-suited they are for a particular position or career. For example, some people, attracted to management consulting by good salaries, early responsibility, and high-level corporate exposure, do not adapt well to the long hours, heavy travel demands, and constant pressure to produce. Be sure to ask yourself how you might adapt to the day-to-day duties and working environment that a specific position entails. Then ask yourself how you might adapt to the demands of that career or industry as a whole.

Choosing Your Strategy

Assuming that you've established your career objectives, the next step of the job search is to develop a strategy. If you don't take the time to develop a plan, you may find yourself going in circles after several weeks of randomly searching for opportunities that always seem just beyond your reach.

The most common jobseeking techniques are:

* following up on help-wanted advertisements (in the newspaper or online)
* using employment services
* relying on personal contacts
* contacting employers directly (the Direct Contact method)

Each of these approaches can lead to better jobs. However, the Direct Contact method boasts twice the success rate of the others. So unless you have specific reasons to employ other strategies, Direct Contact should form the foundation of your job search.

If you choose to use other methods as well, try to expend at least half your energy on Direct Contact. Millions of other jobseekers have already proven that Direct Contact has been twice as effective in obtaining employment, so why not follow in their footsteps?

Setting Your Schedule

Okay, so now that you've targeted a strategy it's time to work out the details of your job search. The most important detail is setting up a schedule. Of course, since job searches aren't something most people do regularly, it may be hard to estimate how long each step will take. Nonetheless, it is important to have a plan so that you can monitor your progress.

When outlining your job search schedule, have a realistic time frame in mind. If you will be job-searching full-time, your search could take at least two months or more. If you can only devote part-time effort, it will probably take at least four months.

You probably know a few people who seem to spend their whole lives searching for a better job in their spare time. Don't be one of them. If you are presently working and don't feel like devoting a lot of energy to jobseeking right now, then wait. Focus on enjoying your present position, performing your best on the job, and storing up energy for when you are really ready to begin your job search.

> **The first step in beginning your job search is to clearly define your objectives.**

Those of you who are currently unemployed should remember that *job-hunting is tough work, both physically and emotionally*. It is also intellectually demanding work that requires you to be at your best. So don't tire yourself out by working on your job campaign around the clock. At the same time, be sure to discipline yourself. The most logical way to manage your time while looking for a job is to keep your regular working hours.

If you are searching full-time and have decided to choose several different strategies, we recommend that you divide up each week, designating some time for each method. By trying several approaches at once, you can evaluate how promising each seems and alter your schedule accordingly. Keep in mind that the *majority of openings are filled without being advertised*. Remember also that positions advertised on the Internet are just as likely to already be filled as those found in the newspaper!

If you are searching part-time and decide to try several different contact methods, we recommend that you try them sequentially. You simply won't have enough time to put a meaningful amount of effort into more than one method at once. Estimate the length of your job search, and then allocate so many weeks or months for each contact method, beginning with Direct Contact. The purpose of setting this schedule is not to rush you to your goal but to help you periodically evaluate your progress.

The Direct Contact Method

Once you have scheduled your time, you are ready to begin your search in earnest. Beginning with the Direct Contact method, the first step is to develop a checklist for categorizing the types of firms for which you'd like to work. You might categorize firms by product line, size, customer type (such as industrial or consumer), growth prospects, or geographical location. Keep in mind, the shorter the list the easier it will be to locate a company that is right for you.

Next you will want to use this *JobBank* book to assemble your list of potential employers. Choose firms where *you* are most likely to be able to find a job. Try matching your skills with those that a specific job demands. Consider where your skills might be in demand, the degree of competition for employment, and the employment outlook at each company.

Separate your prospect list into three groups. The first 25 percent will be your primary target group, the next 25 percent will be your secondary group, and the remaining names will be your reserve group.

After you form your prospect list, begin working on your resume. Refer to the Resumes and Cover Letters section following this chapter for more information.

Once your resume is complete, begin researching your first batch of prospective employers. You will want to determine whether you would be happy working at the firms you are researching and to get a better idea of what their employment needs might be. You also need to obtain enough information to sound highly informed about the company during phone conversations and in mail correspondence. But don't go all out on your research yet! You probably won't be able to arrange interviews with some of these firms, so save your big research effort until you start to arrange interviews. Nevertheless, you should plan to spend several hours researching each firm. Do your research in batches to save time and energy. Start with this book, and find out what you can about each of the firms in your primary target group. For answers to specific questions, contact any pertinent professional associations that may be able to help you learn more about an employer. Read industry publications looking for articles on the firm. (Addresses of associations and names of important publications are listed after each section of employer listings in this book.) Then look up the company on the Internet or try additional resources at your local library. Keep organized, and maintain a folder on each firm.

> **The more you know about a company, the more likely you are to catch an interviewer's eye. (You'll also face fewer surprises once you get the job!)**

Information to look for includes: company size; president, CEO, or owner's name; when the company was established; what each division does; and benefits that are important to you. An abundance of company information can now be found electronically, through the World Wide Web or commercial online services. Researching companies online is a convenient means of obtaining information quickly and easily. If you have access to the Internet, you can search from your home at any time of day.

You may search a particular company's Website for current information that may be otherwise unavailable in print. In fact, many companies that maintain a site update their information daily. In addition, you may also search articles written about the company online. Today, most of the nation's largest newspapers, magazines, trade publications, and regional business periodicals have online versions of their publications. To find additional resources, use a search engine like Yahoo! or Alta Vista and type in the keyword "companies" or "employers."

If you discover something that really disturbs you about the firm (they are about to close their only local office), or if you discover that your chances of getting a job there are practically nil (they have just instituted a hiring freeze), then cross them off your prospect list. If possible, supplement your research efforts by contacting individuals who know the firm well. Ideally you should make an informal contact with someone at that particular firm, but often a direct competitor or a major customer will be able to supply you with just as much information. At the very least, try to obtain whatever printed information the company has available -- not just annual reports, but product brochures, company profiles, or catalogs. This information is often available on the Internet.

Getting the Interview

Now it is time to make Direct Contact with the goal of arranging interviews. If you have read any books on job-searching, you may have noticed that most of these books tell you to avoid the human resources office like the plague. It is said that the human resources office never hires people; they screen candidates. Unfortunately, this is often the case. If you can identify the appropriate manager with the authority to hire you, you should try to contact that person directly.

The obvious means of initiating Direct Contact are:

- Mail (postal or electronic)
- Phone calls

Mail contact is a good choice if you have not been in the job market for a while. You can take your time to prepare a letter, say exactly what you want, and of course include your resume. Remember that employers receive many resumes every day. Don't be surprised if you do not get a response to your inquiry, *and don't spend weeks waiting for responses that may never come.* If you do send a letter, follow it up (or precede it) with a phone call. This will increase your impact, and because of the initial research you did, will underscore both your familiarity with and your interest in the firm. Bear in mind that your goal is to make your name a familiar one with prospective employers, so that when a position becomes available, your resume will be one of the first the hiring manager seeks out.

DEVELOPING YOUR CONTACTS: NETWORKING

Some career counselors feel that the best route to a better job is through somebody you already know or through somebody to whom you can be introduced. These counselors recommend that you build your contact base beyond your current acquaintances by asking each one to introduce you, or refer you, to additional people in your field of interest.

The theory goes like this: You might start with 15 personal contacts, each of whom introduces you to three additional people, for a total of 45 additional contacts. Then each of these people introduces you to three additional people, which adds 135 additional contacts. Theoretically, you will soon know every person in the industry.

Of course, developing your personal contacts does not work quite as smoothly as the theory suggests because some people will not be able to introduce you to anyone. The further you stray from your initial contact base, the weaker your references may be. So, if you do try developing your own contacts, try to begin with as many people that you know personally as you can. Dig into your personal phone book and your holiday greeting card list and locate old classmates from school. Be particularly sure to approach people who perform your personal business such as your lawyer, accountant, banker, doctor, stockbroker, and insurance agent. These people develop a very broad contact base due to the nature of their professions.

If you send a fax, always follow with a hard copy of your resume and cover letter in the mail. Often, through no fault of your own, a fax will come through illegibly and employers do not often have time to let candidates know.

Another alternative is to make a "cover call." Your cover call should be just like your cover letter: concise. Your first statement should interest the employer in you. Then try to subtly mention your familiarity with the firm. Don't be overbearing; keep your introduction to three sentences or less. Be pleasant, self-confident, and relaxed. This will greatly increase the chances of the person at the other end of the line developing the conversation. But don't press. If you are asked to follow up with "something in the mail," this signals the conversation's natural end. Don't try to prolong the conversation once it has ended, and don't ask what they want to receive in the mail. Always send your resume and a highly personalized follow-up letter, reminding the addressee of the phone conversation. *Always* include a cover letter if you are asked to send a resume, and treat your resume and cover letter as a total package. Gear your letter toward the specific position you are applying for and prove why you would be a "good match" for the position.

> **Always include a cover letter if you are asked to send a resume.**

Unless you are in telephone sales, making smooth and relaxed cover calls will probably not come easily. Practice them on your own, and then with your friends or relatives.

DON'T BOTHER WITH MASS MAILINGS OR BARRAGES OF PHONE CALLS

Direct Contact does not mean burying every firm within a hundred miles with mail and phone calls. Mass mailings rarely work in the job hunt. This also applies to those letters that are personalized -- but dehumanized -- on an automatic typewriter or computer. Don't waste your time or money on such a project; you will fool no one but yourself.

The worst part of sending out mass mailings, or making unplanned phone calls to companies you have not researched, is that you are likely to be remembered as someone with little genuine interest in the firm, who lacks sincerity -- somebody that nobody wants to hire.

If you obtain an interview as a result of a telephone conversation, be sure to send a thank-you note reiterating the points you made during the conversation. You will appear more professional and increase your impact. However, unless specifically requested, don't mail your resume once an interview has been arranged. Take it with you to the interview instead.

You should never show up to seek a professional position without an appointment. Even if you are somehow lucky enough to obtain an interview, you will appear so unprofessional that you will not be seriously considered.

HELP WANTED ADVERTISEMENTS

Only a small fraction of professional job openings are advertised. Yet the majority of jobseekers -- and quite a few people not in the job market -- spend a lot of time studying the help wanted ads. As a result, the competition for advertised openings is often very severe.

A moderate-sized employer told us about their experience advertising in the help wanted section of a major Sunday newspaper:

It was a disaster. We had over 500 responses from this relatively small ad in just one week. We have only two phone lines in this office and one was totally knocked out. We'll never advertise for professional help again.

If you insist on following up on help wanted ads, then research a firm before you reply to an ad. Preliminary research might help to separate you from all of the other professionals responding to that ad, many of whom will have only a passing interest in the opportunity. It will also give you insight about a particular firm, to help you determine if it is potentially a good match. That said, your chances of obtaining a job through the want ads are still much smaller than they are with the Direct Contact method.

Preparing for the Interview

As each interview is arranged, begin your in-depth research. You should arrive at an interview knowing the company upside-down and inside-out. You need to know the company's products, types of customers, subsidiaries, parent company, principal locations, rank in the industry, sales and profit trends, type of ownership, size, current plans, and much more. By this time you have probably narrowed your job search to one industry. Even if you haven't, you should still be familiar with common industry terms, the trends in the firm's industry, the firm's principal competitors and their relative performance, and the direction in which the industry leaders are headed.

Dig into every resource you can! Surf the Internet. Read the company literature, the trade press, the business press, and if the company is public, call your stockbroker (if you have one) and ask for additional information. If possible, speak to someone at the firm before the

> **You should arrive at an interview knowing the company upside-down and inside-out.**

interview, or if not, speak to someone at a competing firm. The more time you spend, the better. Even if you feel extremely pressed for time, you should set aside several hours for pre-interview research.

If you have been out of the job market for some time, don't be surprised if you find yourself tense during your first few interviews. It will probably happen every time you re-enter the market, not just when you seek your first job after getting out of school.

Tension is natural during an interview, but knowing you have done a thorough research job should put you more at ease. Make a list of questions that you think might be asked in each interview. Think out your answers carefully and practice them with a friend. Tape record your responses to the problem questions. (*See also in this chapter: Informational Interviews.*) If you feel particularly unsure of your interviewing skills, arrange your first interviews at firms you are not as interested in. (But remember it is common courtesy to seem enthusiastic about the possibility of working for any firm at which you interview.) Practice again on your own after these first few interviews. Go over the difficult questions that you were asked.

Take some time to really think about how you will convey your work history. Present "bad experiences" as "learning experiences." Instead of saying "I hated my position as a salesperson because I had to bother people on the phone," say "I realized that cold-calling was not my strong suit. Though I love working with people, I decided my talents would be best used in a more face-to-face atmosphere." Always find some sort of lesson from previous jobs, as they all have one.

Interview Attire

How important is the proper dress for a job interview? Buying a complete wardrobe, donning new shoes, and having your hair styled every morning are not enough to guarantee you a career position as an investment banker. But on the other hand, if you can't find a clean, conservative suit or won't take the time to wash your hair, then you are just wasting your time by interviewing at all.

Personal grooming is as important as finding appropriate clothes for a job interview. Careful grooming indicates both a sense of thoroughness and self-confidence. This is not the time to make a statement -- take out the extra earrings and avoid any garish hair colors not found in nature. Women should not wear excessive makeup, and both men and women should refrain from wearing any perfume or cologne (it only takes a small spritz to leave an allergic interviewer with a fit of sneezing and a bad impression of your meeting). Men should be freshly shaven, even if the interview is late in the day, and men with long hair should have it pulled back and neat.

Men applying for any professional position should wear a suit, preferably in a conservative color such as navy or charcoal gray. It is easy to get away with wearing the same dark suit to consecutive interviews at the same company; just be sure to wear a different shirt and tie for each interview.

Women should also wear a business suit. Professionalism still dictates a suit with a skirt, rather than slacks, as proper interview garb for women. This is usually true even at companies where pants are acceptable attire for female employees. As much as you may disagree with this guideline, the more prudent time to fight this standard is after you land the job.

The final selection of candidates for a job opening won't be determined by dress, of course. However, inappropriate dress can quickly eliminate a first-round candidate. So while you shouldn't spend a fortune on a new wardrobe, you should be sure that your clothes are appropriate. The key is to dress at least as or slightly more formally and conservatively than the position would suggest.

What to Bring

Be complete. Everyone needs a watch, a pen, and a notepad. Finally, a briefcase or a leather-bound folder (containing extra, *unfolded*, copies of your resume) will help complete the look of professionalism.

Sometimes the interviewer will be running behind schedule. Don't be upset, be sympathetic. There is often pressure to interview a lot of candidates and to quickly fill a demanding position. So be sure to come to your interview with good reading material to keep yourself occupied and relaxed.

The Interview

The very beginning of the interview is the most important part because it determines the tone for the rest of it. Those first few moments are especially crucial. Do you smile when you meet? Do you establish enough eye contact, but not too much? Do you walk into the office with a self-assured and confident stride? Do you shake hands firmly? Do you make small talk easily without being garrulous? It is human nature to judge people by that first impression, so make sure it is a good one. But most of all, try to be yourself.

BE PREPARED:
Some Common Interview Questions

Tell me about yourself.

Why did you leave your last job?

What excites you in your current job?

Where would you like to be in five years?

How much overtime are you willing to work?

What would your previous/present employer tell me about you?

Tell me about a difficult situation that you
faced at your previous/present job.

What are your greatest strengths?

What are your weaknesses?

Describe a work situation where you took initiative
and went beyond your normal responsibilities.

Why should we hire you?

Often the interviewer will begin, after the small talk, by telling you about the company, the division, the department, or perhaps, the position. Because of your detailed research, the information about the company should be repetitive for you, and the interviewer would probably like nothing better than to avoid this regurgitation of the company biography. So if you can do so tactfully, indicate to the interviewer that you are very familiar with the firm. If he or she seems intent on providing you with background information, despite your hints, then acquiesce.

But be sure to remain attentive. If you can manage to generate a brief discussion of the company or the industry at this point, without being forceful, great. It will help to further build rapport, underscore your interest, and increase your impact.

> # The interviewer's job is to find a reason to turn you down; your job is to not provide that reason.
>
> -John L. LaFevre, author,
> *How You Really Get Hired*
>
> Reprinted from the 1989/90 *CPC Annual*, with permission of the National Association of Colleges and Employers (formerly College Placement Council, Inc.), copyright holder.

Soon (if it didn't begin that way) the interviewer will begin the questions, many of which you will have already practiced. This period of the interview usually falls into one of two categories (or somewhere in between): either a structured interview, where the interviewer has a prescribed set of questions to ask; or an unstructured interview, where the interviewer will ask only leading questions to get you to talk about yourself, your experiences, and your goals. Try to sense as quickly as possible in which direction the interviewer wishes to proceed. This will make the interviewer feel more relaxed and in control of the situation.

Remember to keep attuned to the interviewer and make the length of your answers appropriate to the situation. If you are really unsure as to how detailed a response the interviewer is seeking, then ask.

As the interview progresses, the interviewer will probably mention some of the most important responsibilities of the position. If applicable, draw parallels between your experience and the demands of the position as detailed by the interviewer. Describe your past experience in the same manner that you do on your resume: emphasizing results and achievements and not merely describing activities. But don't exaggerate. Be on the level about your abilities.

The first interview is often the toughest, where many candidates are screened out. If you are interviewing for a very competitive position, you will have to make an impression that will last. Focus on a few of your greatest strengths that are relevant to the position. Develop these points carefully, state them again in different words, and then try to summarize them briefly at the end of the interview.

Often the interviewer will pause toward the end and ask if you have any questions. Particularly in a structured interview, this might be the one chance to really show your knowledge of and interest in the firm. Have a list prepared of specific questions that are of real interest to you. Let your questions subtly show your research and your knowledge of the firm's activities. It is wise to have an extensive list of questions, as several of them may be answered during the interview.

Do not turn your opportunity to ask questions into an interrogation. Avoid reading directly from your list of questions, and ask questions that you are fairly certain the interviewer can answer (remember how you feel when you cannot answer a question during an interview).

Even if you are unable to determine the salary range beforehand, do not ask about it during the first interview. You can always ask later. Above all, don't ask about fringe benefits until you have been offered a position. (Then be sure to get all the details.)

Try not to be negative about anything during the interview, particularly any past employer or any previous job. Be cheerful. Everyone likes to work with someone who seems to be happy. Even if you detest your current/former job or manager, do not make disparaging comments. The interviewer may construe this as a sign of a potential attitude problem and not consider you a strong candidate.

Don't let a tough question throw you off base. If you don't know the answer to a question, simply say so -- do not apologize. Just smile. Nobody can answer every question -- particularly some of the questions that are asked in job interviews.

Before your first interview, you may be able to determine how many rounds of interviews there usually are for positions at your level. (Of course it may differ quite a bit even within the different levels of one firm.) Usually you can count on attending at least two or three interviews, although some firms are known to give a minimum of six interviews for all professional positions. While you should be more relaxed as you return for subsequent interviews, the pressure will be on. The more prepared you are, the better.

Depending on what information you are able to obtain, you might want to vary your strategy quite a bit from interview to interview. For instance, if the first interview is a screening interview, then be sure a few of your strengths really stand out. On the other hand, if later interviews are primarily with people who are in a position to veto your hiring, but not to push it forward, then you should primarily focus on building rapport as opposed to reiterating and developing your key strengths.

If it looks as though your skills and background do not match the position the interviewer was hoping to fill, ask him or her if there is another division or subsidiary that perhaps could profit from your talents.

After the Interview

Write a follow-up letter immediately after the interview, while it is still fresh in the interviewer's mind (see the sample follow-up letter format found in the Resumes and Cover Letters chapter). Not only is this a thank-you, but it also gives you the chance to provide the interviewer with any details you may have forgotten (as long as they can be tactfully added in). If you haven't heard back from the interviewer within a week of sending your thank-you letter, call to stress your continued interest in the firm and the position. If you lost any points during the interview for any reason, this letter can help you regain footing. Be polite and make sure to stress your continued interest and competency to fill the position. Just don't forget to proofread it thoroughly. If you are unsure of the spelling of the interviewer's name, call the receptionist and ask.

THE BALANCING ACT:
Looking for a New Job While Currently Employed

For those of you who are still employed, job-searching will be particularly tiring because it must be done in addition to your normal work responsibilities. So don't overwork yourself to the point where you show up to interviews looking exhausted or start to slip behind at your current job. On the other hand, don't be tempted to quit your present job! The long hours are worth it. Searching for a job while you have one puts you in a position of strength.

Making Contact

If you must be at your office during the business day, then you have additional problems to deal with. How can you work interviews into the business day? And if you work in an open office, how can you even call to set up interviews? Obviously, you should keep up the effort and the appearances on your present job. So maximize your use of the lunch hour, early mornings, and late afternoons for calling. If you keep trying, you'll be surprised how often you will be able to reach the executive you are trying to contact during your out-of-office hours. You can catch people as early as 8 a.m. and as late as 6 p.m. on frequent occasions.

Scheduling Interviews

Your inability to interview at any time other than lunch just might work to your advantage. If you can, try to set up as many interviews as possible for your lunch hour. This will go a long way to creating a relaxed atmosphere. But be sure the interviews don't stray too far from the agenda on hand.

Lunchtime interviews are much easier to obtain if you have substantial career experience. People with less experience will often find no alternative to taking time off for interviews. If you have to take time off, you have to take time off. But try to do this as little as possible. Try to take the whole day off in order to avoid being blatantly obvious about your job search, and try to schedule two to three interviews for the same day. (It is very difficult to maintain an optimum level of energy at more than three interviews in one day.) Explain to the interviewer why you might have to juggle your interview schedule; he/she should honor the respect you're showing your current employer by minimizing your days off and will probably appreciate the fact that another prospective employer is interested in you.

> **Try calling as early as 8 a.m. and as late as 6 p.m. You'll be surprised how often you will be able to reach the executive you want during these times of the day.**

References

What do you tell an interviewer who asks for references from your current employer? Just say that while you are happy to have your former employers contacted, you are trying to keep your job search confidential and would rather that your current employer not be contacted until you have been given a firm offer.

IF YOU'RE FIRED OR LAID OFF:
Picking Yourself Up and Dusting Yourself Off

If you've been fired or laid off, you are not the first and will not be the last to go through this traumatic experience. In today's changing economy, thousands of professionals lose their jobs every year. Even if you were terminated with just cause, do not lose heart. Remember, being fired is not a reflection on you as a person. It is usually a reflection of your company's staffing needs and its perception of your recent job performance and attitude. And if you were not performing up to par or enjoying your work, then you will probably be better off at another company anyway.

> **Be prepared for the question "Why were you fired?" during job interviews.**

A thorough job search could take months, so be sure to negotiate a reasonable severance package, if possible, and determine to what benefits, such as health insurance, you are still legally entitled. Also, register for unemployment compensation immediately. Don't be surprised to find other professionals collecting unemployment compensation -- it is for everyone who has lost their job.

Don't start your job search with a flurry of unplanned activity. Start by choosing a strategy and working out a plan. Now is not the time for major changes in your life. If possible, remain in the same career and in the same geographical location, at least until you have been working again for a while. On the other hand, if the only industry for which you are trained is leaving, or is severely depressed in your area, then you should give prompt consideration to moving or switching careers.

Avoid mentioning you were fired when arranging interviews, but be prepared for the question "Why were you fired?" during an interview. If you were laid off as a result of downsizing, briefly explain, being sure to reinforce that your job loss was not due to performance. If you were in fact fired, be honest, but try to detail the reason as favorably as possible and portray what you have learned from your mistakes. If you are confident one of your past managers will give you a good reference, tell the interviewer to contact that person. Do not to speak negatively of your past employer and try not to sound particularly worried about your status of being temporarily unemployed.

Finally, don't spend too much time reflecting on why you were let go or how you might have avoided it. Think positively, look to the future, and be sure to follow a careful plan during your job search.

THE COLLEGE STUDENT:
Conducting Your First Job Search

While you will be able to apply many of the basics covered earlier in this chapter to your job search, there are some situations unique to the college student's job search.

THE GPA QUESTION

You are interviewing for the job of your dreams. Everything is going well: You've established a good rapport, the interviewer seems impressed with your qualifications, and you're almost positive the job is yours. Then you're asked about your GPA, which is pitifully low. Do you tell the truth and watch your dream job fly out the window?

Never lie about your GPA (they may request your transcript, and no company will hire a liar). You can, however, explain if there is a reason you don't feel your grades reflect your abilities, and mention any other impressive statistics. For example, if you have a high GPA in your major, or in the last few semesters (as opposed to your cumulative college career), you can use that fact to your advantage.

Perhaps the biggest problem college students face is lack of experience. Many schools have internship programs designed to give students exposure to the field of their choice, as well as the opportunity to make valuable contacts. Check out your school's career services department to see what internships are available. If your school does not have a formal internship program, or if there are no available internships that appeal to you, try contacting local businesses and offering your services. Often, businesses will be more than willing to have an extra pair of hands (especially if those hands are unpaid!) for a day or two each week. Or try contacting school alumni to see if you can "shadow" them for a few days, and see what their daily duties are like.

Informational Interviews

Although many jobseekers do not do this, it can be extremely helpful to arrange an informational interview with a college alumnus or someone else who works in your desired industry. You interview them about their job, their company, and their industry with questions you have prepared in advance. This can be done over the phone but is usually done in person. This will provide you with a contact in the industry who may give you more valuable information -- or perhaps even a job opportunity -- in the future. Always follow up with a thank you letter that includes your contact information.

The goal is to try to begin building experience and establishing contacts as early as possible in your college career.

What do you do if, for whatever reason, you weren't able to get experience directly related to your desired career? First, look at your previous jobs and see if there's anything you can highlight. Did you supervise or train other employees? Did you reorganize the accounting system, or boost productivity in some way? Accomplishments like these demonstrate leadership, responsibility, and innovation -- qualities that most companies look for in employees. And don't forget volunteer activities and school clubs, which can also showcase these traits.

On-Campus Recruiting

Companies will often send recruiters to interview on-site at various colleges. This gives students a chance to interview with companies that may not have interviewed them otherwise. This is particularly true if a company schedules "open" interviews, in which the only screening process is who is first in line at the sign-ups. Of course, since many more applicants gain interviews in this format, this also means that many more people are rejected. The on-campus interview is generally a screening interview, to see if it is worth the company's time to invite you in for a second interview. So do everything possible to make yourself stand out from the crowd.

The first step, of course, is to check out any and all information your school's career center has on the company. If the information seems out of date, check out the company on the Internet or call the company's headquarters and ask for any printed information.

Many companies will host an informational meeting for interviewees, often the evening before interviews are scheduled to take place. DO NOT MISS THIS MEETING. The recruiter will almost certainly ask if you attended. Make an effort to stay after the meeting and talk with the company's representatives. Not only does this give you an opportunity to find out more information about both the company and the position, it also makes you stand out in the recruiter's mind. If there's a particular company that you had your heart set on, but you weren't able to get an interview with them, attend the information session anyway. You may be able to persuade the recruiter to squeeze you into the schedule. (Or you may discover that the company really isn't the right fit for you after all.)

Try to check out the interview site beforehand. Some colleges may conduct "mock" interviews that take place in one of the standard interview rooms. Or you may be able to convince a career counselor (or even a custodian) to let you sneak a peek during off-hours. Either way, having an idea of the room's setup will help you to mentally prepare.

Arrive at least 15 minutes early to the interview. The recruiter may be ahead of schedule, and might meet you early. But don't be surprised if previous interviews have run over, resulting in your 30-minute slot being reduced to 20 minutes (or less). Don't complain or appear anxious; just use the time you do have as efficiently as possible to showcase the reasons *you* are the ideal candidate. Staying calm and composed in these situations will work to your advantage.

LAST WORDS

A parting word of advice. Again and again during your job search you will face rejection. You will be rejected when you apply for interviews. You will be rejected after interviews. For every job offer you finally receive, you probably will have been rejected many times. Don't let rejections slow you down. Keep reminding yourself that the sooner you go out, start your job search, and get those rejections flowing in, the closer you will be to obtaining the job you want.

RESUMES AND COVER LETTERS

When filling a position, an employer will often have 100-plus applicants, but time to interview only a handful of the most promising ones. As a result, he or she will reject most applicants after only briefly skimming their resumes.

Unless you have phoned and talked to the employer -- which you should do whenever you can -- you will be chosen or rejected for an interview entirely on the basis of your resume and cover letter. *Your cover letter must catch the employer's attention, and your resume must hold it.* (But remember -- a resume is no substitute for a job search campaign. *You* must seek a job. Your resume is only one tool, albeit a critical one.)

RESUME FORMAT:
Mechanics of a First Impression

The Basics

Employers dislike long resumes, so unless you have an unusually strong background with many years of experience and a diversity of outstanding achievements, keep your resume length to one page. If you must squeeze in more information than would otherwise fit, try using a smaller typeface or changing the margins. Watch also for "widows" at the end of paragraphs. You can often free up some space if you can shorten the information enough to get rid of those single words taking up an entire line. Another tactic that works with some word processing programs is to decrease the font size of your paragraph returns and changing the spacing between lines.

Print your resume on standard 8 1/2" x 11" paper. Since recruiters often get resumes in batches of hundreds, a smaller-sized resume may be lost in the pile. Oversized resumes are likely to get crumpled at the edges, and won't fit easily in their files.

First impressions matter, so make sure the recruiter's first impression of your resume is a good one. Never hand-write your resume (or cover letter)! Print your resume on quality paper that has weight and texture, in a conservative color such as white, ivory, or pale gray. Good resume paper is easy to find at many stores that sell stationery or office products. It is even available at some drug stores. Use *matching* paper and envelopes for both your resume and cover letter. One hiring manager at a major magazine throws out all resumes that arrive on paper that differs in color from the envelope!

Do not buy paper with images of clouds and rainbows in the background or anything that looks like casual stationery that you would send to your favorite aunt. Do not spray perfume or cologne on your resume. Do not include your picture with your resume unless you have a specific and appropriate reason to do so.

Another tip: Do a test print of your resume (and cover letter), to make sure the watermark is on the same side as the text so that you can read it. Also make sure it is right-side up. As trivial as this may sound, some recruiters check for this! One recruiter at a law firm in New Hampshire sheepishly admitted this is the first thing he checks. *"I open each envelope and check the watermarks on the resume and cover letter. Those candidates that have it wrong go into a different pile."*

Getting it on Paper

Modern photocomposition typesetting gives you the clearest, sharpest image, a wide variety of type styles, and effects such as italics, bold-facing, and book-like justified margins. It is also too expensive for many jobseekers. The quality of today's laser printers means that a computer-generated resume can look just as impressive as one that has been professionally typeset.

A computer with a word processing or desktop publishing program is the most common way to generate your resume. This allows you the flexibility to make changes almost instantly and to store different drafts on disk. Word processing and desktop publishing programs also offer many different fonts to choose from, each taking up different amounts of space. (It is generally best to stay between 9-point and 12-point font size.) Many other options are also available, such as bold-facing or italicizing for emphasis and the ability to change and manipulate spacing. It is generally recommended to leave the right-hand margin unjustified as this keeps the spacing between the text even and therefore easier to read. It is not wrong to justify both margins of text, but if possible try it both ways before you decide.

For a resume on paper, the end result will be largely determined by the quality of the printer you use. Laser printers will generally provide the best quality. Do not use a dot matrix printer.

Many companies now use scanning equipment to screen the resumes they receive, and certain paper, fonts, and other features are more compatible with this technology. White paper is preferable, as well as a standard font such as Courier or Helvetica. You should use at least a 10-point font, and avoid bolding, italics, underlining, borders, boxes, or graphics.

Household typewriters and office typewriters with nylon or other cloth ribbons are *not* good enough for typing your resume. If you don't have access to a quality word processing program, hire a professional with the resources to prepare your resume for you. Keep in mind that businesses such as Kinko's (open 24 hours) provide access to computers with quality printers.

Don't make your copies on an office photocopier. Only the human resources office may see the resume you mail. Everyone else may see only a copy of it, and copies of copies quickly become unreadable. Furthermore, sending photocopies of your resume or cover letter is completely unprofessional. Either print out each copy individually, or take your resume to a professional copy shop, which will generally offer professionally-maintained, extra-high-quality photocopiers and charge fairly reasonable prices. You want your resume to represent you with the look of polished quality.

Proof with Care

Whether you typed it or paid to have it produced professionally, mistakes on resumes are not only embarrassing, but will usually remove you from consideration (particularly if something obvious such as your name is misspelled). No matter how much you paid someone else to type, write, or typeset your resume, *you* lose if there is a mistake. So proofread it as carefully as possible. Get a friend to help you. Read your draft aloud as your friend checks the proof copy. Then have your friend read aloud while you check. Next, read it letter by letter to check spelling and punctuation.

If you are having it typed or typeset by a resume service or a printer, and you don't have time to proof it, pay for it and take it home. Proof it there and bring it back later to get it corrected and printed.

If you wrote your resume with a word processing program, use the built-in spell checker to double-check for spelling errors. Keep in mind that a spell checker will not find errors such as "to" for "two" or "wok" for "work." Many spell check programs do not recognize missing or misused punctuation, nor are they set to check the spelling of capitalized words. It's important that you still proofread your resume to check for grammatical mistakes and other problems, even after it has been spellchecked. If you find mistakes, do not make edits in pen or pencil or use white-out to fix them on the final copy!

Electronic Resumes

As companies rely increasingly on emerging technologies to find qualified candidates for job openings, you may opt to create an electronic resume in order to remain competitive in today's job market. Why is this important? Companies today sometimes request that resumes be submitted by e-mail, and many hiring managers regularly check online resume databases for candidates to fill unadvertised job openings. Other companies enlist the services of electronic employment database services, which charge jobseekers a nominal fee to have their resumes posted to the database to be viewed by potential employers. Still other companies use their own automated applicant tracking systems, in which case your resume is fed through a scanner that sends the image to a computer that "reads" your resume, looking for keywords, and files it accordingly in its database.

Whether you're posting your resume online, e-mailing it directly to an employer, sending it to an electronic employment database, or sending it to a company you suspect uses an automated applicant tracking system, you must create some form of electronic resume to take advantage of the technology. Don't panic! An electronic resume is simply a modified version of your conventional resume. An electronic resume is one that is sparsely formatted, but filled with keywords and important facts.

In order to post your resume to the Internet -- either to an online resume database or through direct e-mail to an employer -- you will need to change the way your resume is formatted. Instead of a Word, WordPerfect, or other word processing document, save your resume as a plain text, DOS, or ASCII file. These three terms are basically interchangeable, and describe text at its simplest, most basic level, without the formatting such as boldface or italics that most jobseekers use to make their resumes look more interesting. If you use e-mail, you'll notice that all of your messages are written and received in this format. First, you should remove all formatting from your resume including boldface, italics, underlining, bullets, differing font sizes, and graphics. Then, convert and save your resume as a plain text file. Most word processing programs have a "save as" feature that allows you to save files in different formats. Here, you should choose "text only" or "plain text."

Another option is to create a resume in HTML (hypertext markup language), the text formatting language used to publish information on the World Wide Web. However, the real usefulness of HTML resumes is still being explored. Most of the major online databases do not accept HTML resumes, and the vast majority of companies only accept plain text resumes through their e-mail.

Finally, if you simply wish to send your resume to an electronic employment database or a company that uses an automated applicant tracking system, there is no need to convert your resume to a plain text file. The only change you need to make is to organize the information in your resume by keywords. Employers are likely to do keyword searches for information, such as degree held or knowledge of particular types of software. Therefore, using the right keywords or key phrases in your resume is critical to its ultimate success. Keywords are usually nouns or short phrases that the computer searches for which refer to experience, training, skills, and abilities. For example, let's say an employer searches an employment database for a sales representative with the following criteria:

BS/BA
exceeded quota
cold calls
high energy
willing to travel

Even if you have the right qualifications, neglecting to use these keywords would result in the computer passing over your resume. Although there is no way to know for sure which keywords employers are most likely to search for, you can make educated guesses by checking the help-wanted ads or online job postings for your type of job. You should also arrange keywords in a keyword summary, a paragraph listing your qualifications that immediately follows your name and address (see sample letter in this chapter). In addition, choose a nondecorative font with clear, distinct characters, such as Helvetica or Times. It is more difficult for a scanner to accurately pick up the more unusual fonts. Boldface and all capital letters are best used only for major section headings, such as "Experience" and "Education." It is also best to avoid using italics or underlining, since this can cause the letters to bleed into one another.

Types of Resumes

The most common resume formats are the functional resume, the chronological resume, and the combination resume. (Examples can be found at the end of this chapter.) A functional resume focuses on skills and de-emphasizes job titles, employers, etc. A functional resume is best if you have been out of the work force for a long time or are changing careers. It is also good if you want to highlight specific skills and strengths, especially if all of your work experience has been at one company. This format can also be a good choice if you are just out of school or have no experience in your desired field.

Choose a chronological format if you are currently working or were working recently, and if your most recent experiences relate to your desired field. Use reverse chronological order and include dates. To a recruiter your last job and your latest schooling are the most important, so put the last first and list the rest going back in time.

A combination resume is perhaps the most common. This resume simply combines elements of the functional and chronological resume formats. This is used by many jobseekers with a solid track record who find elements of both types useful.

Organization

Your name, phone number, e-mail address (if you have one), and a complete mailing address should be at the top of your resume. Try to make your name stand out by using a slightly larger font size or all capital letters. Be sure to spell out everything. Never abbreviate St. for Street or Rd. for Road. If you are a college student, you should also put your home address and phone number at the top. Change your message on your answering machine if necessary – RUSH blaring in the background or your sorority sisters screaming may not come across well to all recruiters. If you think you may be moving within six months then include a second address and phone number of a trusted friend or relative who can reach you no matter where you are.

Remember that employers will keep your resume on file and
may contact you months later if a position opens that fits your qualifications.
All too often, candidates are unreachable because they have moved and had not
previously provided enough contact options on their resume.

Next, list your experience, then your education. If you are a recent graduate, list your education first, unless your experience is more important than your education. (For example, if you have just graduated from a teaching school, have some business experience, and are applying for a job in business, you would list your business experience first.)

Keep everything easy to find. Put the dates of your employment and education on the left of the page. Put the names of the companies you worked for and the schools you attended a few spaces to the right of the dates. Put the city and state, or the city and country, where you studied or worked to the right of the page.

The important thing is simply to break up the text in some logical way that makes your resume visually attractive and easy to scan, so experiment to see which layout works best for your resume. However you set it up, *stay consistent*. Inconsistencies in fonts, spacing, or tenses will make your resume look sloppy. Also, be sure to use tabs to keep your information vertically lined up, rather than the less precise space bar.

RESUME CONTENT:
Say it with Style
Sell Yourself

You are selling your skills and accomplishments in your resume, so it is important to inventory yourself and know yourself. If you have achieved something, say so. Put it in the best possible light, but avoid subjective statements, such as "I am a hard worker" or "I get along well with my coworkers." Just stick to the facts.

While you shouldn't hold back or be modest, don't exaggerate your achievements to the point of misrepresentation. <u>Be honest</u>. Many companies will immediately drop an applicant from consideration (or fire a current employee) upon discovering inaccurate or untrue information on a resume or other application material.

Write down the important (and pertinent) things you have done, but do it in as few words as possible. Your resume will be scanned, not read, and short, concise phrases are much more effective than long-winded sentences. Avoid the use of "I" when emphasizing your accomplishments. Instead, use brief phrases beginning with action verbs.

While some technical terms will be unavoidable, you should try to avoid excessive "technicalese." Keep in mind that the first person to see your resume may be a human resources person who won't necessarily know all the jargon -- and how can they be impressed by something they don't understand?

Keep it Brief

Also, try to hold your paragraphs to six lines or less. If you have more than six lines of information about one job or school, put it in two or more paragraphs.

A short resume will be examined more carefully. Remember: Your resume usually has between eight and 45 seconds to catch an employer's eye. So make every second count.

Job Objective

A functional resume may require a job objective to give it focus. One or two sentences describing the job you are seeking can clarify in what capacity your skills will be best put to use. Be sure that your stated objective is in line with the position you're applying for.

Examples:

> An entry-level editorial assistant position in the publishing industry.
> A senior management position with a telecommunications firm.

Don't include a job objective on a chronological resume unless your previous work experiences are <u>completely</u> unrelated to the position for which you're applying. The presence of an overly specific job objective might eliminate you from consideration for other positions that a recruiter feels are a better match for your qualifications. But even if you don't put an objective on paper, having a career goal in mind as you write can help give your resume a solid sense of direction.

USE ACTION VERBS

How you write your resume is just as important as *what* you write. In describing previous work experiences, the strongest resumes use short phrases beginning with action verbs. Below are a few you may want to use. (This list is not all-inclusive.)

achieved	developed	integrated	purchased
administered	devised	interpreted	reduced
advised	directed	interviewed	regulated
arranged	distributed	launched	represented
assisted	established	managed	resolved
attained	evaluated	marketed	restored
budgeted	examined	mediated	restructured
built	executed	monitored	revised
calculated	expanded	negotiated	scheduled
collaborated	expedited	obtained	selected
collected	facilitated	operated	served
compiled	formulated	ordered	sold
completed	founded	organized	solved
computed	generated	participated	streamlined
conducted	headed	performed	studied
consolidated	identified	planned	supervised
constructed	implemented	prepared	supplied
consulted	improved	presented	supported
controlled	increased	processed	tested
coordinated	initiated	produced	trained
created	installed	proposed	updated
determined	instructed	published	wrote

Some jobseekers may choose to include both "Relevant Experience" and "Additional Experience" sections. This can be useful, as it allows the jobseeker to place more emphasis on certain experiences and to de-emphasize others.

Emphasize continued experience in a particular job area or continued interest in a particular industry. De-emphasize irrelevant positions. It is okay to include one opening line providing a general description of each company you've worked at. Delete positions that you held for less than four months (unless you are a very recent college grad or still in school). Stress your results and your achievements, elaborating on how you contributed in your previous jobs. Did you increase sales, reduce costs, improve a product, implement a new program? Were you promoted? Use specific numbers (i.e., quantities, percentages, dollar amounts) whenever possible.

Education

Keep it brief if you have more than two years of career experience. Elaborate more if you have less experience. If you are a recent college graduate, you may choose to include any high school activities that are directly relevant to your career. If you've been out of school for a while you don't need to list your education prior to college.

Mention degrees received and any honors or special awards. Note individual courses or projects you participated in that might be relevant for employers. For example, if you are an English major applying for a position as a business writer, be sure to mention any business or economics courses. Previous experience such as Editor-in-Chief of the school newspaper would be relevant as well.

If you are uploading your resume to an online job hunting site such as CareerCity.com, action verbs are still important, but the key words or key nouns that a computer would search for become more important. For example, if you're seeking an accounting position, key nouns that a computer would search for such as "Lotus 1-2-3" or "CPA" or "payroll" become very important.

Highlight Impressive Skills

Be sure to mention any computer skills you may have. You may wish to include a section entitled "Additional Skills" or "Computer Skills," in which you list any software programs you know. An additional skills section is also an ideal place to mention fluency in a foreign language.

Personal Data

This section is optional, but if you choose to include it, keep it brief. A one-word mention of hobbies such as fishing, chess, baseball, cooking, etc., can give the person who will interview you a good way to open up the conversation.

Team sports experience is looked at favorably. It doesn't hurt to include activities that are somewhat unusual (fencing, Akido, '70s music) or that somehow relate to the position or the company to which you're applying. For instance, it would be worth noting if you are a member of a professional organization in your industry of interest. Never include information about your age, alias, date of birth, health, physical characteristics, marital status, religious affiliation, or political/moral beliefs.

References

The most that is needed is the sentence "References available upon request" at the bottom of your resume. If you choose to leave it out, that's fine. This line is not really necessary. It is understood that references will most likely be asked for and provided by you later on in the interviewing process. Do not actually send references with your resume and cover letter unless specifically requested.

HIRING A RESUME WRITER:
Is it the Right Choice for You?

If you write reasonably well, it is to your advantage to write your own resume. Writing your resume forces you to review your experiences and figure out how to explain your accomplishments in clear, brief phrases. This will help you when you explain your work to interviewers. It is also easier to tailor your resume to each position you're applying for when you have put it together yourself.

If you write your resume, everything will be in your own words; it will sound like you. It will say what you want it to say. If you are a good writer, know yourself well, and have a good idea of which parts of your background employers are looking for, you should be able to write your own resume better than someone else. If you decide to write your resume yourself, have as many people as possible review and proofread it. Welcome objective opinions and other perspectives.

When to Get Help

If you have difficulty writing in "resume style" (which is quite unlike normal written language), if you are unsure which parts of your background to emphasize, or if you think your resume would make your case better if it did not follow one of the standard forms outlined either here or in a book on resumes, then you should consider having it professionally written.

Even some professional resume writers we know have had their resumes written with the help of fellow professionals. They sought the help of someone who could be objective about their background, as well as provide an experienced sounding board to help focus their thoughts.

If You Hire a Pro

The best way to choose a writer is by reputation: the recommendation of a friend, a personnel director, your school placement officer, or someone else knowledgeable in the field.

Important questions:
· "How long have you been writing resumes?"
· "If I'm not satisfied with what you write, will you go over it with me and change it?"
· "Do you charge by the hour or a flat rate?"

There is no sure relation between price and quality, except that you are unlikely to get a good writer for less than $50 for an uncomplicated resume and you shouldn't have to pay more than $300 unless your experience is very extensive or complicated. There will be additional charges for printing. Assume nothing no matter how much you pay. It is your career at stake if there are mistakes on your resume!

Few resume services will give you a firm price over the phone, simply because some resumes are too complicated and take too long to do for a predetermined price. Some services will quote you a price that applies to almost all of their customers. Once you decide to use a specific writer, you should insist on a firm price quote *before* engaging their services. Also, find out how expensive minor changes will be.

COVER LETTERS:
Quick, Clear, and Concise

Always mail a cover letter with your resume. In a cover letter you can show an interest in the company that you can't show in a resume. You can also point out one or two of your skills or accomplishments the company can put to good use.

Make it Personal

The more personal you can get, the better, so long as you keep it professional. If someone known to the person you are writing has recommended that you contact the company, get permission to include his/her name in the letter. If you can get the name of a person to send the letter to, address it directly to that person (after first calling the company to verify the spelling of the person's name, correct title, and mailing address). Be sure to put the person's name and title on both the letter and the envelope. This will ensure that your letter will get through to the proper person, even if a new person now occupies this position. It will not always be possible to get the name of a person. Always strive to get at least a title.

Be sure to mention something about why you have an interest in the company -- *so many candidates apply for jobs with no apparent knowledge of what the company does!* This conveys the message that they just want any job.

Type cover letters in full. Don't try the cheap and easy ways, like using a computer mail merge program or photocopying the body of your letter and typing in the inside address and salutation. You will give the impression that you are mailing to a host of companies and have no particular interest in any one.

Print your cover letter on the same color and same high-quality paper as your resume.

Cover letter basic format

Paragraph 1: State what the position is that you are seeking. It is not always necessary to state how you found out about the position -- often you will apply without knowing that a position is open.
Paragraph 2: Include what you know about the company and why you are interested in working there. Mention any prior contact with the company or someone known to the hiring person if relevant. Briefly state your qualifications and what you can offer. (Do not talk about what you cannot do).
Paragraph 3: Close with your phone number and where/when you can be reached. Make a request for an interview. State when you will follow up by phone (or mail or e-mail if the ad requests no phone calls). Do not wait long -- generally five working days. If you say you're going to follow up, then actually do it! This phone call can get your resume noticed when it might otherwise sit in a stack of 225 other resumes.

Cover letter do's and don'ts

- *Do* keep your cover letter brief and to the point.
- *Do* be sure it is error-free.
- *Do* accentuate what you can offer the company, not what you hope to gain.

- *Do* be sure your phone number and address is on your cover letter just in case it gets separated from your resume (this happens!).
- *Do* check the watermark by holding the paper up to a light -- be sure it is facing forward so it is readable -- on the same side as the text, and right-side up.
- *Do* sign your cover letter (or type your name if you are sending it electronically). Blue or black ink are both fine. Do not use red ink.
- *Don't* just repeat information verbatim from your resume.
- *Don't* overuse the personal pronoun "I."
- *Don't* send a generic cover letter -- show your personal knowledge of and interest in that particular company.

THANK YOU LETTERS:
Another Way to Stand Out

As mentioned earlier, *always* send a thank you letter after an interview (see the sample later in this section). So few candidates do this and it is yet another way for you to stand out. Be sure to mention something specific from the interview and restate your interest in the company and the position.

It is generally acceptable to handwrite your thank you letter on a generic thank you card (but *never* a postcard). Make sure handwritten notes are neat and legible. However, if you are in doubt, typing your letter is always the safe bet. If you met with several people it is fine to send them each an individual thank you letter. Call the company if you need to check on the correct spelling of their names.

Remember to:
- Keep it short.
- Proofread it carefully.
- Send it *promptly*.

FUNCTIONAL RESUME

C.J. RAVENCLAW
129 Pennsylvania Avenue
Washington DC 20500
202/555-6652
e-mail: ravenclaw@dcpress.net

Objective
A position as a graphic designer commensurate with my acquired skills and expertise.

Summary
Extensive experience in plate making, separations, color matching, background definition, printing, mechanicals, color corrections, and personnel supervision. A highly motivated manager and effective communicator. Proven ability to:

- **Create Commercial Graphics**
- **Produce Embossed Drawings**
- **Color Separate**
- **Control Quality**
- **Resolve Printing Problems**
- **Analyze Customer Satisfaction**

Qualifications
Printing:
Knowledgeable in black and white as well as color printing. Excellent judgment in determining acceptability of color reproduction through comparison with original. Proficient at producing four- or five-color corrections on all media, as well as restyling previously reproduced four-color artwork.

Customer Relations:
Routinely work closely with customers to ensure specifications are met. Capable of striking a balance between technical printing capabilities and need for customer satisfaction through entire production process.

Specialties:
Practiced at creating silk screen overlays for a multitude of processes including velo bind, GBC bind, and perfect bind. Creative design and timely preparation of posters, flyers, and personalized stationery.

Personnel Supervision:
Skillful at fostering atmosphere that encourages highly talented artists to balance high-level creativity with maximum production. Consistently beat production deadlines. Instruct new employees, apprentices, and students in both artistry and technical operations.

Experience
Graphic Arts Professor, Ohio State University, Columbus OH (1997-2001).
Manager, Design Graphics, Washington DC (2002-present).

Education
Massachusetts Conservatory of Art, Ph.D. 1995
University of Massachusetts, B.A. 1993

CHRONOLOGICAL RESUME

HARRY SEABORN
557 Shoreline Drive
Seattle, WA 98404
(206) 555-6584
e-mail: hseaborn@centco.com

EXPERIENCE

THE CENTER COMPANY   Seattle, WA
Systems Programmer   2001-present
• Develop and maintain customer accounting and order tracking
database using a Visual Basic front end and SQL server.
• Plan and implement migration of company wide transition from
mainframe-based dumb terminals to a true client server environment
using Windows NT Workstation and Server.
• Oversee general local and wide area network administration
including the development of a variety of intranet modules to
improve internal company communication and planning across
divisions.

INFO TECH, INC.   Seattle, WA
Technical Manager   1995-2001
• Designed and managed the implementation of a network providing
the legal community with a direct line to Supreme Court cases
across the Internet using SQL Server and a variety of Internet tools.
• Developed a system to make the entire library catalog available on
line using PERL scripts and SQL.
• Used Visual Basic and Microsoft Access to create a registration
system for university registrar.

EDUCATION

SALEM STATE UNIVERSITY   Salem, OR
      M.S. in Computer Science.   1998
      B.S. in Computer Science.   1996

COMPUTER SKILLS

• Programming Languages: Visual Basic, Java, C++, SQL, PERL
• Software: SQL Server, Internet Information Server, Oracle
• Operating Systems: Windows NT, UNIX, Linux

FUNCTIONAL RESUME

Donna Hermione Moss
703 Wizard's Way
Chicago, IL 60601
(312) 555-8841
e-mail: donna@cowfire.com

OBJECTIVE:
To contribute over five years of experience in promotion, communications, and administration to an entry-level position in advertising.

SUMMARY OF QUALIFICATIONS:
- Performed advertising duties for small business.
- Experience in business writing and communications skills.
- General knowledge of office management.
- Demonstrated ability to work well with others, in both supervisory and support staff roles.
- Type 75 words per minute.

SELECTED ACHIEVEMENTS AND RESULTS:
Promotion:
Composing, editing, and proofreading correspondence and public relations materials for own catering service. Large-scale mailings.

Communication:
Instruction; curriculum and lesson planning; student evaluation; parent-teacher conferences; development of educational materials. Training and supervising clerks.

Computer Skills:
Proficient in MS Word, Lotus 1-2-3, Excel, and Filemaker Pro.

Administration:
Record-keeping and file maintenance. Data processing and computer operations, accounts receivable, accounts payable, inventory control, and customer relations. Scheduling, office management, and telephone reception.

PROFESSIONAL HISTORY:
Teacher; Self-Employed (owner of catering service); Floor Manager; Administrative Assistant; Accounting Clerk.

EDUCATION:
Beloit College, Beloit, WI, BA in Education, 1996

CHRONOLOGICAL RESUME

PERCY ZIEGLER
16 Josiah Court
Marlborough CT 06447
203/555-9641 (h)
203/555-8176, x14 (w)

EDUCATION

Keene State College, Keene NH
Bachelor of Arts in Elementary Education, 2002
• Graduated *magna cum laude*
• English minor
• Kappa Delta Pi member, inducted 2000

EXPERIENCE
September 2002-
Present

Elmer T. Thienes Elementary School, Marlborough CT
Part-time Kindergarten Teacher
• Instruct kindergartners in reading, spelling, language arts, and
   music.
• Participate in the selection of textbooks and learning aids.
• Organize and supervise class field trips and coordinate in-class
   presentations.

Summers
1999-2001

Keene YMCA, Youth Division, Keene NH
Child-care Counselor
• Oversaw summer program for low-income youth.
• Budgeted and coordinated special events and field trips,
   working with Program Director to initiate variations in the
   program.
• Served as Youth Advocate in cooperation with social worker to
   address the social needs and problems of participants.

Spring 2001

Wheelock Elementary School, Keene NH
Student Teacher
• Taught third-grade class in all elementary subjects.
• Designed and implemented a two-week unit on Native
   Americans.
• Assisted in revision of third-grade curriculum.

Fall 2000

Child Development Center, Keene NH
Daycare Worker
• Supervised preschool children on the playground and during art
   activities.
• Created a "Wishbone Corner," where children could quietly
   look at books or take a voluntary "time-out."

ADDITIONAL INTERESTS

Martial arts, Pokemon, politics, reading, skiing, writing.

ELECTRONIC RESUME

GRIFFIN DORE
69 Dursley Drive
Cambridge, MA 02138
(617) 555-5555

KEYWORD SUMMARY

Senior financial manager with over ten years experience in Accounting and Systems Management, Budgeting, Forecasting, Cost Containment, Financial Reporting, and International Accounting. MBA in Management. Proficient in Lotus, Excel, Solomon, and Windows.

EXPERIENCE

COLWELL CORPORATION, Wellesley, MA
Director of Accounting and Budgets, 1995 to present
   Direct staff of twenty in General Ledger, Accounts Payable, Accounts Receivable, and International Accounting.
   Facilitate month-end closing process with parent company and auditors.
   Implemented team-oriented cross-training program within accounting group, resulting in timely month-end closings and increased productivity of key accounting staff.
   Developed and implemented a strategy for Sales and Use Tax Compliance in all fifty states.
   Prepare monthly financial statements and analyses.

FRANKLIN AND DELANEY COMPANY, Melrose, MA
Senior Accountant, 1992-1995
   Managed Accounts Payable, General Ledger, transaction processing, and financial reporting. Supervised staff of five.

Staff Accountant, 1990-1992
   Managed Accounts Payable, including vouchering, cash disbursements, and bank reconciliation.
   Wrote and issued policies.
   Maintained supporting schedules used during year-end audits.
   Trained new employees.

EDUCATION

MBA in Management, Northeastern University, Boston, MA, 1994
BS in Accounting, Boston College, Boston, MA, 1990

ASSOCIATIONS

National Association of Accountants

GENERAL MODEL
FOR A COVER LETTER

Your mailing address
Date

Contact's name
Contact's title
Company
Company's mailing address

Dear Mr./Ms. _____:

Immediately explain why your background makes you the best candidate for the position that you are applying for. Describe what prompted you to write (want ad, article you read about the company, networking contact, etc.). Keep the first paragraph short and hard-hitting.

Detail what you could contribute to this company. Show how your qualifications will benefit this firm. Describe your interest in the corporation. Subtly emphasizing your knowledge about this firm and your familiarity with the industry will set you apart from other candidates. Remember to keep this letter short; few recruiters will read a cover letter longer than half a page.

If possible, your closing paragraph should request specific action on the part of the reader. Include your phone number and the hours when you can be reached. Mention that if you do not hear from the reader by a specific date, you will follow up with a phone call. Lastly, thank the reader for their time, consideration, etc.

Sincerely,

(signature)

Your full name (typed)

Enclosure (use this if there are other materials, such as your resume, that are included in the same envelope)

SAMPLE COVER LETTER

16 Josiah Court
Marlborough CT 06447
January 16, 2005

Ms. Leona Malfoy
Assistant Principal
Laningham Elementary School
43 Mayflower Drive
Keene NH 03431

Dear Ms. Malfoy:

Toby Potter recently informed me of a possible opening for a third grade teacher at Laningham Elementary School. With my experience instructing third-graders, both in schools and in summer programs, I feel I would be an ideal candidate for the position. Please accept this letter and the enclosed resume as my application.

Laningham's educational philosophy that every child can learn and succeed interests me, since it mirrors my own. My current position at Elmer T. Thienes Elementary has reinforced this philosophy, heightening my awareness of the different styles and paces of learning and increasing my sensitivity toward special needs children. Furthermore, as a direct result of my student teaching experience at Wheelock Elementary School, I am comfortable, confident, and knowledgeable working with third-graders.

I look forward to discussing the position and my qualifications for it in more detail. I can be reached at 203/555-9641 evenings or 203/555-8176, x14 weekdays. If I do not hear from you before Tuesday of next week, I will call to see if we can schedule a time to meet. Thank you for your time and consideration.

Sincerely,

Percy Ziegler

Percy Ziegler

Enclosure

GENERAL MODEL FOR A
THANK YOU/FOLLOW-UP LETTER

Your mailing address
Date

Contact's name
Contact's title
Company
Company's mailing address

Dear Mr./Ms._____:

Remind the interviewer of the reason (i.e., a specific opening, an informational interview, etc.) you were interviewed, as well as the date. Thank him/her for the interview, and try to personalize your thanks by mentioning some specific aspect of the interview.

Confirm your interest in the organization (and in the opening, if you were interviewing for a particular position). Use specifics to re-emphasize that you have researched the firm in detail and have considered how you would fit into the company and the position. This is a good time to say anything you wish you had said in the initial meeting. Be sure to keep this letter brief; a half page is plenty.

If appropriate, close with a suggestion for further action, such as a desire to have an additional interview, if possible. Mention your phone number and the hours you can be reached. Alternatively, you may prefer to mention that you will follow up with a phone call in several days. Once again, thank the person for meeting with you, and state that you would be happy to provide any additional information about your qualifications.

Sincerely,

(signature)

Your full name (typed)

PRIMARY EMPLOYERS

ACCOUNTING & MANAGEMENT CONSULTING

You can expect to find the following types of companies in this section:
Consulting and Research Firms • Industrial Accounting Firms • Management Services • Public Accounting Firms • Tax Preparation Companies

---

ECKERT, INGRUM, TINKLER, OLIPHANT, & FEATHERSTON, L.L.P.
P.O. Box 5821, San Angelo TX 76902-5821. 915/944-3571. **Fax:** 915/942-1093. **Contact:** Hiring Partner. **Description:** An accounting firm involved in bookkeeping, taxes, and auditing of various institutions including schools, governments, and banks. **NOTE:** Entry-level positions are offered. **Corporate headquarters location:** This location.

PAYCHEX, INC.
4242 Woodcock Drive, Suite 100, San Antonio TX 78228. 512/469-0550. **Contact:** Human Resources. **World Wide Web address:** http://www.paychex.com. **Description:** A payroll accounting firm. It also offers services to help employers track attendance. **NOTE:** Jobseekers should apply at the corporate website which lists openings and contact e-mail addresses. **Other area locations:** Houston TX; Dallas TX; Fort Worth TX; Austin TX. **Corporate headquarters location:** Rochester NY. **Listed on:** NASDAQ. **Stock exchange symbol:** PAYX.

ADVERTISING, MARKETING, AND PUBLIC RELATIONS

You can expect to find the following types of companies in this section:
Advertising Agencies • Direct Mail Marketers • Market Research Firms • Public Relations Firms

---

BRSG (BLACK ROGERS SULLIVAN GOODNIGHT)
701 Brazos, Suite, 1010 Austin TX 78701. 512/320-8511. **Fax:** 512/320-8990. **Fax:** 713/783-1592. **World Wide Web address:** http://www.brsg.com. **Contact:** Employment. **Description:** A marketing communications firm. **Special programs:** Internships. **Office hours:** Monday - Friday, 8:00 a.m. - 5:00 p.m. **Corporate headquarters location:** This location. **Operations at this facility include:** Administration; Research and Development.

COX MEDIA
401 Cantu Road, Suite D, Del Rio TX 78840. 830/774-5538. **Fax:** 830/774-5438. **Contact:** Human Resources. **World Wide Web address:** http://www.coxmedia.com. **Description:** Provides advertising services for businesses through major cable networks such as CNN. **NOTE:** Please visit website to search for jobs and apply online. **Corporate headquarters location:** Macon GA. **Other area locations:** Statewide. **Other U.S. locations:** Nationwide. **Parent company:** Cox Communications. **Number of employees nationwide:** 1,400.

GSD&M ADVERTISING
828 West Sixth Street, Austin TX 78703. 512/427-4736. **Contact:** Marci Rogers, Recruiting Coordinator; at 512/242-5932. **E-mail address:** marci_rogers@gsdm.com. Human Resources. **World Wide Web address:** http://www.gsdm.com. **Description:** An advertising agency. **Positions advertised include:** Media Supervisor; Broadcast Supervisor; Media Research Analyst; Administrative Assistant. **Corporate headquarters location:** This location.

HARTE-HANKS, INC.
P.O. Box 269, San Antonio TX. **Physical address:** 200 Concord Plaza Drive, San Antonio TX 78216. 210/829-9000. **Contact:** Human Resources. **World Wide Web address:** http://www.harte-hanks.com. **Description:** Provides direct marketing services for various companies and publishes a weekly shopping guide. **NOTE:** Interested jobseekers should apply online at the corporate website. **Corporate headquarters location:** This location. **Other U.S. locations:** Nationwide.

LEAD DOGS
2433 Rutland Drive, Suite 210, Austin TX 78758. **Toll-free phone:** 800/336-2616. **Fax:** 512/990-8999. **Contact:** Tina Tripoli, Human Resources Director, ext. 106. **E-mail address:** Ttripoli@leaddogs.com.

World Wide Web address: http://www.leaddogs.com. **Description:** Provides direct marketing services for high-tech companies including event management and database development. **Positions advertised include:** Marketing Pre-Sales Representative; Account Manager; Call Center Manager.

TL MARKETING INC.
4407 Bee Caves Road, Building 6, 2nd Floor, Suite 622, Austin TX 78746. 512/371-7272. **Fax:** 512/371-0727. **Contact:** Human Resources. **Description:** A marketing firm representing manufacturers within the electrical industry. **Corporate headquarters location:** Dallas TX.

AEROSPACE

You can expect to find the following types of companies in this section:
Aerospace Products and Services • Aircraft Equipment and Parts

THE BOEING COMPANY

9566 Railroad Drive, El Paso TX 79924. 915/834-1000. **Contact:** Human Resources. **World Wide Web address:** http://www.boeing.com. **Description:** The Boeing Company is one of the largest aerospace firms in the United States, one of the nation's top exporters, and one of the world's leading manufacturers of commercial jet transports. The company is a major U.S. government contractor, with capabilities in missile and space, electronic systems, military aircraft, helicopters, and information systems management. **NOTE:** Please visit website to search for jobs and apply online. Resumes are only accepted online. **Corporate headquarters location:** Chicago IL. **Other U.S. locations:** Nationwide. Navy. **Listed on:** New York Stock Exchange. **Stock Exchange symbol:** BA.

CFAN COMPANY

1000 Technology Way, San Marcos TX 78666. 512/353-2832. **Fax:** 512/353-2838. **Contact:** Human Resources. **World Wide Web address:** http://www.c-fan.com. **Description:** CFAN Company manufactures composite fan blades for G.E. Aircraft Engines.

DERCO AEROSPACE, INC.

22 Ocean Drive, Corpus Christi TX 78419. 361/937-8334. **Contact:** Human Resources. **E-mail address:** resumes@dercoaerospace.com. **World Wide Web address:** http://www.dercoaerospace.com. Description: Military aircraft parts distributor and repair company. **NOTE:** To apply, write to Derco Aerospace, Inc., Human Resources, P.O. Box 250970, Milwaukee, WI 53225; or fax a resume to 414/214-2040. Resumes may also be e-mailed. **Positions advertised include:** Warehouse Professionals.

ENGINE COMPONENTS INC.

9503 Middlex Drive, San Antonio TX 78217. 210/820-8100. **Contact:** Human Resources. **World Wide Web address:** http://www.eci2fly.com. **Description:** Manufactures and repairs engine components for aircraft. **Corporate headquarters location:** This location. **Other U.S. locations:** Bradenton FL; Aurora OR.

GOODRICH AEROSPACE AEROSTRUCTURES GROUP

2005 Technology Way, San Marcos TX 78666. 512/754-3600. **Contact:** Human Resources. **World Wide Web address:** http://www.goodrich.com. **Description:** Designs, integrates, manufactures, sells, and supports aircraft engine nacelle systems and components for large commercial and military aircraft. **Positions advertised include:** Quality Inspector; Tooler; Manufacturing Engineer; Administrative Assistant; Aerospace Assembler. **Corporate headquarters location:** Charlotte NC. **Parent company:** Goodrich Company provides aircraft systems, components, and services and manufactures a wide range of specialty chemicals. The business units comprising the aerospace division of Goodrich consist of landing systems; sensors and integrated systems; safety systems; and maintenance, repair, and overhaul. Specialty chemical business units include specialty plastics; specialty additives; sealants, coatings, and adhesives; and water systems and services. **Listed on:** New York Stock Exchange. **Stock Exchange Symbol:** GR. **Number of employees nationwide:** 23,000.

M7 AEROSPACE
P.O. Box 790490, San Antonio TX 78279-0490. 210/824-9421. **Fax:** 210/824-9476. **Contact:** Human Resources. **E-mail address:** employment@m7aerospace. **World Wide Web address:** http://www.m7aerospace.com. **Description:** Manufactures aircraft and provides a wide range of aviation services. **Corporate headquarters location:** This location.

NEW SYSTEMS
1201 North Industrial Boulevard, Round Rock TX 78681. 512/388-4806. **Contact:** Human Resources.**:** Engineers and manufactures kits used for installing navigational equipment in commercial aircraft.

SAN ANTONIO AEROSPACE, L.P.
9800 John Saunders Road, San Antonio TX 78216. 210/293-3200. **Contact:** Steve Klein, SAA Recruiting Department. **Description:** Repairs, modifies, and designs aircraft.

APPAREL, FASHION, AND TEXTILES

You can expect to find the following types of companies in this section:
Broadwoven Fabric Mills • Knitting Mills • Yarn and Thread Mills • Curtains and Draperies • Footwear • Nonwoven Fabrics • Textile Goods and Finishing

BORDER APPAREL LAUNDRY LTD.
6969-B Industrial Avenue, El Paso TX 79915. 915/772-7170. **Fax:** 915/772-4527. **Contact:** Employment. **E-mail address:** mflores@tramexdelnorte.com. **World Wide Web address:** http://www.blaundry.com. **Description:** Manufactures jeans for Levi and CK. **NOTE:** There are three facilities located in El Paso. **Corporate headquarters location:** This location. **International locations:** Toreon Mexico.

TONY LAMA COMPANY
1137 Tony Lama Street, El Paso TX 79915. 915/778-8311. **Fax:** 915/778-5237. **Contact:** Human Resources. **World Wide Web address:** http://www.tonylama.com. **Description:** A manufacturer of men's and women's cowboy boots. **Corporate headquarters location:** Fort Worth TX. **Parent company:** Berkshire Hathaway. **Operations at this facility:** Manufacturing.

LUCCHESE BOOT COMPANY
40 Walter Jones Boulevard, El Paso TX 79906. 915/778-3066. **Contact:** Human Resources. **World Wide Web address:** http://www.lucchese.com. **Description:** A manufacturer, retailer, and marketer of men's and women's cowboy boots. **NOTE:** This company also has an outlet store in El Paso TX.

SAVANE INTERNATIONAL CORPORATION
P.O. Box 13800, 4171 North Mesa Building D, El Paso TX 79902. 915/496-7000. **Contact:** Human Resources. **World Wide Web address:** http://www.savane.com. **Description:** A manufacturer of men's wear for department stores. **Corporate headquarters location:** Tampa FL. **Parent company:** Tropical Sportswear International Corporation. **Listed on:** NASDAQ. **Stock exchange symbol:** TSIC.

STITCHES INC.
1144 Vista De Oro Drive, El Paso TX 79935. 915/593-2990. **Contact:** Human Resources. **Description:** A textile sewing and cutting contractor. **Corporate headquarters location:** This location.

TEX TAN WESTERN LEATHER COMPANY
808 South U.S. Highway 77A, Yoakum TX 77995. 361/293-2314. **Fax:** 361/293-2369. **Contact:** Human Resources. **World Wide Web address:**

http://www.textan.com. **Description:** Tex Tan Western Leather Company is a manufacturer of various leather products including saddles, riding equipment, belts, and other sundry products. Tex Tan Western Leather Company provides these products to dealers worldwide. **Listed on:** Privately held.

TEXACE CORPORATION
402 West Nueva, San Antonio TX 78207-0429. 210/227-7551. **Toll-free phone:** 800/835-8973. **Fax:** 210/227-4237. **Contact:** Minerva Martinez, Human Resources. **World Wide Web address:** http://www.texace.com. **Description:** Texace Corporation manufactures a variety of headwear including golf caps and visors.

WALLS INDUSTRIES, INC.
P.O. Box 196, Sweetwater TX 79556-0196. 915/235-5456. **Fax:** 915/235-8512. **Contact:** Human Resources. **World Wide Web address:** http://www.wallsoutdoors.com. **Description:** Manufactures outerwear for men, women, and children. This location is an outlet store. **Corporate headquarters location:** Cleburne TX.

WILLIAMSON-DICKIE MANUFACTURING COMPANY
P.O. Box 295, Weslaco TX 78596. 956/968-1567. **Contact:** Human Resources. **World Wide Web address:** http://www.dickies.com. **Description:** Williamson-Dickie Manufacturing Company manufactures apparel for men and boys including casual slacks and work pants. **NOTE:** Apply online at this company's website. **Corporate headquarters location:** Fort Worth TX. **Operations at this facility include:** This location is primarily engaged in apparel sewing.

WILLIAMSON-DICKIE MANUFACTURING COMPANY
6110 South 42nd Street, McAllen TX 78503. 956/686-6541. **Contact:** Human Resources. **World Wide Web address:** http://www.dickies.com. **Description:** Williamson-Dickie Manufacturing Company manufactures apparel for men and boys including casual slacks and work pants. **NOTE:** Apply online at this company's website. **Corporate headquarters location:** Fort Worth TX. **Operations at this facility include:** This location manufactures men's work pants.

ARCHITECTURE, CONSTRUCTION, AND ENGINEERING

You can expect to find the following types of companies in this section:
Architectural and Engineering Services • Civil and Mechanical Engineering Firms • Construction Products, Manufacturers, and Wholesalers • General Contractors/Specialized Trade Contractors

J.D. ABRAMS LP
111 Congress Avenue, Suite 2400, Austin TX 78701-4083. 512/322-4000. **Fax:** 512/322-4018. **Contact:** Mr. Dean Bernal, Vice President of Human Resources. **E-mail address:** dbernal@jdabrams.com. **World Wide Web address:** http://www.jdabrams.com. **Description:** A heavy, civil construction company specializing in public works infrastructure projects. Founded 1966. **Positions advertised include:** Estimator; Project Manager; Project Engineer; Field Engineer; Scheduler; Accountant; Human Resources Representative; Clerk. **Corporate headquarters location:** This location. **Other area locations:** Dallas TX; El Paso TX; Houston TX. **President:** Jon Abrams.

BAY LTD.
P.O. Box 9908 Corpus Christi TX 78469. 361/693-2100. **Physical address:** 401 Corn Products Road, Corpus Christi TX 78409. **Fax:** 361/289-5005. **Contact:** Porfilio Silva, Personnel. **E-mail address:** silvap@bayltd.com. **World Wide Web address:** http://www.bayltd.com. **Description:** Provides construction and fabrication services to the petroleum industry. **NOTE:** Contact Personnel directly at 361/289-2400. **Corporate headquarters location:** This location. **Other area locations:** Friendswood TX. **Other U.S. locations:** Amerlia LA. **International location:** Mexico. **Parent company:** Berry Contracting Inc.

BELDON ROOFING COMPANY
P.O. Box 13380, San Antonio TX 78213. 210/341-3100. **Physical address:** 5039 West Avenue, San Antonio TX 78213. **Toll-free phone:** 800/688-7663. **Fax:** 210/341-2959. **Contact:** Human Resources. **E-mail address:** greatjob@beldon.com. **World Wide Web address:** http://www.beldon.com. **Description:** A construction company that specializes in roofing and sheet metal work for all types of buildings. Founded in 1946. **NOTE:** Please visit website to view job listings and access online application. Please note whether your desired position requires an online application. Resumes are not kept on file. **Positions advertised include:** Roofer; Sheet Metal Installer. **Office hours:** Monday - Friday, 8:00 a.m. - 5:00 p.m.

BERNARD JOHNSON YOUNG, INC.
9050 North Capital of Texas Highway, Building 3, Suite 170, Austin TX 78759. 512/231-8900. **Fax:** 512/231-9052. **Contact:** Human Resources. **World Wide Web address:** http://www.bjy.com/phoenix. **Description:**

An architectural engineering firm. The company also provides technical services, using the Internet to provide a full-time video link to customers. **Special programs:** Internships. **Corporate headquarters location:** This location. **Other area locations:** Dallas TX; Houston TX. **Other U.S. locations:** Rockville MD; Washington D.C.; Peoria IL; Phoenix AZ; American Fork UT; Pleasanton CA. **Operations at this facility include:** Administration; Regional Headquarters; Research and Development; Sales. **Listed on:** Privately held.

J.C. EVANS CONSTRUCTION COMPANY
P.O. Box 9647, Leander TX 78641. **Physical address:** 301 County Road 271, Leander TX 78646, 512/244-1400. **Fax:** 512/244-1900. **Contact:** Human Resources. **World Wide Web address:** http://www.jcevans.com. **Description:** A general contracting company. **Positions advertised include:** Concrete Finisher. **Corporate headquarters location:** This location.

FINSA INDUSTRIAL PARKS
973 South Minnesota, Brownsville TX 78521. 956/550-9017. **Contact:** Human Resources. **World Wide Web address:** http://www.finsa.net. **Description:** A company that constructs, owns, sells, and leases industrial park property.

LAUREN ENGINEERS & CONSTRUCTORS
901 South First Street, Abilene TX 79602. 915/670-9660. **Fax:** 915/670-9663. **Contact:** Human Resources. **E-mail address:** hr@laurenec.com. **World Wide Web address:** http://www.laurenec.com. **Description:** Designs and builds power plants, refineries, and related large-scale projects. **Positions advertised include:** Process Engineering Manager; Senior Mechanical Engineer. **Corporate headquarters location:** This location.

LYDA COMPANY
P.O. Box 680907, San Antonio TX 78268. 210/684-1770. **Contact:** Human Resources. **Description:** One of the largest general commercial contractors in Texas. Past projects included the Alamo Dome.

O'HAIR SHUTTERS
P.O. Box 2764, Lubbock TX 79408. 806/765-5791. **Toll-free phone:** 800/582-2625. **Fax:** 888/765-7140. **Contact:** Human Resources. **World Wide Web address:** http://www.ohair.com. **Description:** Manufactures outdoor shutters for homes. **Corporate headquarters location:** This location.

H.B. ZACHRY COMPANY
537 Logwood, San Antonio TX 78221. 210/475-8000. **Fax:** 210/475-8775. **Recorded jobline:** 800/JOB-SUSA. **Contact:** Larry Cantwell, Professional Employment Manager. **World Wide Web address:** http://www.zachry.com. **Description:** A construction management company operating through the following seven divisions: Process, Power, Heavy, Maintenance & Service, Commercial, International, and

Pipeline. The company primarily builds power plants, highways, and pipelines in the southern United States, as well as in foreign countries. H.B. Zachry Company does not handle residential construction contracts. Founded in 1923. **NOTE:** Entry-level positions are offered. This company's website has a complete job listings on its website. Apply online. **Positions advertised include:** Documents Controls; Legal Secretary; Construction Electrical Facilitator; Design Technician; Mechanical Equipment Reliability Improvement Coordinator; Maintenance Supervisor; Civil Field Superintendents; Secretary **Special programs:** Summer Jobs. **Corporate headquarters location:** This location. **Listed on:** Privately held.

ARTS, ENTERTAINMENT, SPORTS, AND RECREATION

**You can expect to find the following types of companies
in this section:**
Botanical and Zoological Gardens • Entertainment Groups • Motion
Picture and Video Tape Production and Distribution • Museums and Art
Galleries • Physical Fitness Facilities • Professional Sports Clubs;
Sporting and Recreational Camps • Public Golf Courses and Racing and
Track Operations • Theatrical Producers and Services

AUSTIN MUSEUM OF ART
823 Congress Avenue, Austin TX 78701. 512/495-9224. **Fax:** 512/496-
9159. **Contact:** Human Resources. **E-mail address:** jobs@aoma.org.
World Wide Web address: http://www.amoa.org. **Description:** This
museum's collection includes outdoor sculptures. Paintings, photos, and
drawings are also on display. The property for this location was donated
in 1970s. It also houses an art school.

AUSTIN NATURE CENTER
301 Nature Center Drive, Austin TX 78746. 512/327-8181. **Fax:** 512/306-
8470. **Contact:** Personnel. **World Wide Web address:**
http://www.ci.austin.tx.us/ansc/ http://www.ci.austin.tx.us/ansc.
Description: An indoor/outdoor nature center housing exhibits, live
animals, interactive games, and discovery labs. Austin Nature Center is
situated on an 80-acre preserve, with more than two miles of hiking trails.
NOTE: Volunteer positions are also available.

CERUTTI PRODUCTIONS
3410 Saddle Point, San Antonio TX 78259-3625. 210/403-0800.
Contact: Mark Cerutti, President. **E-mail address:** Marc@Cerutti.org.
World Wide Web address: http://www.filcro.com/cerutti.html.
Description: A video production studio offering talent, engineering, and
technical services. **NOTE:** See website for instructions about how to
submit resumes and portfolio items. **Positions advertised include:**
Production Assistants; Writers; Post Production Assistants; Marketing
Assistants; Sales Representatives; Voice-over talent. **Listed on:**
Privately held.

EL PASO ASSOCIATION FOR THE PERFORMING ARTS
P.O. Box 31340, El Paso TX 79931. 915/565-6900. **Contact:** Human
Resources. **World Wide Web address:** http://www.viva-ep.org.
Description: Hosts various Shakespeare productions in conjunction with
the McKelligon Canyon Amphitheater (also at this location).

GREATER TUNA CORPORATION
3660 Stone Ridge Road, Suite C101, Austin TX 78746. 512/328-8862.
Fax: 512/347-8975. **Contact:** Human Resources. **World Wide Web**

address: http://www.greatertuna.com. **Description:** Produces a variety of comedic theater performances including *Greater Tuna,* a political satire shown in theaters nationwide. Other shows have included *A Tuna Christmas* and *Red, White and Tuna.*

LADY BIRD JOHNSON WILDFLOWER CENTER
4801 La Crosse Avenue, Austin TX 78739. 512/292-4200. **Contact:** Human Resources. **World Wide Web address:** http://www.wildflower.org. **Description:** A nonprofit organization that serves to educate people on the value and beauty of native plants. Lady Bird Johnson Wildflower Center also houses Wild Ideas: The Store, a retail store offering books, art, and clothing dedicated to generating an interest in plant life; and The Wildflower Cafe, a coffee shop and eatery. **Special programs:** Internships. **Corporate headquarters location:** This location.

SEA WORLD OF TEXAS
10500 Sea World Drive, San Antonio TX 78251-3002. 210/523-3198. **Contact:** Human Resources. **World Wide Web address:** http://www.seaworld.com. **Description:** Sea World is home to all types of marine life, and includes such entertainment as shows, exhibits, and a water park. **NOTE:** Seasonal, professional and hourly positions offered. Apply at the nearest Sea World location. **Special programs:** Student and Senior Employment.

SIX FLAGS FIESTA TEXAS
17000 Interstate Highway 10 West, San Antonio TX 78257. 210/697-5000. **Contact:** Human Resources. **World Wide Web address:** http://www.sixflags.com. **Description:** A theme park offering attractions, shows, and a water park. **NOTE:** Full-time, part-time and seasonal positions offered. Apply in person or online at the company's website. **Positions advertised include:** Admissions Attendant; Food Services Assistant; Merchandise Host Assistant; Technician. **Office hours:** Monday – Sunday, 9:00 a.m. – 5:00 p.m. **Parent company:** Premier Parks (OK) owns and operates 35 theme parks nationwide.

WESTERN PLAYLAND INC.
6900 Delta Drive, El Paso TX 79905. 915/772-3953. **Contact:** Human Resources. **World Wide Web address:** http://www.westernplayland.com. **Description:** An amusement park. **NOTE:** A completed application is required for any position. Download application online and mail it.

ZILKER BOTANICAL GARDEN
2220 Barton Springs Road, Austin TX 78746. 512/477-8672. **Contact:** Human Resources. **World Wide Web address:** http://www.zilkergarden.org. **Description:** Covering 22 acres of land, Zilker Botanical Garden is comprised of a multitude of individual gardens including Xeriscape Garden, Herb and Fragrance Garden, and Rose Garden. **Special programs:** Volunteer.

AUTOMOTIVE

You can expect to find the following types of companies in this section:
Automotive Repair Shops • Automotive Stampings • Industrial Vehicles and Moving Equipment • Motor Vehicles and Equipment • Travel Trailers and Campers

---

PAK-MORLTD.
2191 Rudeloff Road, Seguin TX 781055. 830/303-7256. **Contact:** Human Resources. **Description:** A manufacturer of refuse trucking equipment. **Corporate headquarters location:** This location.

TRICO TECHNOLOGIES
1995 Billy Mitchell Boulevard, Brownsville TX 78521. 956/544-2722. **Fax:** 956/827-3272. **Contact:** Human Resources. **World Wide Web address:** http://www.tricoproducts.com. **Description:** A manufacturer of windshield wipers. **Special programs:** Training. **Corporate headquarters location:** Rochester Hills MI.

BANKING, SAVINGS & LOANS, AND OTHER DEPOSITORY INSTITUTIONS

You can expect to find the following types of companies in this section:
Banks • Bank Holding Companies and Associations • Lending Firms/Financial Services Institutions

---

AMERICAN BANK
P.O. Box 6469, Corpus Christi TX 78466-6469. 361/992-9901. **Recorded jobline:** 361/653-5391. **Contact:** Human Resources. **E-mail address:** internetbanking@americanbank.com. **World Wide Web address:** http://www.americanbank.com. **Description:** A full-service bank with 10 locations. This location is its corporate office and main branch. Founded in 1971. **Positions advertised include:** E-Branch Officer; Teller Supervisor; Teller. **Other area locations include:** Port Aransas TX; Austin TX.

AMARILLO NATIONAL BANK
P.O. Box 1, Amarillo TX 79105. 806/378-8000. **Physical address:** 410 South Taylor, Amarillo TX 79101. **Fax:** 806/378-8066. **Contact:** Personnel. **World Wide Web address:** http://www.anb.com. **Description:** A full-service bank with 12 locations. Services include intra-bank funds transfers, mortgages, and online banking. **Corporate headquarters location:** This location. **Other area locations:** Statewide.

BANK OF AMERICA
303 West Wall Street, Midland TX 79701. 432/685-2000. **Contact:** Human Resources. **World Wide Web address:** http://www.bankofamerica.com. **Description:** Bank of America is a full-service banking and financial institution. The company operates through four business segments: Global Corporate and Investment Banking, Principal Investing and Asset Management, Commercial Banking, and Consumer Banking. **NOTE:** Please visit website to search for jobs and apply online. **Positions advertised include:** Teller. **Corporate headquarters location:** Charlotte NC. **Other area locations:** Statewide. **Operations at this facility include:** This location is a bank. **Listed on:** New York Stock Exchange. **Stock exchange symbol:** BAC.

CITICORP US SERVICE CENTER
100 Citibank Drive, San Antonio TX 78245-3214. 210/677-6500. **Fax:** 210/677-7047. **Contact:** Human Resources. **World Wide Web address:** http://careers.citibank.com/sanantonio. **Description:** A data and customer service center for the nationwide banking company.

FARM CREDIT BANK OF TEXAS
P.O. Box 15919, 6210 Highway 290 East, Austin TX 78723-1023. 512/465-0400. **Contact:** Human Resources. **World Wide Web address:**

http://www.farmcreditbank.com. **Corporate headquarters location:** This location. **Other area locations:** McKinney, Bowie, Mulesoe, Kenedy, Weatherford, Lubbock, and Robstown TX. **Description:** A bank that provides loans to the agricultural industry. **Positions advertised include:** Junior Loan Processor; Office/Clerical Assistant; Debt and Investment Accounting Analyst; Relationship Manager Trainee.

FIRST NATIONAL BANK OF ABILENE

P.O. Box 701, Abilene TX 79604. 915/627-7000. **Recorded jobline:** 325/627-7356. **Contact:** Pam Mann, Human Resources Director. **World Wide Web address:** http://www.fnbabilene.com. **Description:** A full-service bank that offers online banking, loan, and investment services. **NOTE:** Applicants should apply in person at the company's Human Resources offices at 400 Pine Street, Abilene TX. Online application can be found on the company's website. **Positions advertised include:** Teller; Cashier; Infrastructure Support Technician.

FROST NATIONAL BANK
CULLEN/FROST BANKERS, INC.

P.O. Box 1600, San Antonio TX 78296-1400. 210/220-4011. **Recorded jobline:** 210/220-5627. **Contact:** Human Resources. **World Wide Web address:** http://www.frostbank.com. **Description:** A bank that offers online banking, financial management, and loan services. There are 81 locations in major Texas cities. **NOTE:** Human Resources office hours vary from bank location. Check company's website for office hours and scheduling pre-employment tests. **Corporate headquarters location:** This location. **Other area locations:** Statewide. **Parent company:** Cullen/Frost Bankers, Inc.. **Listed on:** New York Stock Exchange. **Stock exchange symbol:** CFR.

INTERNATIONAL BANK OF COMMERCE

P.O. Box 1359, Laredo TX 78042-1359. 956/722-7611. **Physical address:** 1200 San Bernardo Avenue, Laredo TX 78042-1359. **Contact:** Human Resources. **World Wide Web address:** http://www.iboc.com. **Description:** A full-service bank with locations throughout Texas that offers checking and savings accounts, CDs, wire transfers, mortgage loans, ATMs, and Right Checking Accounts. **Corporate headquarters location:** This location.

LAREDO NATIONAL BANK

700 San Bernardo Avenue, Laredo TX 78040. 956/723-1151. **Contact:** Human Resources. **E-mail address:** lnbhr@lnb.com. **World Wide Web address:** http://www.lnb.com. **Description:** A full-service bank that markets its services to the Hispanic community. The bank offers checking and savings accounts, CDs, mortgages, and wire transfers. **NOTE:** This company requires its employees to speak English and Spanish. **Positions advertised include:** Teller. **Other area locations:** Austin TX; Brownsville TX; Corpus Christi TX; Houston TX: Dallas TX: McAllen TX.

WELLS FARGO BANK
P.O. Box 1241, Lubbock TX 79408-1241. 806/765-8861. **Physical address:** 1500 Broadway Street, Lubbock TX 79401. **Contact:** Human Resources. **World Wide Web address:** http://www.wellsfargo.com. **Description:** A diversified financial institution with more than $200 billion in assets. Wells Fargo serves more than 17 million customers through 5,000 independent locations worldwide. The company also maintains several stand-alone ATMs and branches within other retail outlets. Services include community banking, credit and debit cards, home equity and mortgage loans, online banking, student loans, and insurance. Wells Fargo also offers a complete line of commercial and institutional financial services. Founded in 1852. This location provides notary service and Spanish-speaking tellers. **Positions advertised include:** Banker; Teller. **NOTE:** Jobseekers are encouraged to submit resumes via the Website: http://www.wfjobs.com. **Corporate headquarters location:** San Francisco CA. **Other U.S. locations:** Nationwide. **International locations:** Worldwide. **Listed on:** New York Stock Exchange. **Stock exchange symbol:** WFC. **Number of employees worldwide:** 123,000.

WELLS FARGO BANK
P.O. Box 1891, San Angelo TX 76902. 915/657-8600. **Physical address:** 36 West Beauregard Avenue, San Angelo TX 76903. **Contact:** Human Resources. **World Wide Web address:** http://www.wellsfargo.com. **Description:** A main branch location of Wells Fargo, a diversified financial institution billions of dollars in assets. In addition to commercial and institutional financing, this location offers its customers Spanish-speaking services and a notary public. **Positions advertised include:** Banker; Teller. **NOTE:** Jobseekers are encouraged to submit resumes via the Website: http://www.wfjobs.com. **Corporate headquarters location:** San Francisco CA. **Other U.S. locations:** Nationwide. **International locations:** Worldwide. **Listed on:** New York Stock Exchange. **Stock exchange symbol:** WFC. **Number of employees worldwide:** 123,000.

WELLS FARGO BANK
P.O. Box 1790, Alice TX 78333. 361/668-2400. **Physical address:** 601 East Main Street, Alice TX 78332. **Contact:** Human Resources. **World Wide Web address:** http://www.wellsfargo.com. **Description:** A worldwide diversified financial institution. Services at this location include: A talking ATM; Spanish-speaking tellers; a notary; and wheelchair access. **Positions advertised include:** Banker; Teller. **NOTE:** Jobseekers are encouraged to submit resumes via the Website: http://www.wfjobs.com. **Corporate headquarters location:** San Francisco CA. **Other U.S. locations:** Nationwide. **International locations:** Worldwide. **Listed on:** New York Stock Exchange. **Stock exchange symbol:** WFC. **Number of employees worldwide:** 123,000.

WELLS FARGO BANK
P.O. Box 699, Laredo TX 78042. 956/726-8200. **Physical address:** 1100 Matamoros Street, Laredo TX 78040. **Contact:** Human Resources. **World Wide Web address:** http://www.wellsfargo.com. **Description:** A

diversified financial institution with more than 17 million customers through 5,300 independent locations worldwide. The company also maintains several stand-alone ATMs and branches. Wells Fargo also offers a complete line of commercial and institutional financial services. Founded in 1852. Services at this location include cashier checks; notary services; traveler's checks and Spanish-speaking tellers. This location is also wheelchair accessible. **Positions advertised include:** Banker; Teller. **NOTE:** Jobseekers are encouraged to submit resumes via the Website: http://www.wfjobs.com. **Corporate headquarters location:** San Francisco CA. **Other U.S. locations:** Nationwide. **International locations:** Worldwide. **Listed on:** New York Stock Exchange. **Stock exchange symbol:** WFC. **Number of employees worldwide:** 123,000.

BIOTECHNOLOGY, PHARMACEUTICALS, AND SCIENTIFIC R&D

You can expect to find the following types of companies in this section:
Clinical Labs • Lab Equipment Manufacturers • Pharmaceutical Manufacturers and Distributors

---

DPT LABORATORIES INC.
307 East Josephine Street, San Antonio TX 78215. 210/223-3281. **Fax:** 210/476-0794. **Contact:** Human Resources. **E-mail address:** hr.sa@dptlabs.com. **World Wide Web address:** http://www.dptlabs.com. **Description:** Provides pharmaceutical manufacturing and development services from prototype development to worldwide distribution. **NOTE:** Entry-level positions and second and third shifts are offered. Corporate headquarters location: 318 McCullough Street, San Antonio TX. **Positions advertised include:** Packaging Engineer; Industrial Engineer; Account Coordinator; Administrative Assistant.

LABORATORY CORPORATION OF AMERICA (LABCORP)
4207 James Casey Street, Suite 101, Austin TX 78745. 512/443-0538. **Fax:** 210/735-0512. **Contact:** Human Resources. **World Wide Web address:** http://www.labcorp.com. **Description:** One of the nation's leading clinical laboratory companies, providing services primarily to physicians, hospitals, clinics, nursing homes, and other clinical labs nationwide. LabCorp performs tests on blood, urine, and other body fluids and tissue, aiding the diagnosis of disease. **NOTE:** This company has locations in Houston and Dallas. For a complete list of jobs and locations, see the company's website. **Corporate headquarters location:** Burlington NC. **Other U.S. locations:** Nationwide. **Operations at this facility include:** This location is a blood-drawing facility. **Listed on:** New York Stock Exchange. **Stock exchange symbol:** LH. **Number of employees nationwide:** 19,600.

McNEIL CONSUMER & SPECIALTY PHARMACEUTICALS
4001 North Interstate Highway 35, Round Rock TX 78664. 512/255-4111. **Contact:** Human Resources. **Description:** A scientific research and development company that is also involved in the manufacturing of pharmaceutical products. McNeil is a subsidiary of Johnson and Johnson. **NOTE:** Interested jobseekers should apply online at Johnson and Johnson's corporate website: http://www.jnj.com/careers.

PPD DEVELOPMENT
4009 Banister Lane, Austin TX 78704. 512/447-2663. **Contact:** Human Resources. **World Wide Web address:** http://www.ppdi.com. **Description:** Provides research and development services for companies in the biotechnology and pharmaceutical industries.

Positions advertised include: Clinical Data Associate; Project Manager; Clinical Research Associate; Project Manager; Medical Writer; Senior Scientist. **Parent company:** PPD, Inc. **Listed on:** NASDAQ. **Stock exchange symbol:** PPDI.

PHARMERICA
3019 Interstate Drive, San Antonio TX 78219. 210/227-5262. **Contact:** Human Resources. **World Wide Web address:** http://www.pharmerica.com. **Description:** A supplier of pharmaceuticals and related products to long-term care facilities, hospitals, and assisted living communities. PharMerica also provides nurse consultant services, infusion therapy and training, medical records consulting, and educational programs. This company has locations throughout Texas and the United States. **NOTE:** PharMerica lists its Texas locations on its website and job listings for each location. Interested jobseekers are encouraged to visit the website and apply online. **Corporate headquarters location:** Tampa FL.

SOUTHWEST RESEARCH INSTITUTE
P.O. Drawer 28510, San Antonio TX 78228-0510. 210/522-2223. **Physical address:** 6220 Culebra Road, San Antonio TX 78238. **Fax:** 210/522-3990. **Contact:** Human Resources. **E-mail address:** humanresources@swri.org. **World Wide Web address:** http://www.swri.org. **Description:** An independent, nonprofit, applied engineering and physical science research and development organization. Research is conducted in areas such as automation, intelligent systems, and advanced computer technology; biosciences/bioengineering; nuclear waste regulatory analyses; electronic systems and instrumentation; encapsulation and polymer research; engines, fuels, and lubricants; environmental science; fire technology; fluid and machinery dynamics; engineering and materials sciences; nondestructive evaluation research and development; and space sciences. **Special programs:** Internships. **Corporate headquarters location:** This location. **Listed on:** Privately held. **Number of employees nationwide:** 2,800.

TEXAS VETERINARY MEDICAL DIAGNOSTIC LABORATORY
P.O. Box 3200, Amarillo TX 79116-3200. 806/353-7478. **Physical address:** 6610 Amarillo Boulevard West, Amarillo TX 79106. **Toll-free phone:** 888/646-5624. **Fax:** 806/359-0636. **Contact:** Human Resources. **World Wide Web address:** http:// tvmdl.tamu.edu. **Description:** A diagnostic laboratory that performs medical testing on animals to assist veterinarians with diagnosis and prognosis. Test fields include chemistry, hematology, urology, toxicology, serology, histology, bacteriology, and necropsies. **Office hours:** Monday - Friday, 8:00 a.m. - 5:00 p.m.; Saturday, 8:00 a.m. - 12:00 p.m. **Other U.S. locations:** College Station TX; Gonzales TX; Center TX.

BUSINESS SERVICES & NON-SCIENTIFIC RESEARCH

You can expect to find the following types of companies in this section:
Adjustment and Collection Services • Cleaning, Maintenance, and Pest Control Services • Credit Reporting Services • Detective, Guard, and Armored Car Services • Security Systems Services • Miscellaneous Equipment Rental and Leasing • Secretarial and Court Reporting Services

ADT SECURITY SERVICES
1817 West Breaker Lane, Suite 400, Austin TX 78758-3605. 512/832-0122. **Fax:** 512/832-2988. **Contact:** Paul Ebersol, Human Resources. **World Wide Web address:** http://www.adtsecurityservices.com. **Description:** Designs, installs, sells, and monitors fire and burglar alarm systems for commercial and industrial retail customers. ADT Security also offers armed and unarmed security guards. **Corporate headquarters location:** Boca Raton FL. **Parent company:** Tyco International, Ltd. **Listed on:** New York Stock Exchange. **Stock exchange symbol:** TYC. **Number of employees nationwide:** 15,000.

ADT SECURITY SERVICES
140 Heimer Road, Suite 100, San Antonio TX 78232. 210/491-0300. **Fax:** 210/491-3259. **Contact:** Sandy McDonald, Human Resources. **World Wide Web address:** http://www.adtsecurityservices.com. **Description:** Designs, installs, sells, and monitors fire and burglar alarm systems for commercial and industrial retail customers. ADT Security also offers armed and unarmed security guards. **NOTE:** Contact Human Resources directly at 310/491-3231. **Corporate headquarters location:** Boca Raton FL. **Parent company:** Tyco International, Ltd. **Listed on:** New York Stock Exchange. **Stock exchange symbol:** TYC. **Number of employees nationwide:** 15,000.

ALLIED SECURITY INC.
9027 North Gate Boulevard, Suite 110, Austin TX 78758. 512/836-8599. **Fax:** 512/836-8579. **Contact:** Human Resources. **World Wide Web address:** http://www.alliedsecurity.com. **Description:** One of the largest contract security officer companies in the nation. Allied Security provides loss prevention services to private businesses and government agencies. **NOTE:** Please visit website to fill out online application form. **Corporate headquarters location:** King of Prussia PA. **Other area locations:** Dallas TX; Houston TX; San Antonio TX. **Other U.S. locations:** Nationwide.

ALLIED SECURITY INC.
1635 NE Loop 410, Suite 206, San Antonio TX 78209. 210/829-1711. **Fax:** 210/829-1731. **Contact:** Human Resources. **World Wide Web address:** http://www.alliedsecurity.com. **Description:** One of the largest

contract security officer companies in the nation. Allied Security provides loss prevention services to private businesses and government agencies. **NOTE:** Please visit website to fill out online application form. **Corporate headquarters location:** King of Prussia PA. **Other area locations:** Dallas TX; Houston TX; San Antonio TX. **Other U.S. locations:** Nationwide.

THE BENCHMARK COMPANY
907 South Congress Avenue, Suite 7, Austin TX 78704. 512/707-7500. **Fax:** 512/707-7757. **Contact:** Human Resources Department. **E-mail address:** thebenc@earthlink.net. **World Wide Web address:** http://www.thebenchmarkcompany.net. **Description:** Gathers data and research about radio listeners. Benchmark is also involved in researching broadcasting companies. **President/CEO:** Dr. Robert E. Balon.

FIRST AMERICAN FLOOD DATA SERVICES
11902 Burnet Road, Suite 400, Austin TX 78758. 512/834-9595. **Toll-free number:** 800/447-1772. **Fax:** 800/447-2258. **Contact:** Judy Ellison, Human Resources Director. **World Wide Web address:** http://floodcert.com. **Description:** Determines whether properties are in a flood zone for mortgage companies and banks.

HOOVER'S, INC.
5800 Airport Boulevard, Austin TX 78752. 512/374-4500. **Fax:** 512/374-4501. **Contact:** Human Resources. **World Wide Web address:** http://www.hoovers.com. **Description:** A leading provider of business information for sales, marketing, business development, and other professionals who need intelligence on U.S. and global companies, industries, and people. This information is available through an online service, corporate intranets and distribution agreements with licensees, as well as via print and CD-ROM products. **NOTE:** Search and apply for positions online. **Positions advertised include:** Applications Manager; Direct Marketing Program Coordinator; Director of Retention Marketing; Editorial Operations Analyst; Industry Editor; Product Marketing Specialist - Large Accounts; Product Training Manager; Sales Manager; Sales Operations Analyst; Saleslogix Programmer; VP Acquisition Marketing; VP Managing Editor. **Parent company:** Dun & Bradstreet.

INITIAL SECURITY
3355 Cherry Ridge, Suite 200, San Antonio TX 78230. 210/349-6321. **Toll-free phone:** 800/683-7771. **Fax:** 210/349-0213. **Contact:** Human Resources. **E-mail address:** initial@initialsecurity.com. **World Wide Web address:** http://www.initialsecurity.com. **Description:** Offers security guard services throughout the greater San Antonio area. **NOTE:** This company offers entry-level positions and training.

LOOMIS, FARGO & COMPANY
611 South Presa Street, San Antonio TX 78210. 210/226-0195. **Contact:** Human Resources. **World Wide Web address:** http://www.loomisfargo.com. **Description:** Provides armored

transportation, cash vault, and ATM services. **NOTE:** This company has locations throughout Texas and the United States. See the company's website for job listings by location and for mailing addresses. **Corporate headquarters location:** Houston TX. **Other U.S. locations:** Nationwide.

MANN & MANN MEDIA SERVICES, INC.
84 NE Loop 410, Suite 126, San Antonio TX 78216. 210/525-8148. **Fax:** 210/525-8246. **Contact:** Wanda Mann, President. **Description:** A media buying firm. Mann & Mann Media Services serves as a negotiator between advertisers and radio and television stations, newspapers, and magazines. Founded in 1986. **Corporate headquarters location:** This location. **Listed on:** Privately held.

QUANTUM RESEARCH INTERNATIONAL
7505B Lockheed Drive, El Paso TX 79925. 915/772-2700. **Fax:** 915/772-2250. **Contact:** Human Resources. **World Wide Web address:** http://www.quantum-intl.com. **Description:** Engaged in weapons research and general engineering for the army. **NOTE:** Mail resumes to 991 Discovery Drive, Huntsville, AL 35806; or fax them to 256/971-1802; or e-mail them to personnel@quantum-intl.com. **Corporate headquarters location:** Huntsville AL.

SECURITAS
5825 Callaghan, Suite 107, San Antonio TX 78228. 210/647-9770. **Fax:** 210/543-1102. **Contact:** Melissa Perze, Human Resources. **World Wide Web address:** http://www.securitasinc.com. **Description:** A security service that sends guards to secure various locations and functions. **Corporate headquarters location:** Chicago IL. **Parent company:** Securitas AB (Sweden). **Number of employees nationwide:** 93,000.

WEST TELESERVICES
10931 Laureate Drive, Building 3000, San Antonio TX 78249. 210/690-6900. **Toll-free phone:** 800/521-6000. **Contact:** Human Resources. **World Wide Web address:** http://www.west.com. **Description:** A telemarketing company that deals with both outbound (phone sales) and inbound (phone orders) calls. This location handles inbound and outbound calling for *Fortune* 500 companies. **NOTE:** This company requires that interested jobseekers apply in person. The website provides job listings for each location as well as location addresses and office hours. **Positions advertised include:** Customer Service Representative; Interactive Sales Representative; Marketing Representative; Teleservices Representative. **Special programs:** Internships. **Other area locations:** Beaumont TX; El Paso TX; Harlingen TX; Killeen TX; Lubbock TX; Universal City TX; Waco TX; Sherman TX. **Listed on:** NASDAQ. **Stock exchange symbol:** WSTC.

CHARITIES AND SOCIAL SERVICES

You can expect to find the following types of companies in this section:
Social and Human Service Agencies • Job Training and Vocational Rehabilitation Services • Nonprofit Organizations

AIDS SERVICES OF AUSTIN
P.O. Box 4874, Austin TX 78765. 512/458-2437. **Fax:** 512/452-3299. **Contact:** Personnel. **E-mail address:** asa.mail@asaustin.org. **World Wide Web address:** http://www.asaustin.org. **Description:** This organization has 600 volunteers that work together to assist the community and individuals who are HIV-positive. AIDS Services of Austin is involved in philanthropy, wellness educational programs, safe sex seminars, counseling, and financial aid for HIV-positive individuals. **NOTE:** Volunteer positions are also available. **Special programs:** Internship. **Office hours:** Monday – Friday, 8:30 a.m. – 5:30 p.m.

AMERICAN RED CROSS
3642 East Houston Street, San Antonio TX 78219. 210/224-5151. **Toll-free phone:** 800/775-6803. Fax: 210/226-9973. **Contact:** Human Resources. **E-mail address:** infosatx@usa.redcross.org. **World Wide Web address:** http://www.saredcross.org. **Description:** A humanitarian organization that aids disaster victims, gathers blood for crisis distribution, trains individuals to respond to emergencies, educates individuals on various diseases, and raises funds for other charitable establishments. **NOTE:** Please visit website to view job listings and to fill out online job application. **Positions advertised include:** Instructor; Associate Director of Financial Development. **Corporate headquarters location:** Washington D.C.

BETTY HARDWICK CENTER
2616 South Clack, Abilene TX 79606. 325/690-5100. **Fax:** 325/690-5136. **Contact:** Human Resources. **World Wide Web address:** http://bhcmhmr.org. **Description:** An outpatient counseling facility for mentally challenged people. **NOTE:** Please visit website to view jobs listings and apply online. **Positions advertised include:** Contract Foster Care Provider; HCS Trainer; Skills Trainer.

HARMONY FAMILY SERVICES
1111 Industrial Boulevard, Abilene TX 79602. 915/691-2800. **Contact:** Human Resources. **Description:** A social services agency that offers many programs including a residential treatment center for runaway and homeless youths.

MARTIN LUTHER HOMES OF TEXAS INC.
332 South Loop 123 Business, Suite 400, Seguin TX 78155. 830/372-3075. **Contact:** Human Resources. **World Wide Web address:**

http://www.mosiacinfo.org. **Description:** An agency that provides housing and support services for individuals with mental retardation. This company is now part of Mosaic, an organization created by the Lutheran Church.

OAKS TREATMENT CENTER
1407 West Stassney Lane, Austin TX 78745. 512/464-0200. **Toll-free phone:** 800/843-6257. **Fax:** 512/464-0439. **Contact:** Human Resources. **World Wide Web address:** http://www.psysolutions.com/facilities/oaks. **Description:** A residential and treatment center for children and young adults with behavioral, emotional, or developmental disabilities. **NOTE:** See website for job listings. **Positions advertised include:** Speech/Language Pathologist; Occupational Therapist; Collector; RN. **Corporate headquarters location:** This location. **Parent company:** Psychiatric Solutions Inc. (PSI).

PANHANDLE COMMUNITY SERVICES
P.O. Box 763, Clarendon TX 79226. 806/874-2573. **Contact:** Human Resources. **Description:** Offers housing, energy, transportation, and food banks for homeless and low-income families.

CHEMICALS, RUBBER, AND PLASTICS

You can expect to find the following types of companies in this section:
Adhesives, Detergents, Inks, Paints, Soaps, Varnishes • Agricultural Chemicals and Fertilizers • Carbon and Graphite Products • Chemical Engineering Firms • Industrial Gases

CAPROCK MANUFACTURING, INC.
2303 120th Street, Lubbock TX 79423. 806/745-6454. **Fax:** 806/745-9441. **Contact:** Human Resources. **E-mail address:** caprock@caprock-mfg.com. **World Wide Web address:** http://www.caprock-mfg.com. **Description:** A plastic injection molding company that manufactures plastic parts for cellular phones including phone windows and battery cases. Founded 1983. **NOTE:** Second and third shifts are offered. **Corporate headquarters location:** This location. **Listed on:** Privately held. **President:** Ryan Provenzano. **Number of employees at this location:** 160.

CELANESE AG
Highway 77 South, P.O. Box 428, Bishop TX 78343. 361/584-6000. **Fax:** 361/584-6606. **Contact:** Human Resources. **World Wide Web address:** http://www.celanese.com. **Description:** A manufacturing plant producing chemicals and plastics. Celanese AG is an industrial chemical company operating in five business segments: Acetyl Products; Chemical Intermediates; Celanese Acetate Textiles; Ticona Technical Polymers; and Nutrovina Performance Products. **Special programs:** Internships; Co-ops. **Other area locations:** Bay City TX; Corpus Christi TX; Dallas TX; Pampa TX; Pasadena TX. **Other U.S. locations:** Nationwide. **Listed on:** New York Stock Exchange. **Stock exchange symbol:** CZ. **Number of employees worldwide:** 9,500.

E.I. DUPONT DE NEMOURS & COMPANY
P.O. Box 2626, Victoria TX 77902-2626. 361/572-1111. **Physical address:** 2695 Old Bloomington Road North, Victoria TX 77905. **Contact:** Human Resources. **World Wide Web address:** http://www.dupont.com. **Description:** E.I. DuPont de Nemours & Company's activities include the manufacturing of biomedical, industrial, and consumer products (such as photographic, data-recording, and video devices); the production of man-made fiber products (with applications in a variety of consumer and commercial industries); polymer products (such as plastic resins, elastomers, and films); agricultural and industrial chemicals (such as herbicides and insecticides, pigments, fluorochemicals, petroleum additives, and mineral acids); the exploration and production of crude oil and natural gas; the refining, marketing, and downstream transportation of petroleum; and the mining and distribution of steam and metallurgical coals. The company supplies the aerospace, agricultural, apparel, transportation, health care,

and printing and publishing industries. **NOTE:** Job openings and online application can be found at http://www.careers.DuPont.com. **Corporate headquarters location:** Wilmington DE. **Operations at this facility include:** This location is a chemical processing plant. **Listed on:** New York Stock Exchange. **Listed on:** New York Stock Exchange. **Stock exchange symbol:** DD. **Number of employees worldwide:** 77,000.

FLINT HILLS RESOURCES LP
P.O. Box 2608, Corpus Christi TX 78403-2608. 361/241-4811. **Physical address:** 2825 Suntide Road, Corpus Christi TX 78410. **Contact:** Human Resources. **World Wide Web address:** http://www.fhr.com. **Description:** A manufacturer of chemicals. **Positions advertised include:** Product Specialist; Senior Process Engineer. **Corporate headquarters location:** Wichita KS. **Other area locations:** Austin TX; Ft. Worth TX. **Parent company:** Koch Industries.

INDUSTRIAL MOLDING CORPORATION
616 East Slaton Road, Lubbock TX 79404. 806/474-1000. **Contact:** Keri Mathews, Human Resources Manager. **World Wide Web address:** http://www.indmolding.com. **Description:** Manufactures injection molded plastics. **Corporate headquarters location:** This location.

TORO IRRIGATION
9455 Railroad Drive, El Paso TX 79924-6702. 915/757-2586. **Contact:** Human Resources. **Description:** Manufactures and assembles plastic molding injections for the irrigation industry. **Corporate headquarters location:** Riverside CA.

COMMUNICATIONS:TELECOMMUNICATIONS AND BROADCASTING

You can expect to find the following types of companies in this section:
Cable/Pay Television Services • Communications Equipment • Radio and Television Broadcasting Stations • Telephone, Telegraph, and Other Message Communications

CLEAR CHANNEL COMMUNICATIONS
200 Basse Road, San Antonio TX 78209. 210/822-2828. **Fax:** 210/822-2299. **Contact:** Personnel. **World Wide Web address:** http://www.clearchannel.com. **Description:** A nationwide television and radio broadcasting company. Clear Channel Communications operates approximately 1,225 radio and 37 television stations in the United States. **NOTE:** Please visit http://www.clearcareers.com to search for jobs and apply online. Clear Channel also has a location in Corpus Christi TX. To apply or for more information, e-mail the company at corpuschristijobs@clearchannel.com. **Positions advertised include:** Treasury Analyst; Photographer – Part-time; Production Assistant; Traffic Anchor; Traffic Department; Payroll Tax Specialist. **Corporate headquarters location:** This location. **Listed on:** New York Stock Exchange. **Stock exchange symbol:** CCU.

KFDA-TV
NEWS CHANNEL 10
P.O. Box 10, Amarillo TX 79105. 806/383-1010. **Contact:** Human Resources. **World Wide Web address:** http://www.newschannel10.com. **Description:** A CBS-affiliated television broadcasting station.

KLBK-TV
7403 South University Avenue, Lubbock TX 79423. 806/745-2345. **Contact:** Human Resources. **World Wide Web address:** http://www.klbk.com. **Description:** A CBS-affiliated television broadcasting station.

KVII-TV
One Broadcast Center, Amarillo TX 79101. 806/373-1787. **Contact:** Human Resources. **World Wide Web address:** http://www.kvii.com. **Description:** An ABC-affiliated television broadcasting station.

QVC INC.
9855 West Stover Hills Boulevard, San Antonio TX 78251. 210/522-4300. **Recorded jobline:** 866/782-4473. **Contact:** Human Resources. **World Wide Web address:** http://www.qvc.com. **Description:** A nationwide home shopping television network. **NOTE:** QVC has offices throughout the U.S. See website for job listings. **Operations at this location:** Service center.

SBC COMMUNICATIONS INC.
SOUTHWESTERN BELL
175 East Houston Street, San Antonio TX 78205. 210/821-4105. **Recorded jobline:** 210/820-6832. **Contact:** Human Resources. **World Wide Web address:** http://www.sbc.com. **Description:** Provides telecommunications products and services throughout the United States and internationally. **NOTE:** SBC's website provides job listings for all its Texas locations. See website for listings and application information. **Corporate headquarters location:** This location. **Subsidiaries include:** Ameritech, CellularOne, Nevada Bell, Pacific Bell, SBC Telecom, SNET, and Southwestern Bell (also at this location) provides local telephone and cellular services. **Listed on:** New York Stock Exchange. **Stock exchange symbol:** SBC. **Number of employees worldwide:** 168,000.

VTEL CORPORATION
9208 Waterford Centre Boulevard, Austin TX 78758. 512/821-7000. **Contact:** Human Resources. **World Wide Web address:** http://www.vtel.com. **Description:** A leading provider of interactive videoconferencing systems in the distance learning and health care markets. VTEL products are distributed primarily through resellers and co-marketers. **NOTE:** Fax resumes to Amanda in Human Resources at 512/821-7133. **Corporate headquarters location:** This location. **Listed on:** Privately held.

VERIZON COMMUNICATIONS
LAW ENFORCEMENT ASSISTANCE
2701 South Johnson Street, San Angelo TX 76904. **Toll-free phone:** 888/483-2600. **Contact:** Human Resources. **World Wide Web address:** http://www.verizon.com. **Description:** A full-service communications services provider. **NOTE:** Resumes must be submitted via the Website: http://www.verizon.com/careers. **Corporate headquarters location:** New York NY. **Listed on:** New York Stock Exchange. **Stock exchange symbol:** VZ.

XEROX OMNIFAX
9715 Burnet Road, Austin TX 78758. **Toll-free phone:** 800/221-5566. **Fax:** 512/719-5567 **Contact:** Human Resources. **World Wide Web address:** http://www.omnifax.com. **Description:** Manufactures communications systems, telewriters, and facsimile recording devices. **NOTE:** Apply online at the parent company's website: http://www.xerox.com. **Parent company:** Xerox Corporation. **Listed on:** New York Stock Exchange. **Stock exchange symbol:** XRX.

COMPUTER HARDWARE, SOFTWARE, AND SERVICES

You can expect to find the following types of companies in this section:
Computer Components and Hardware Manufacturers • Consultants and Computer Training Companies • Internet and Online Service Providers • Networking and Systems Services • Repair Services/Rental and Leasing • Resellers, Wholesalers, and Distributors • Software Developers/Programming Services • Web Technologies

AT&T BUSINESS SOLUTIONS
6100 Bandera Road, Suite 505, San Antonio TX 78238. 210/520-7878. **Fax:** 210/520-7881. **Contact:** Human Resources. **World Wide Web address:** http://www.att.com/hr/gvtsol.html. **Description:** AT&T Business Solutions (formerly GRC International) creates large-scale, decision-support systems and software engineering environments; applies operations research and mathematical modeling to business and management systems; and implements advanced database technology. GRC International also provides studies and analysis capabilities for policy development and planning; modeling and simulation of hardware and software used in real-time testing of sensor, weapon, and battlefield management command, control, and communication systems; and testing and evaluation. GRC International's services are offered primarily to government and commercial customers. **NOTE:** Job listings by location can be found at http://www.att.hire.com. **Corporate headquarters location:** Vienna VA. **Other U.S. locations:** Nationwide. **Operations at this facility include:** This location is involved in technical research. **Parent company:** AT&T Corporation. **Listed on:** New York Stock Exchange. **Stock exchange symbol:** T.

ACCENTURE
1501 South MoPac Expressway, Suite 300, Austin TX 78746. 512/476-2323. **Fax:** 512/476-7765. **Contact:** Human Resources. **World Wide Web address:** http://www.accenture.com. **Description:** A management and technology consulting firm. Accenture offers a wide range of services including business re-engineering, customer service system consulting, data system design and implementation, Internet sales systems research and design; and strategic planning. **NOTE:** Please visit website to search for jobs and apply online. **Corporate headquarters location:** Hamilton, Bermuda. **Other area locations:** Houston TX; Dallas TX. **Other U.S. locations:** Nationwide. **International locations:** Worldwide. **Listed on:** New York Stock Exchange. **Stock exchange symbol:** ACN. **Number of employees worldwide:** 90,000.

ANALYSTS INTERNATIONAL CORPORATION (AIC)
7000 North Mopac Expressway, Suite 220, Austin TX 78731. 512/206-2700. **Toll-free phone:** 800/654-8194. **Fax:** 512/206-2720. **Contact:** Human Resources. **World Wide Web address:** http://www.analysts.com. **Description:** An international computer

consulting firm. The company assists clients in developing systems in a variety of industries using diverse programming languages and software. Founded in 1966. **NOTE:** Please visit website to register, search for jobs, and apply online. **Positions advertised include:** Cisco Consultant. **Corporate headquarters location:** Minneapolis MN. **Other U.S. locations:** Nationwide. **International locations:** Canada; England. **Listed on:** NASDAQ. **Stock exchange symbol:** ANLY. **President/CEO:** Mike LaVelle.

APPLE COMPUTER, INC.
2420 Ridgepoint Drive, Austin TX 78754. 512/674-2000. **Contact:** Employment. **World Wide Web address:** http://www.apple.com. **Description:** Apple Computer manufactures personal computers and computer-related products for home, business, scientific, industrial, professional, and educational use. **NOTE:** Please visit https://jobs.apple.com to search for jobs and apply online. **Positions advertised include:** Inside Software Sales Account Executive; K12 Education Inside Account Executive; Product Administration Specialist; Professional Video Technical Support Representative; Senior Tax Accountant. **Special programs:** Internships. **Corporate headquarters location:** Cupertino CA. **Operations at this facility include:** This location offers sales and technical support to companies and educational institutions. **Listed on:** NASDAQ. **Stock exchange symbol:** AAPL.

AQUENT
8140 North Mopac, Building I Suite 150, Austin TX 78759. 512/442-0992. **Fax:** 512/442-2462. **Contact:** Human Resources. **World Wide Web address:** http://www.aquent.com. **Description:** Engaged in software consulting, training, and staffing. Founded 1986. **Corporate headquarters location:** Boston MA. **Other area locations:** Dallas TX; Houston TX. **Other U.S. locations:** Nationwide. **International locations:** Worldwide. **Operations at this facility include:** This office is part of the Marketing and Creative Services division.

AVNET, INC.
1130 Rutherford Lane, Building 2 Suite 208, Austin TX 78753. 512/835-1152. **Recorded jobline:** 800/459-1225. **Contact:** Human Resources. **E-mail address:** avnet.staffing@avnet.com. **World Wide Web address:** http://www.avnet.com. **Description:** Avnet is the world's largest distributor of semiconductors, interconnect, passive, and electromechanical components, computer products, and embedded systems from leading manufacturers. **NOTE:** Contact the corporate information line, at 800/882-8638 option 4, for more information on applying for jobs. Please visit website to view job listings and apply online. Online applications are preferred. **Positions advertised include:** Field Application Engineer. **Corporate headquarters location:** Phoenix AZ. **Other U.S. locations:** Nationwide. **International locations:** Worldwide. **Listed on:** New York Stock Exchange. **Stock exchange symbol:** AVT. **Number of employees worldwide:** 10,000.

CIRRUS LOGIC, INC.
2901 Via Fortuna, Austin TX 78746. 512/851-4000. **Contact:** Human Resources. **World Wide Web address:** http://www.cirrus.com. **Description:** Designs, markets, and tests computer chips for audio, digital, multimedia, and telecommunication products. Cirrus Logic also supplies high-performance analog circuits. **Positions advertised include:** Operations Production Control Planner Product Marketing Manager; Senior Digital Design Engineer; Analog Design Engineer; Applications Engineer; Senior Internal Auditor; Digital Design Engineer; Staff Design Engineer. **Special programs:** Internships. **Corporate headquarters location:** This location. **International locations:** Hong Kong China; Tokyo Japan; Henley-on-Thames United Kingdom.

COMPUTER SCIENCES CORPORATION (CSC)
400 West Cesar Chavez Street, Austin TX 78701. 512/345-5700. **Contact:** Sherry Reese, Recruiter. **World Wide Web address:** http://www.csc.com. **Description:** Develops software and provides related services for the financial services industry. **NOTE:** Please visit http://careers.csc.com to search for jobs and apply online. **Positions advertised include:** Programmer Analyst; HR Generalist. **Corporate headquarters location:** El Segundo CA. **Other area locations:** Dallas TX; El Paso TX; Fort Hood TX; Fort Worth TX; Houston TX; Irving TX; McKinney TX. **Other U.S. locations:** Nationwide. **International locations:** Worldwide. **Listed on:** New York Stock Exchange. **Stock exchange symbol:** CSC. **Number of employees worldwide:** 90,000.

COMPUTER SCIENCES CORPORATION (CSC)
4606 Centerview, Suite 170, San Antonio TX 78228. 210/737-0721. **Fax:** 210/737-3273. **Contact:** Human Resources. **World Wide Web address:** http://www.csc.com. **Description** Develops software and provides related services for the financial services industry. **NOTE:** Please visit http://careers.csc.com to search for jobs and apply online. **Positions advertised include:** Third Party Administrator; Life Claims Examiner; Data Entry Clerk; Data Imaging Processor; Business Developer. **Corporate headquarters location:** El Segundo CA. **International locations:** Worldwide. **Operations at this facility include:** This location is a sales office. **Listed on:** New York Stock Exchange. **Stock exchange symbol:** CSC. **Number of employees worldwide:** 68,000.

CYBERBASIN INTERNET SERVICES
407 North Big Spring Street, Midland TX 79701. 432/620-0051. **Contact:** Human Resources. **E-mail address:** info@cyberbasin.com. **World Wide Web address:** http://www.cyberbasin.com. Description: This company is an Internet Service Provider. Provides Network and hosting services. **NOTE:** E-mail resumes to this company. **Parent company:** Southwest Royalties, Inc. **Listed on:** Privately held.

DELL INC.
One Dell Way, Round Rock TX 78682. 512/338-4400. **Fax:** 800/816-4643. **Contact:** Human Resources. **World Wide Web address:** http://www.dell.com. **Description:** Designs, develops, manufactures,

markets, services, and supports personal computer systems and related equipment including servers, workstations, notebooks, and desktop systems. The company also offers over 4,000 software packages and peripherals. **Special programs:** Dell for MBA's; Dell for Undergrad/Masters; Internships. **Corporate headquarters location:** This location. **International locations:** Ireland; United Kingdom. **Listed on:** NASDAQ. **Stock exchange symbol:** DELL. **Number of employees worldwide:** 46,000.

EPSIIA CORPORATION
1101 Capital of Texas Highway South, Building K, Suite 200, Austin TX 78746. 512/329-0081. **Toll-free phone:** 800/401-4774. Fax: 512/329-0086. **Contact:** Human Resources. **E-mail address:** jobs@EPSIIA.com. **World Wide Web address:** http://www.epsiia.com. **Description:** Develops retrieval and conversion software. **Positions advertised include:** Sales Account Executive. **Corporate headquarters location:** This location. **International locations:** United Kingdom; Brazil. **Parent company:** Fiserv Resources.

FARSIGHT COMPUTER
1219 West University Boulevard, Odessa TX 79764-7119. 915/335-0879. **Fax:** 915/335-8411. **Contact:** Human Resources. **World Wide Web address:** http://www.farsweb.com. **Description:** A computer wholesaler, specializing in custom-built PCs.

GALACTIC TECHNOLOGIES, INC.
400 North Loop 1604 East, Suite 210, San Antonio TX 78232. 210/496-7250. **Fax:** 210/490-6790. **Contact:** Cynthia J. Chatelain, Vice President of Operations. **World Wide Web address:** http://www.galactictech.com. **Description:** Provides computer hardware and software engineering, PC support, and networking services. Galactic Technologies also operates as a value-added reseller. **Positions advertised include:** Software Engineer; PC Technician. **Office hours:** Monday - Friday, 7:30 a.m. - 5:00 p.m. **Corporate headquarters location:** This location.

IBM CORPORATION
11400 Burnett Road, Austin TX 78758. 512/823-0000. **Toll-free phone:** 800/796-7876. **Contact:** Human Resources. **World Wide Web address:** http://www.ibm.com. **Description:** IBM Corporation is a developer, manufacturer, and marketer of advanced information processing products including computers and microelectronic technology, software, networking systems, and information technology-related services. **NOTE:** Jobseekers should apply online via the company's website.. **Corporate headquarters location:** Armonk NY. **International locations:** Worldwide. **Operations at this facility include:** This location is a sales office. **Subsidiaries include:** IBM Global; IBM Financing; IBM Technology; IBM Personal Servers; IBM Research; IBM Servers; IBM Software. **Listed on:** New York Stock Exchange. **Stock exchange symbol:** IBM.

LIANT SOFTWARE CORPORATION
8911 North Capital of Texas Highway, Austin TX 78759. 512/343-1010. **Toll-free phone:** 800/349-9222. **Fax:** 512/371-7609. **Contact:** Human Resources. **World Wide Web address:** http://www.liant.com. **Description:** Develops software including Relativity, an SQL relational access through ODBC to COBOL managed data for client/server Windows applications, and Open PL/I, which offers transitions of PL/I mainframe and minicomputer applications from legacy systems to open, client/server environments. **Corporate headquarters location:** Framingham MA. **Operations at this facility include:** This location is engaged in software packaging and distribution. **Listed on:** Privately held.

MESQUITE SOFTWARE, INC.
8500 North Mopac, Suite 825, Austin TX 78759. 512/338-9153. **Contact:** Human Resources. **World Wide Web address:** http://www.mesquite.com. **Description:** Develops software and provides support services for the system simulation market. The company's product line includes CSIM18-The Simulation Engine. **Corporate headquarters location:** This location.

METROWERKS INC.
7700 West Parmer Lane, Austin TX 78729. 512/996-5300. **Fax:** 512/996-4910. **Contact:** Human Resources. **World Wide Web address:** http://www.metrowerks.com. **Description:** Develops and markets software development and programming tools for computers, Internet, and wireless applications as well as games. Founded in 1985. **Corporate headquarters location:** This location. **Other U.S. locations:** CA; MA; WA: UT; TX. **International locations:** Worldwide.

NETQOS
6504 Bridge Point Parkway, Suite 501, Austin TX 78730. 512/407-8629. **Toll-free phone:** 877/835-9575. **Fax:** 512/407-8629. **Contact:** Cristina Jaramillo, Human Resources. **E-mail address:** careers@netqos.com. **World Wide Web address:** http://www.netqos.com. **Description:** Develops software and consulting services to manage the performance of enterprise computer networks of Fortune 1000 companies. **NOTE:** Send resume and cover letter to the company. **Positions advertised include:** Software Engineer; Account Manager; WAN Network Engineer; Sales Executive (New York City area).

NEWTEK INC.
5131 Beckwith Boulevard, San Antonio TX 78249. 210/370-8000. **Contact:** Human Resources. **World Wide Web address:** http://www.newtek.com. **Description:** Designs and develops software used for animation and graphics. **Positions advertised include:** Video Software Engineer. **Corporate headquarters location:** This location.

PERVASIVE SOFTWARE INC.
12365 Riata Trace Parkway, Building Two, Austin TX 78727. 512/231-6000. **Toll-free phone:** 800/287-4383. **Fax:** 512/231-6010. **Contact:**

Human Resources. **E-mail address:** greatjobs@pervasive.com. **World Wide Web address:** http://www.pervasive.com. **Description:** Develops embedded database software. **Positions advertised include:** Quality Technician; Engineering Consultant; Senior Marketing Programs Specialist; Senior Developer. **Corporate headquarters location:** This location. **International locations:** Belgium; Canada; England; France; Germany; Hong Kong; Ireland; Japan. **Listed on:** NASDAQ. **Stock exchange symbol:** PVSW.

TECHWORKS, INC.
4030 West Braker Lane, Suite 120, Austin TX 78759. 512/794-8533. **Fax:** 512/794-8520. **Contact:** Human Resources. **World Wide Web address:** http://www.techworks.com. **Description:** Manufactures and sells computer memory.

TRILOGY DEVELOPMENT GROUP
5001 Plaza on the Lake, Austin TX 78746. 512/874-3100. **Fax:** 512/874-8900. **Contact:** Human Resources. **E-mail address:** recruit_US@trilogy.com. **World Wide Web address:** http://www.trilogy.com. **Description:** A developer of configuration software for a variety of industries including automotive, utilities, insurance, shipping, and computers.

VIGNETTE CORPORATION
1301 South Mopac Expressway, Building 3, Austin TX 78746-5776. 512/741-4300. **Toll-free phone:** 888/608-9900. **Fax:** 512/741-1403. **Contact:** Human Resources. **World Wide Web address:** http://www.vignette.com. **Description:** Supplies e-business applications to online business clients. **NOTE:** Apply online at this company's website. **Positions advertised include:** Customer Support Engineer; Technical Writer; Systems Administrator; Copywriter/Editor; Customer Reference Specialist; Marketing Programs Manager; Financial Analyst. **Corporate headquarters location:** This location. **Listed on:** NASDAQ. **Stock exchange symbol:** VIGN.

EDUCATIONAL SERVICES

**You can expect to find the following types of companies
in this section:**
Business/Secretarial/Data Processing Schools •
Colleges/Universities/Professional Schools • Community
Colleges/Technical Schools/Vocational Schools • Elementary and
Secondary Schools • Preschool and Child Daycare Services

ABILENE CHRISTIAN UNIVERSITY
ACU Station, Box 29106, Abilene TX 79699-9106. 915/674-2000.
Physical address: Abilene Christian University, Hardin Administration
Building, Room 213, Abilene TX. **Fax:** 915/674-6899. **Contact:** Human
Resources. **Recorded jobline:** 325/674-5621. **World Wide Web
address:** http://www.acu.edu. **Description:** A Church of Christ-affiliated
university with 117 undergraduate programs, 39 graduate fields of study,
and one doctoral program in theology. Approximately 4,700 students are
enrolled in the university. **NOTE:** Please visit website to view job listings
and download application form. **Positions advertised include:**
Landscaping Coordinator; Assistant Registrar and Record Technology
Coordinator; Residence Director; Program Coordinator; Library
Technician and Assistant Cataloger; Career Services Specialist;
Administrative Associate; Faculty – Various Departments.

AMARILLO COLLEGE
P.O. Box 447, Amarillo TX 79178-0001. 806/371-5040. **Contact:** Human
Resources. **World Wide Web address:** http://www.actx.edu/hr.
Description: A two-year community college. Approximately 7,300
students are enrolled at this location. Amarillo College has three other
campuses in Amarillo. **NOTE:** Please visit website to view job listings
and to download application forms. Resumes are not accepted online;
you must mail your resume. The Human Resources office is located at
the Washington Street Campus, on the second floor of the Student
Service Center, Suite 280. **Positions advertised include:** Instructor –
Various Departments; Director of Human Resources; Director of
Broadcasting Operations; Associate Director – Center for Continuing
Healthcare Education; Dean of Student Services; Police Officer; Staff
Assistant; Student Services and Outreach Representative; Senior
Programmer/Analyst; Maintenance Mechanic.

ANGELO STATE UNIVERSITY
P.O. Box 11009, ASU Station, San Angelo TX 76909. 325/942-2168.
Physical address: 2601 West Avenue North, San Angelo TX 76909.
Contact: Office of Human Resources. **E-mail address:**
laura.billings@angelo.edu. **World Wide Web address:**
http://www.angelo.edu. **Description:** A state university offering 45
bachelor's degree and 21 master's degree programs. Angelo State
University has an enrollment of approximately 6,300 students. Founded

in 1976. **NOTE:** Please visit website to view job listings and access application forms. **Positions advertised include:** Assistant Professor – Various Departments; Head – Department of Computer Science; Head – Department of Physical Therapy; Physical Therapy Faculty; Professional Specialist; Director of Institutional Effectiveness; Assistant Director – Recreation and Intramurals; Assistant Manager of Infrastructure Services; Area Coordinator.

AUSTIN COMMUNITY COLLEGE
5930 Middle Fiskville Road, Austin TX 78752. 512/223-7000. Recorded jobline: 512/223-5621. **Contact:** Human Resources. **World Wide Web address:** http://www.austin.cc.tx.us. **Description:** A two-year community college. **NOTE:** Call the enrollment office at 512/223-7534 or -7573. Please visit website to search for jobs and download employment application. **Positions advertised include:** Coordinator – Internal Audit; Coordinator – Texas Success Initiative Program; Clerk; Associate Vice President for Institutional Effectiveness; Web Development Specialist; Safety Officer; Internal Programs Manager; Technical Office Assistant; Construction Buyer; Evening Supervisor; Specialist – Student Recruitment; Counselor – Part-time; Child Care Assistant; Senior Computer Support Technician; Online Application Software Administrator; Account Executive; Instructor – Various Departments; Faculty – Various Departments. Office hours: Monday – Friday, 8:00 a.m. – 5:00 p.m.

AUSTIN INDEPENDENT SCHOOL DISTRICT
1111 West Sixth Street, Austin TX 78703. 512/414-1700. **Contact:** Human Resources. **World Wide Web address:** http://www.austin.isd.tenet.edu. **Description:** This location serves as the administrative offices for the entire Austin K-12 school system. **NOTE:** This website has job listings for all of the schools in the Austin district. See website and apply online. **Positions advertised include:** Accounting Clerk; Art Teacher; Assistant Band Director; Bilingual Behavior Specialist; Biology/Athletics Teacher; Elementary Special Education Teacher; Geography Teacher; French Teacher; High School Librarian; History Teacher; Housekeeping Services Specialist.

CISCO JUNIOR COLLEGE
717 East Industrial, Abilene TX 79602. 915/673-4567. **Contact:** Personnel. **World Wide Web address:** http://www.cisco.cc.tx.us. **Description:** A junior college. **NOTE:** Please visit website to view job listings and download application form. **Positions advertised include:** Custodian; Plant/Operations Supervisor. **Other area locations:** Cisco TX.

HARCOURT ASSESSMENT, INC.
19500 Bulverde, San Antonio TX 78259. 800/872-1726. **Contact:** Human Resources. **World Wide Web address:** http://www.marketplace.psychcorp.com. **Description:** One of the oldest and largest commercial test publishers in the nation. The company provides tests (e.g. the Stanford Achievement Test Series, the

Metropolitan Achievement Tests, and Wechsler Intelligence Scales for Children and Adults) and related services to schools and colleges, clinicians and professional organizations, businesses, and public entities. The company's services include test research and development, printing, marketing, distribution, administration, and scoring. **NOTE:** This company also seeks people test administrators and test writers. See website for contact information. **Positions advertised include:** Requirements Analyst; Production Coordinator-Planning; Senior Associate, Sampling; Psychometrician; Test Development Manager; Senior Programmer Analyst. **Corporate headquarters location:** This location.

HARDIN-SIMMONS UNIVERSITY
HSU Box 16030, Abilene TX 79698. 915/670-1507. **Physical address:** 2200 South Hickory Street, Abilene TX 79601. **Fax:** 915/670-5874. **Contact:** Earl T. Garrett, Human Resources. **World Wide Web address:** http://www.hsutx.edu. **Description:** A Southern Baptist university offering both graduate and undergraduate degrees. This university also offers a nursing program. **NOTE:** Job listings for faculty and staff are listed on the company's website. Applicants interested in faculty positions should send resumes to the contact names provided in the listings. **Positions advertised include:** Faculty Positions; University Communications Director; Financial Aid Director. Recruiting Director; Campus Recreation Director; Visitor Coordinator. **Corporate headquarters location:** This location. **Operations at this facility include:** Administration. **Number of employees at this location:** 300.

LAREDO COMMUNITY COLLEGE
West End Washington Street, Laredo TX 78040. 956/721-5138. **Fax:** 956/721-5367. **Contact:** Human Resources. **World Wide Web address:** http://www.laredo.cc.tx.us. **Description:** Offers a variety of Associate's degrees in programs including business, computers, electronics, and nursing. Approximately 6,900 students attend the college. Founded in 1947. **NOTE:** An application must be submitted via mail for any position. The application can be downloaded on the college's website. **Positions advertised include:** Catalog Librarian; Chemistry Instructor; ENSL Spanish Instructor; Government Instructor; Mathematics Instructor; Music/Strings; Speech/Theater; Assistant Plumber.

LUBBOCK CHRISTIAN UNIVERSITY
5601 Nineteenth Street, Lubbock TX 79407. 806/720-7215. **Contact:** Human Resources. **E-mail address:** careers@lcu.edu. **World Wide Web address:** http://www.lcu.edu. **Description:** A private institution offering courses in divinity, kinesiology and environmental science. **NOTE:** To apply, mail resume or visit the Human Resources in person in Room 112 of the Administration Building. **Positions advertised include:** Human Resources Director; Continuing Education Specialist.

McMURRY UNIVERSITY
McMurry Station, P.O. Box 308, Abilene TX 79697. 915/793-3800. **Contact:** Human Resources. **World Wide Web address:**

http://www.mcm.edu. **Description:** A four-year university offering undergraduate degrees. Approximately 1,425 students attend McMurry University **NOTE:** This company lists all job listings and specific contact information on its website. **Positions advertised include:** Instructor; Night Custodian; Assistant Professor.

THE NATIONAL ALLIANCE FOR INSURANCE EDUCATION & RESEARCH
P.O. Box 27027, Austin TX 78755-1027. 512/345-7932. **Fax:** 512/343-2167. **Contact:** Amy Schott, Human Resources Director. **World Wide Web address:** http://www.scic.com. **Description:** A nonprofit insurance education organization offering the Certified Insurance Counselors (CIC) designation, the Certified Insurance Service Representatives (CISR) designation, and the Certified Risk Manager (CRM) designation. The Academy of Producers Insurance Studies is the research arm of The National Alliance.

ST. EDWARD'S UNIVERSITY
Campus Mailbox 1042, 3001 South Congress Avenue, Austin TX 78748. 512/448-8587. **Fax:** 512/464-8813. **Recorded jobline:** 512/448-8541. **Contact:** Human Resources. **World Wide Web address:** http://www.stedwards.edu/humr/jobs.htm. **Description:** A private university affiliated with the Catholic Church. St. Edward's University offers a liberal arts program to undergraduate and graduate students interested in business or human services. **NOTE:** See website for job listings and contact information. **Positions advertised include:** Dean, School of Business; Assistant Professor, Finance; Assistant Professor, Bioinformatics; Library Instruction Coordinator; Adjunct Faculty; Residence Hall Director; Senior Secretary; Public Relations Assistant; Groundskeeper; Graduate Internship; Office Specialist. **Corporate headquarters location:** This location. **Operations at this facility include:** Administration. **Listed on:** Privately held.

ST. MARY'S UNIVERSITY
One Camino Santa Maria, San Antonio TX 78228-8565. 210/436-3725. **Fax:** 210/431-2223. **Recorded jobline:** 210/436-3343. **Contact:** Human Resources Director. **World Wide Web address:** http://www.stmarytx.edu. **Description:** A liberal arts university affiliated with the Catholic Church. St. Mary's University has three undergraduate programs and two graduate programs including a law school. The school is one of the oldest and largest Catholic universities in the Southwest. Founded in 1852. **NOTE:** An application is required for certain positions. See the university's website for additional information. **Special programs:** Internships. **Positions advertised include:** Systems Manager; Counselor/Assistant Director; Physician Assistant. **Corporate headquarters location:** This location. **Operations at this facility include:** Administration; Research and Development; Service. **Listed on:** Privately held.

SAN ANTONIO INDEPENDENT SCHOOL DISTRICT
141 Lavaca Street, San Antonio TX 78210. 210/299-5500. **Contact:**

Human Resources. **World Wide Web address:** http://www.saisd.net. **Description:** Administrative offices for the K-12 school system in San Antonio. **NOTE:** See the district's website for job listings for all schools in San Antonio and apply online. **Positions advertised include:** Librarian; Food Service Accounting Director; Assistant Principal; Special Education/Educational Diagnostician; Curriculum Lead Teacher; Technology Grant Specialist; Campus Social Worker; Data Clerk; Head Golf Coach; Head Soccer Coach; General Assistant Coach; Scheduler; Bus Driver; Head Custodian; Electrician; Police Officer.

SOUTH PLAINS COLLEGE
1401 South College Avenue, Levelland TX 79336. 806/894-9611. **Fax:** 806/894-6880. **Contact:** Human Resources. **World Wide Web address:** http://www.spc.cc.tx.us. **Description:** A two-year, state-funded college. South Plains College offers majors in education, arts and sciences, nursing, and continuing education. The college has an enrollment of approximately 5,400 students. **NOTE:** An application is required for any position. See website for job listings and application information.

SOUTHWEST COLLEGIATE INSTITUTE FOR THE DEAF
3200 Avenue C, Big Spring TX 79720-9960. 915/264-3700. **Fax:** 915/264-3707. **Contact:** Dr. Ron Brasel, Provost. **World Wide Web address:** http://www.hc.cc.tx.us. **Description:** A college for the deaf with an enrollment of approximately 105 students. The institute offers courses in liberal arts, technical, vocational/occupational, and developmental studies. The institute also offers numerous support services such as career advisement and job placement assistance. Founded in 1980. **NOTE:** An application must be submitted for any position. See website for job listings and applications. **Positions advertised include:** Men's Residence Hall Supervisor; Preparatory English Instructor; Fitness Center Director; Utility Maintenance Technician; Speech Instructor.. **Parent company:** Howard County Junior College.

TEXAS STATE UNIVERSITY—SAN MARCOS
601 University Drive, J.C. Kellam Building, Suite 340, San Marcos TX 78666. 512/245-2557. **Fax:** 512/245-3911. **Contact:** Human Resources. **E-mail address:** hr@txstate.edu. **World Wide Web address:** http://www.humanresources.swt.edu. **Description:** A college offering undergraduate, graduate and doctoral degrees. **NOTE:** For more information about the university, visit http://www.txstate.edu. To apply for staff positions, a completed application must accompany a resume. Download application at the website. For faculty and other positions, see website for application procedures. Walk-in applications are accepted in the Human Resources office during regular business hours. **Positions advertised include:** Administrative Assistant; Grant Secretary; Data Entry Operator; Residence Hall Director; Business Manager, Microcomputer Lab Assistant; Professor (Various). **Office hours:** Monday – Friday, 8:00 a.m. – 5:00 p.m.

TEXAS TECH UNIVERSITY
P.O. Box 41093, Lubbock TX 79409-1093. 806/742-3851. **Contact:** James A. Brown, Managing Director. **E-mail address:** employment@ttu.edu. **World Wide Web address:** http://www.ttu.edu. **Description:** A state university. The university offers undergraduate and graduate degrees in liberal arts, law, applied health, and medicine. **NOTE:** Texas Tech University has campus locations throughout Texas. See website for locations, job listings and application requirements. **Positions advertised include:** Administrative Assistant; Analyst; Professor (Various); Chief Accountant; Chief of Police; Coordinator; Custodian; Development Officer; Lead Advisor; Medical Lab Technician; Patient Services Supervisor; Proposal Writer; Section Manager. **Corporate headquarters location:** This location.

TRINITY UNIVERSITY
One Trinity Place, Box 91, San Antonio TX 78212-7200. 210/999-7507. **Fax:** 210/999-7542. **Recorded jobline:** 210/999-7510. **Contact:** Human Resources. **E-mail address:** humanresources@trinity.edu. **World Wide Web address:** http://www.trinity.edu. **Description:** A four-year college with majors including education, biology, communications, business administration, and engineering. The current enrollment is approximately 2,400. Founded in 1869. **NOTE:** Full-time, part-time and temporary positions offered. A completed application is required for certain positions. See website for job listings and application information. **Positions advertised include:** Senior Data Entry Clerk; Senior Secretary; Degree Audit Coordinator; Associate Director of Development; Information Resources Communications Officer; Assistant Director of Financial Aid; Assistant Director of Admissions, Professor (Various); Molecular Biologist. **Office hours:** Monday – Friday, 8:00 a.m. – 5:00 p.m.

UNIVERSITY OF TEXAS AT AUSTIN
P.O. Box Drawer V, Austin TX 78713-8922. 512/471-3656. **Physical address:** University of Texas at Austin, Austin TX 78712.. **Toll-free phone:** 800/687-8086. **Contact:** Human Resources. **World Wide Web address:** http://www.utexas.edu. **Description:** One location of the state university. **NOTE:** Interested jobseekers can mail their applications; apply online at the school's website, or visit the Human Resources. See the website for staff job listings, additional application procedures and requirements. **Office hours:** Monday, Tuesday, Thursday, and Friday, 8:00 a.m. – 5:00 p.m. Wednesday, 9:00 a.m. – 5:00 p.m. **Operations at this facility include:** Administration; Research and Development; Service.

UNIVERSITY OF TEXAS AT BROWNSVILLE
80 Fort Brown Street, Brownsville TX 78520. 956/544-8205. **Fax:** 956/982-0175. **Contact:** Human Resources. **World Wide Web address:** http://www.utb.edu. **Description:** University of Texas at Brownsville and Texas Southmost College are partner institutions offering the following programs of study: College of Liberal Arts, College of Science, Mathematics & Technology, School of Business, School of Education,

and School of Health Sciences. Founded in 1973. **NOTE:** A completed application is required for any position. See website for job listings and application procedures. Applications and resumes may be mailed, faxed or delivered to the Human Resources Office located in the Cortez Building, Suite 129. **Positions advertised include:** Accounting Clerk; Accounting Group Supervisor; Chemistry Lab Coordinator; Child Care Assistant; Maintenance Worker; Librarian; Staff Nurse; Lecturer (Various); Professor (Various).

UNIVERSITY OF TEXAS AT EL PASO

Human Resources Services, Administration Building, Room 216, El Paso TX 79968-0507. 915/747-5202. **Recorded jobline:** 915/747-8837.. **Contact:** Human Resources. **World Wide Web address:** http://www.utep.edu. **Description:** One location of the state university with more than two-thirds of the student population representing the area's strong Mexican-American community. Bachelors, masters, and doctoral degrees offered in liberal arts and science fields. **NOTE:** See website for job listings, contact information and application requirements and procedures. **Positions advertised include:** Horticulturist; Coach (Various); Special Projects Manager; Database Administrator; Professor (Various); Lecturer (Various); Literacy Coordinator; Research Associate.

UNIVERSITY OF THE INCARNATE WORD

4301 Broadway Street, Box 320, San Antonio TX 78209. 210/829-6019. **Fax:** 210/829-3847. **Contact:** Human Resources. **E-mail address:** uiwhr@university.uiwtx.edu. **World Wide Web address:** http://www.uiw.edu. **Description:** A Catholic, co-educational, four-year university offering liberal arts and professional studies. The university offers such majors as fine arts, nursing, pre-professional studies, business, and education. The enrollment for the college is approximately 3,000 undergraduate and graduate students. Founded in 1881. **NOTE:** An application is required for every position. See website for application. **Positions advertised include:** Dean (Various); Academic Counselor; Director of Student Services; Professor (Various); Librarian; Admissions Secretary; Office Assistant; Resident Director. **Office hours:** Monday – Friday, 8:00 a.m. – 5:00 p.m.

ELECTRONIC/INDUSTRIAL ELECTRICAL EQUIPMENT AND COMPONENTS

You can expect to find the following types of companies in this section:
Electronic Machines and Systems • Semiconductor Manufacturers

ADVANCED MICRO DEVICES, INC. (AMD)
5204 East Ben White Boulevard, Mail Stop 556, Austin TX 78741. 512/602-1000. **Contact:** Employment. **World Wide Web address:** http://www.amd.com. **Description:** Designs, develops, manufactures, and markets complex, monolithic integrated circuits for use by electronic equipment and systems manufacturers, primarily in instrument applications and products for computation and communication. **NOTE:** Please mail resumes to corporate office at 1 AMD Place, P.O. Box 3453, MS 935, Sunnyvale CA 947088. **Positions advertised include:** Administrative Assistant; Applications Manager; Advanced Process Control Engineer; Business Controller; Business Development Manager; Business Operations Manager; Compiler Optimization Engineer; Corporate Manufacturing Competitive Intelligence Project Manager; Design Engineer; Executive Assistant; Global Advertising Manager; Inside Sales Representative; Marketing Manager; Senior Design Engineer. **Corporate headquarters location:** Sunnyvale CA. **Other area locations:** Dallas TX; Houston TX. **Other U.S. locations:** Nationwide. **International locations:** Worldwide. **Operations at this facility include:** This location manufactures semiconductors. **Listed on:** New York Stock Exchange. **Stock exchange symbol:** AMD. **President/CEO:** Hector de J. Ruiz. **Number of employees nationwide:** 14,000.

BAE SYSTEMS
6500 Tracor Lane, Austin TX 78725-2070. 512/926-2800. **Contact:** Human Resources. **World Wide Web address:** http://www.na.baesystems.com. **Description:** Provides a full spectrum of systems engineering and technical services in the areas of systems development, operation, and maintenance. Technical services include system design, integration, and testing; software development, engineering, and maintenance; and integrated logistics support including safety, reliability, and quality assurance engineering. **NOTE:** Please visit website to search for jobs. Unsolicited resumes are not accepted; you must submit a resume for a particular listed job. **Positions advertised include:** Accounting Supervisor; Quality Engineer; Reliability Engineer; SW Test Engineer; Systems Engineer; Business Unit Analyst; Contract Administrator. Special programs: Internships. **Corporate headquarters location:** Rockville MD. **Other U.S. locations:** Nationwide. **International locations:** Worldwide. **Number of employees worldwide:** 90,000.

CYPRESS SEMICONDUCTOR TEXAS INCORPORATED

17 Cypress Boulevard, Round Rock TX 78664. 512/244-7789. **Contact:** Human Resources. **World Wide Web address:** http://www.cypress.com. **Description:** Manufactures semiconductors. **NOTE:** Apply on-line. Positions advertised include: Equipment Maintenance Technician and Test Engineer. **Corporate headquarters location:** San Jose CA. **Listed on:** New York Stock Exchange. **Stock exchange symbol:** CY.

ETS LINDGREN

1301 Arrow Point Drive, Cedar Park TX 78613. 512/531-6400. **Fax:** 512/531-6578. **Contact:** Human Resources. **E-mail address:** resumes@ets-lindgren.com. **World Wide Web address:** http://www.ets-lindgren.com. **Description:** Designs, manufactures, and maintains products that measure, contain, and suppress electromagnetic, RF, and microwave energy. The company markets its products under the names Rantec, EMCO, Rayproof, and Enroshield. Founded in 1995. **Other U.S. locations:** Illinois. **International locations:** United Kingdom; Finland; Singapore; France; Japan; China. **Parent company:** ESCO Technologies Corporation is a diversified producer of commercial products. ESCO's products include electronic equipment, valves and filters, filtration and fluid flow components, automatic test equipment, utility load management equipment, and anechoic/shielding systems. ESCO's other operating subsidiaries include PTI Technologies, Inc.; VACCO Industries; Distribution Control Systems, Inc.; Rantec Microwave & Electronics; Lindgren RF Enclosures; Comtrak Technologies, Inc.; and Filtertek Inc. **Listed on:** New York Stock Exchange. **Stock exchange symbol:** ESE.

EMERSON PROCESS MANAGEMENT

8301 Cameron Road, Austin TX 78754-3895. 512/835-2190. **Contact:** Human Resources. **World Wide Web address:** http://www.emersonprocess.com. **Description:** Offers a wide variety of process control and assess management solutions. **Parent company:** Emerson Electric. **Listed on:** New York Stock Exchange. **Stock exchange symbol:** EMR.

HARRIS CORPORATION

5727 Farinon Drive, San Antonio TX 78249. 210/561-7300. **Fax:** 210/561-7499. **Contact:** Human Resources. **World Wide Web address:** http://www.harris.com. **Description:** Harris Corporation is a communications equipment company that provides broadcast, network, government, and wireless support products and systems. Founded in 1895. **Corporate headquarters location:** Melbourne FL. **Operations at this facility include:** This location develops and manufactures wireless microwave radios. **Listed on:** New York Stock Exchange. **Stock exchange symbol:** HRS. **Number of employees nationwide:** 10,000.

INTERNATIONAL SEMATECH

2706 Montopolis Drive, Austin TX 78741. 512/356-3588. **Fax:** 512/356-3086. **Contact:** Human Resources. **E-mail address:** staffing@sematech.com. **World Wide Web address:**

http://www.sematech.org. **Description:** International SEMATECH is a consortium of U.S. semiconductor manufacturers, working with government and academia, to sponsor and conduct research in semiconductor manufacturing technology for the United States. Results are transferred to consortium members including the Department of Defense for both military and commercial applications. **NOTE:** See website for job listings and contact information. **Operations at this facility include:** This location develops advanced semiconductor manufacturing methods, materials, and equipment.

LEPCO
5204 North Expressway, Brownsville TX 78597. 956/350-5650. **Contact:** Human Resources. **World Wide Web address:** http://www.ies.net/lepco. **Description:** A manufacturer of transformers and conductors. **Corporate headquarters location:** This location.

MKS INSTRUMENTS
3019 Alvin Debane Boulevard, Suite 210, Austin TX 78714. 512/385-1800. **Contact:** Human Resources. **World Wide Web address:** http://www.mksinst.com. **Description:** Manufactures, sells, and services RS generators used in the semiconductor industry. **NOTE:** Interested jobseekers should apply online at the company's website. **Operations at this facility:** Sales; Customer Service. **Listed on:** New York Stock Exchange. **Stock exchange symbol:** MKSI.

NATIONAL ELECTRIC COIL
3330 East 14th Street, Brownsville TX 78521. 956/541-1759. **Fax:** 956/982-7525. **Contact:** Edward K. Rice, Human Resources Manager. **World Wide Web address:** http://www.national-electric-coil.com. **Description:** Manufactures and installs high-voltage generator windings. **Corporate headquarters location:** Nashville TN. **Operations at this facility include:** Administration; Manufacturing; Sales; Service. **Number of employees nationwide:** 850.

NATIONAL INSTRUMENT CORPORATION
11500 North Mopac Expressway, Austin TX 78759-3504. 512/794-0100. **Fax:** 512/683-8745. **Contact:** Human Resources. **World Wide Web address:** http://www.ni.com. **Description:** Manufactures interface boards for the test measurement industry. **Corporate headquarters location:** This location. **International locations:** Worldwide. **Listed on:** NASDAQ. **Stock exchange symbol:** NATI.

O&M SALES, INC.
8705 Shoal Creek Boulevard, Suite 103, Austin TX 78757-6839. 512/453-0275. **Contact:** Human Resources. **World Wide Web address:** http://www.o-m-sales.com. **Description:** A wholesaler of semiconductors and other electronic components.

SAMSUNG AUSTIN SEMICONDUCTOR
12100 Samsung Boulevard, Austin TX 78754. 512/672-1000. **Contact:** Human Resources. **World Wide Web address:**

http://www.samsungusa.com. **Description:** Manufactures semiconductors. This is Samsung's only production plant located outside of Korea. **NOTE:** For job listings and contact information, apply online at the corporate website, http://www.samsungusa.com. **Positions advertised include:** Environmental Engineer; Facilities Electrical Engineer; Human Resources Specialist; Manufacturing Supervisor; Procurement Assistant; Senior Administrative Assistant. **Corporate headquarters location:** Seoul, Korea. **Other U.S. locations:** Nationwide. **International locations:** Worldwide. **Parent company:** Samsung USA, a subsidiary of Samsung Electronics Co. Ltd. **Subsidiaries include:** Samsung Information Technology; Samsung Consumer Electronics Division; **Operations at this facility include:** Sales; Marketing.

SIEMENS INTELLIGENT TRANSPORTATION SYSTEMS
8004 Cameron Road, Austin TX 78754. 512/837-8310. **Fax:** 512/837-0196. **Contact:** Human Resources. **World Wide Web address:** http://www.eagletcs.com. **Description:** Manufactures traffic control systems and lights. **Parent company:** Siemens Energy & Automation, Inc.

SILICON HILLS DESIGN, INC.
8504 Cross Park Drive, Austin TX 78754. 512/836-1088. **Fax:** 512/835-0404. **Contact:** Human Resources. **E-mail address:** Humanresources@siliconhills.com. **World Wide Web address:** http://www.siliconhills.com. **Description:** Designs printed circuit boards for computers as well as for the space and satellite markets.

ENVIRONMENTAL & WASTE MANAGEMENT SERVICES

**You can expect to find the following types of companies
in this section:**
Environmental Engineering Firms • Sanitary Services

SEVERN TRENT LABORATORIES, INC.
14046 Summit Drive, Suite 111, Austin TX 78728. 512/244-0855. **Fax:** 512/244-0160. **Contact:** Human Resources. **World Wide Web address:** http://www.stl-inc.com. **Description:** Provides a complete range of environmental testing services to private industry, engineering consultants, and government agencies in support of federal and state environmental regulations. The company also possesses analytical capabilities in the fields of air toxins, field analytical services, radiochemistry/mixed waste, and advanced technology. **Corporate headquarters location:** United Kingdom. **Other area locations:** Corpus Christi TX; Houston TX; Baytown TX. **Other U.S. locations:** Nationwide. **Number of employees worldwide:** 2,800.

TANKNOLOGY-NDE INTERNATIONAL, INC.
8900 Shoal Creek Boulevard, Building 200, Austin TX 78757. 512/451-6334. **Toll-free phone:** 800/964-0010x119. **Contact:** Human Resources Department. **E-mail address:** thebestjobsare@tankology.com. **World Wide Web address:** http://www.tanknde.com. **Description:** Through its subsidiaries, Tanknology-NDE provides environmental compliance, information, and management services to owners and operators of underground storage tanks. The company has three principal lines of business: domestic underground storage tank testing; domestic tank management; and international underground storage tank testing. The company's primary service is tank tightness testing, tank integrity testing, or precision testing. This service involves testing underground storage tanks and associated piping to determine if they are leaking. **NOTE:** See company's website for job listings and contact information.

URS CORPORATION
P.O. Box 201088, Austin TX 78720-1088. 512/454-4797. **Contact:** Human Resources. **World Wide Web address:** http://www.urscorp.com. **Description:** An architectural, engineering, and environmental consulting firm that specializes in air transportation, environmental solutions, surface transportation, and industrial environmental and engineering concerns. Founded in 1969. **NOTE:** See this company's website for all job listings in Texas. Apply online. **Positions advertised include:** Accounting Clerk; Contract Administrator; Environmental Engineer; Geologist; Scientist; Senior Chemical Engineer; Technical Assistant. **Corporate headquarters location:** This location. **Other area locations:** Dallas TX; Freeport TX; Houston TX; San Antonio TX. **Listed on:** New York Stock Exchange. **Stock exchange symbol:** URS.

WAID AND ASSOCIATES

14205 Burnet Road, Suite 600, Austin TX 78728. 512/255-9999. **Fax:** 512/255-8780. **Contact:** Human Resources. **E-mail address:** waid@waid.com. **World Wide Web address:** http://www.waid.com. **Description:** An engineering and environmental services firm. The company specializes in air quality services for industrial clients, particularly involving emissions control; permitting and compliance. Waid and Associates also provides services in waste and wastewater management, environmental management, and environmental information systems. Founded in 1978. **NOTE:** Entry-level positions are offered. **Office hours:** Monday - Friday, 8:00 a.m. - 5:00 p.m. **Corporate headquarters location:** This location. **Other area locations:** Houston TX; Midland TX. **Parent company:** Waid Corporation. **Listed on:** Privately held.

FABRICATED METAL PRODUCTS AND PRIMARY METALS

You can expect to find the following types of companies in this section:
Aluminum and Copper Foundries • Die-Castings • Iron and Steel Foundries • Steel Works, Blast Furnaces, and Rolling Mills

ALAMO IRON WORKS, INC.
P.O. Box 231, San Antonio TX 78291. 210/223-6161. **Physical address:** 943 Coliseum Road, San Antonio TX 78219. **Toll-free phone:** 800/292-7817. **Fax:** 210/704-8409. **Contact:** Vice President of Human Resources. **Recorded jobline:** 210/704-8491. **E-mail address:** aiw@aiwnet.com. **World Wide Web address:** http://www.aiwnet.com. **Description:** Distributes industrial supplies and operates a foundry and a steel service center. **Positions advertised include:** Welder; Rebar Laborer; Driver; Fleet Mechanic. **Office hours:** Monday, Wednesday, Friday, 8:30 a.m. – 11:00 a.m.; 1:30 p.m. – 4:00 p.m. **Corporate headquarters location:** This location. **Other area locations:** Corpus Christi TX; Brownsville TX; San Angelo TX; El Paso TX; Houston TX. **Other U.S. locations:** Albuquerque NM. **Operations at this facility include:** Administration; Manufacturing; Sales. **Listed on:** Privately held.

ALCOA (ALUMINUM COMPANY OF AMERICA)
P.O. Box 101, Point Comfort TX 77978. 361/987-2631. **Physical address:** State Highway 35, Point Comfort TX 77978. **Fax:** 361/987-6431. **Contact:** Human Resources. **World Wide Web address:** http://www.alcoa.com. **Description:** Engaged in all aspects of the aluminum industry including mining, refining, smelting, fabricating, and recycling. ALCOA also manufactures ceramic packaging for the semiconductor industry, alumina chemicals, plastic bottle closures, vinyl siding, packaging machinery, and electrical distribution systems for automobiles. **NOTE:** Please visit website to search for jobs and apply online. **Special programs:** Internships; Co-ops. **Corporate headquarters location:** Pittsburgh PA. **Other area locations:** Statewide. **Other U.S. locations:** Nationwide. **International locations:** Worldwide. **Operations at this facility include:** Manufacturing. **Listed on:** New York Stock Exchange. **Stock exchange symbol:** AA. **CEO:** Alain Belda. **Annual sales/revenues:** More than $22 billion. **Number of employees worldwide:** 120,000.

AMFELS, INC.
P.O. Box 3107, Brownsville TX 78523-3107. 956/831-8220. **Physical address:** 20000 South Highway 48, Brownsville TX 75821. **Fax:** 956/831-6220. **Contact:** Human Resources. **World Wide Web address:** http://www.keppelfelsamfels.com. **Description:** A shipyard that fabricates steel. **Other area locations:** Houston TX. **Other U.S. locations:** New Providence NJ. **International locations:** Singapore;

Brazil; Azerbaijan; Norway; Bulgaria; India; Vietnam; China; Australia; the Netherlands. **Parent company:** KeppelFELS.

ASARCO INC.
P.O. Box 1111, El Paso TX 79999-1111. 915/541-1800. **Physical address:** 2301 West Paisano Drive, El Paso TX 79922. **Fax:** 915/541-1866. **Contact:** Human Resources. **World Wide Web address:** http://www.asarco.com. **Description:** Asarco is one of the world's leading producers of nonferrous metals, primarily copper, lead, zinc, and silver, from its own mines and through its interest in Southern Peru Copper Corporation. Asarco also produces specialty chemicals and construction aggregates and provides environmental services. Asarco's copper operations consist of its Mission and Ray mines in Arizona, smelters in Hayden AZ and El Paso TX, and a refinery in Amarillo TX. In Missouri, the company operates an integrated lead circuit consisting of West Fork and Sweetwater mines, which provide over 90 percent of the feed for the nearby Glover smelter and refinery. The Tennessee mines division accounts for 57 percent of the total zinc concentrates produced by the company. The remaining 43 percent is produced as a coproduct at the West Fork and Sweetwater lead mines in Missouri and at the Leadville mine in Colorado. **Corporate headquarters location:** Phoenix AZ. **International locations:** Australia; Mexico; Peru. **Operations at this facility include:** This location smelts copper. **Parent Company:** Grupo Mexico S.A. de C.V. **Number of employees at this location:** 5.

PARKVIEW METAL PRODUCTS INC.
400 Barnes Drive, San Marcos TX 78666. 512/754-0200. **Contact:** Human Resources. **E-mail address:** hrsanmarcos@parkv.com. **World Wide Web address:** http://www.parkviewmetal.com. **Description:** A manufacturer of metal stamping and metal parts for computers, radios, and VCRs. **Other U.S. locations:** IL; NM. **International locations:** Mexico.

SAFETY STEEL SERVICE INC.
P.O. Box 2298, Victoria TX 77902. 361/575-4561. **Contact:** Human Resources. **Description:** Provides a variety of services for the steel industry including manufacturing rebar and structural pipes.

SEMCO DOT METAL PRODUCTS
18757 Bracken Drive, San Antonio TX 78266. 210/651-6331. **Toll-free phone:** 800/331-9966. **Fax:** 210/651-5825. **Contact:** Human Resources. **World Wide Web address:** http://www.gibraltar1.com. **Description:** Manufactures a variety of metal products including metal edging. **Corporate headquarters location:** Buffalo NY. **Other area locations:** Houston TX. **Parent company:** Gibraltar. **Listed on:** NASDAQ. **Stock exchange symbol:** ROCK.

FINANCIAL SERVICES

You can expect to find the following types of companies in this section:
Consumer Financing and Credit Agencies • Investment Specialists • Mortgage Bankers and Loan Brokers • Security and Commodity Brokers, Dealers, and Exchanges

---

AMERICAN EXPRESS FINANCIAL ADVISORS
9442 Capital of Texas Highway North, Plaza One Suite 800, Austin TX 78759. 512/346-5400. **Fax:** 512/338-1705. **Contact:** Katie Froelich. **E-mail address:** advisor.resumes@aexp.com. **World Wide Web address:** http://www.americanexpress.com/advisors. **Description:** Offers financial planning, annuities, mutual funds, insurance, investment certificates, and institutional investment advisory trust, tax preparation, and retail securities brokerage services. **NOTE:** Reach listed contact at Ext. 320. Learn more about financial advisor careers at http://americanexpress.com/advisorcareers, **Corporate headquarters location:** Minneapolis MN. **Other U.S. locations:** Nationwide. **Parent company:** American Express Company (New York NY).

AMERICAN PHYSICIANS SERVICE GROUP, INC. (APS)
1301 South Capital of Texas Highway, Suite C-300, Austin TX 78746. 512/328-0888. **Fax:** 512/314-4398. **Contact:** Bill Hayes, Chief Financial Officer. **World Wide Web address:** http://www.amph.com. **Description:** A management and financial services firm with subsidiaries and affiliates that provide medical malpractice insurance services for doctors, brokerage and investment services to institutions and individuals, lithotripsy services in 34 states, refractive vision surgery, and dedicated care facilities for Alzheimer's patients. **Corporate headquarters location:** This location. **Subsidiaries include:** APS Financial Corporation; AMPC Insurance Services; American Physicians Insurance Exchange. **Listed on:** NASDAQ. **Stock exchange symbol:** AMPH.

CHARLES SCHWAB
115 Wild Basin Road, Austin TX 78746. **Toll-free phone:** 877/729-2379. **Contact:** Human Resources. **World Wide Web address:** http://www.schwab.com. Founded in 1974, this company is a large financial firm marketing its services to individuals, institutions, and financial professionals. This location manages the operations for its online trading subsidiary, Cybertrader. **NOTE:** To read more about Cybertrader, visit its website at http://www.cybertrader.com. Apply online. **Positions advertised include:** Technology Solutions Staff; Staff Software Developer; Reporter Developer; Associate Web Application Developer. **Listed on:** New York Stock Exchange. **Stock exchange symbol:** SCH. **Number of employees worldwide:** 19,000.

MERRILL LYNCH
701 South Taylor Street, Suite 100, Amarillo TX 79101. 806/376-4861. **Contact:** Human Resources. **World Wide Web address:** http://www.ml.com. **Description:** Brokers in securities, option contracts, commodities, financial futures contracts, and insurance. **NOTE:** Interested jobseekers must apply online at the corporate website. **Positions advertised include:** Commercial Banking Professionals; Financial Advisor. **Other U.S. locations:** Nationwide. **Listed on:** New York Stock Exchange. **Stock exchange symbol:** MER.

RAYMOND JAMES & ASSOCIATES
6034 West Courtyard Drive, Suite 305, Austin TX 78730. 512/418-1700. **Contact:** Human Resources. **World Wide Web address:** http://www.raymondjames.com. **Description:** An investment brokerage firm offering financial planning, investment banking, asset management, and trust services. Founded in 1962. **NOTE:** This company has 10 other locations in the Austin area. See website for additional addresses and contact information.

VALERO ENERGY CORPORATION
CREDIT CARD CENTER
P.O. Box 300, Amarillo TX 79105. 806/324-4601. **Contact:** Human Resources. **World Wide Web address:** http://www.valero.com. **Description:** Valero Energy Corporation, an energy refining system, operates its own credit card program with more than 500,000 active accounts. NOTE: Apply online at the company's website for all positions. **Corporate headquarters location:** San Antonio TX. **Operations at this facility include:** Accounting; Sales.

WORLD FINANCIAL GROUP
2600 Via Fortuna, Suite 220, Austin TX 78746. 512/328-4220. **Contact:** Human Resources. **World Wide Web address:** http://www.wfg-online.com. **Description:** Offers a wide variety of financial services including mutual funds, debt consolidation, securities, mortgages, health insurance, and life insurance. **Parent company:** AEGON.

WUKASCH COMPANY
1810 Guadalupe Street, Austin TX 78701. 512/472-4700. **Contact:** Don C. Wukasch, President. **Description:** A diversified real estate and securities investment company providing real estate property management and securities portfolio management. **Special programs:** Internships. **Corporate headquarters location:** This location. **Listed on:** Privately held.

FOOD AND BEVERAGES/AGRICULTURE

You can expect to find the following types of companies in this section:
Crop Services and Farm Supplies • Dairy Farms • Food Manufacturers/Processors and Agricultural Producers • Tobacco Products

---

BRUCE FOODS CORPORATION
8000 Ashley Road, El Paso TX 79934. 915/821-2500. **Fax:** 915/821-1744. **Contact:** Human Resources. **World Wide Web address:** http://www.brucefoods.com. **Description:** Processes a wide range of foods. Products include Bruce's Yams, Cajun King, Casa Fiesta, Louisiana Gold, Louisiana Hot Sauce, and Mexene Chili Products. **NOTE:** For information about employment, please call 915/821-1323. **Corporate headquarters location:** New Iberia LA. **Number of employees nationwide:** 1,200.

CACTUS FEEDERS INC.
P.O. Box 3050, Amarillo TX 79116. 806/373-2333. **Physical address:** 22309 West 7th Avenue, Amarillo TX 79106. **Contact:** Kevin Hazelwood, Director of Employment. **E-mail address:** jobs@cactusfeeders.com. **World Wide Web address:** http://www.cactusfeeders.com. **Description:** Feeds and prepares cattle for delivery to meat packing plants and slaughterhouses. **NOTE:** Contact Employment directly at 806/371-4751. **Corporate headquarters location:** This location. **Other area locations:** Cactus TX; Spearman TX; Hereford TX; Hale Center TX; Stratford TX; Perryton TX; Tulia TX. **Other U.S. locations:** KS. **Number of employees nationwide:** 500.

COCA-COLA BOTTLING COMPANY
2400 West Expressway 83, McAllen TX 78501. 956/632-3700. **Fax:** 956/632-3719. **Contact:** Employee Relations Manager. **World Wide Web address:** http://www.coca-cola.com. **Description:** This location is packages Coca-Cola, Barq's, and Dr. Pepper. **Corporate headquarters location:** Atlanta GA. **Other U.S. locations:** Nationwide. **Parent company:** Coca-Cola Company is one of the world's largest marketers, distributors, and producers of bottle and can products. Coca-Cola Enterprises, part of the Coca-Cola Company, is in the liquid nonalcoholic refreshment business, which includes traditional carbonated soft drinks, still and sparkling waters, juices, isotonics, and teas. The company operates in 38 states, the District of Columbia, the U.S. Virgin Islands, the Islands of Tortola and Grand Cayman, and the Netherlands. Including recent acquisitions, Coca-Cola Enterprises franchise territories encompass a population of over 154 million people, representing 54 percent of the population of the United States. Coca-Cola Enterprises operates 268 facilities, approximately 24,000 vehicles, and over 860,000 vending machines, beverage dispensers, and coolers used to market,

distribute, and produce the company's products. **Listed on:** New York Stock Exchange. **Stock exchange symbol:** KO. **Number of employees worldwide:** 49,000.

COCA-COLA BOTTLING COMPANY
2311 Denton Drive, Austin TX 78758. 512/836-9051. **Contact:** Human Resources. **World Wide Web address:** http://www.coca-cola.com. **Description:** A distribution plant that bottles and ships Coca-Cola products to the surrounding area. **Corporate headquarters location:** Atlanta GA. **Other U.S. locations:** Nationwide. **Parent company:** Coca-Cola Company is one of the world's largest marketers, distributors, and producers of bottle and can products. Coca-Cola Enterprises, part of the Coca-Cola Company, is in the liquid nonalcoholic refreshment business, which includes traditional carbonated soft drinks, still and sparkling waters, juices, isotonics, and teas. The company operates in 38 states, the District of Columbia, the U.S. Virgin Islands, the Islands of Tortola and Grand Cayman, and the Netherlands. Including recent acquisitions, Coca-Cola Enterprises franchise territories encompass a population of over 154 million people, representing 54 percent of the population of the United States. Coca-Cola Enterprises operates 268 facilities, approximately 24,000 vehicles, and over 860,000 vending machines, beverage dispensers, and coolers used to market, distribute, and produce the company's products. **Listed on:** New York Stock Exchange. **Stock exchange symbol:** KO. **Number of employees worldwide:** 49,000.

COCA-COLA BOTTLING COMPANY OF THE SOUTHWEST
P.O. Box 58, San Antonio TX 78291. 210/225-2601. **Recorded jobline:** 210/229-0485. **Contact:** Human Resources. **World Wide Web address:** http://www.cokecce.com. **Description:** A bottling company packaging Coca-Cola, Barq's, and Dr. Pepper. **Parent company:** Coca-Cola Enterprises, Inc. is a public and independent company from Coca-Cola, Inc. Coca-Cola Enterprises markets, bottles and distributes Coke and other non-alcoholic beverages, such as still and sparkling waters, juices, isotonics, and teas. This company has facilities in most of the major metropolitan Texas cities. **NOTE:** See website for Coca-Cola Bottling Company of the Southwest job listings and application information. **Listed on:** New York Stock Exchange. **Stock exchange symbol:** CCE.

DANKWORTH PACKAGING
1609 Eubank Street, Ballinger TX 76821. 325-/365-3553. **Fax:** 325/365-2367. **Contact:** Danny Hamilton, Plant Manager. **Description:** A meat packaging plant. **Corporate headquarters location:** This location.

DEL MONTE FOODS
2205 Old Uvalde Highway, Crystal City TX 78839. 830/374-3451. **Contact:** Human Resources. **World Wide Web address:** http://www.delmonte.com. **Description:** Del Monte Foods is an international processor and distributor of foods, operating in the following business segments: Processed Foods, Fresh Fruit, Transportation, and Institutional Services. The Processed Foods Division processes canned,

frozen, dried, and chilled foods. Del Monte's operations include can manufacturing, label printing, seed production, and agricultural and scientific research. The company's products are distributed in more than 60 countries under the brand names Del Monte, Granny Goose, and Award. **Corporate headquarters location:** San Francisco CA. **Operations at this facility include:** This location cans a variety of vegetables such as spinach, carrots, peas, tomatoes, and tomato paste. **Listed on**: New York Stock Exchange. **Stock exchange symbol:** DLM. **Number of employees worldwide:** 17,600.

GANDY'S DAIRIES INC.
201 University Avenue, Lubbock TX, 79415. 806/765-8833.**Contact:** Judy Gooch, Human Resources Director. **Description:** A milk distribution company. **Parent company:** Dean Foods.

C.H. GUENTHER & SON, INC.
128 E. Guenther Street, San Antonio TX 78291. 210/227-1401. **Fax:** 210/227-1409. **Contact:** Human Resources. **World Wide Web address:** http://www.chguenther.com. **Description:** A mill that produces baked goods, mixes and tortillas. It has also food services and frozen baked good divisions.. **Corporate headquarters location:** This location.

HOLLY SUGAR CORPORATION
P.O. Drawer 1778, Hereford TX 79045. 806/364-2590. **Contact:** Human Resources Manager. **World Wide Web address:** http://www.dixiecrystals.com. **Description:** Grows, harvests, and processes sugar beets into granulated sugar. Sugar is packaged at this location year round. **NOTE:** See the corporate website for job listing information. **Parent company:** Imperial Holly Corporation (Sugar Land TX). **Subsidiaries include:** Dixie Crystals.

INSTITUTIONAL SALES ASSOCIATES
3827 Promontory Point Drive, Austin TX 78744. 512/447-1245. **Contact:** Debbie Lampson, Human Resources Manager. **E-mail address:** dlampson@isaonline.net. **World Web address:** http://www.isaonline.net. **Description:** Provides institutional food distribution services. **Note:** Resumes should be mailed to P.O. Box 8938, Houston Texas 77249. **Corporate headquarters location:** Houston.

PABST BREWING COMPANY
P.O. Box 1661, San Antonio TX 78296. 210/226-0231. **Contact:** Human Resources. **E-mail address:** hr@pabst.com. **World Wide Web address:** http://www.pabst.com. **Description:** Produces a line of widely distributed beers and malt beverages including Pabst Blue Ribbon, Pabst Light, and Pabst Extra Light.

PRICE'S CREAMERIES
600 North Piedras Street, El Paso TX 79923. 915/565-2711. **Fax:** 915/724-3605. **Contact:** Bernice Estrada, Human Resources Manager. **World Wide Web address:** http://www.pricesmilk.com. **Description:** A

creamery that manufactures and distributes ice cream, milk, and fruit juices.

SEED RESOURCE, INC.
P.O. Box 326, Tulia TX 79088. 806/995-3882. **Contact:** Gary Regner, Manager. **World Wide Web address:** http://www.seedresource.com. **Description:** Distributes forage seed including Sorghum Sudans, which it produces, alfalfa, turf grass seed, and wheat seed. The company also produces wheat. **Parent company:** AgriBioTech, Inc. (ABT) is a specialized distributor of forage (hay crops) and turf grass seed. The forage and turf grass seed industry supplies seed to the forage and turf cash crop sectors. The company also distributes non-seed products including Bloatenz Plus, a liquid bloat preventative administered to the drinking water of cattle, permitting them to graze on alfalfa safely; and PDS-1000, marketed in conjunction with Bloatenz Plus, is a microprocessor-controlled precision dispensing system designed to dispense solutions into the drinking water of livestock at a preset dosage rate. Other subsidiaries of ABT include Scott Seed Company; Hobart Seed Company; Halsey Seed Company; and Sphar & Company. Combined, these companies cover the following distribution territories: IN; KY; NM; NY; OK; OR; PA; TX; WA.

STERLING FOODS INC.
1075 Arion Parkway, San Antonio TX 78216. 210/490-1669. **Contact:** Jim Keuhl, Human Resources Manager. **World Wide Web address:** http://www.sterlingfoodsusa.com. **Description:** Manufacturers of ready-to-eat bakery foods and snacks. **Number of employees at this location:** 250.

TYSON FRESH MEATS, INC.
P.O. Box 30500, Amarillo TX 79187. 806/335-1531. **Contact:** Human Resources Department. **World Wide Web address:** http://www.tysonfoodsinc.com **Description:** A beef and pork meat processor. **NOTE:** See company's website for job listings.

GOVERNMENT

You can expect to find the following types of companies in this section:
Courts • Executive, Legislative, and General Government • Public Agencies (Firefighters, Military, Police) • United States Postal Service

AUSTIN, CITY OF
EMPLOYMENT SERVICES DIVISION
P.O. Box 1088, Austin TX 78767. 512/974-3210. **Toll-free phone:** 800/526-9159. **Fax:** 512/974-3321. **Contact:** Human Resources. **E-mail address:** employment.services@ci.austin.tx.us. **World Wide Web address:** http://www.ci.austin.tx.us/cityjobs. **Description:** Administrative offices for the City of Austin. **NOTE:** Interested jobseekers may send their resumes, apply online or in person at the Employment Services Division office during business hours. The City of Austin has another location for employment located at 2209 Rosewood Avenue, Suite 205, Austin TX 78702. See website for the location's office hours. **Positions advertised include:** Assistant Police Monitor; Chief Financial Officer; Dental Assistant; Electrical Systems Controller; Energy Marketer; Polygraph Examiner; Police Dispatcher; Production Specialist. **Office hours:** Monday – Thursday, 7:30 a.m. – 6:30 p.m.; Friday, 8:00 a.m. – 5:00 p.m.; Saturday, 9:00 a.m. – 1:00 p.m.

CORPUS CHRISTI, CITY OF
1201 Leopard, Corpus Christi TX 78401. 361/880-3300. **Toll-free phone:** 800/735-2989. **Recorded jobline:** 361/886-4848. **Contact:** Human Resources. **E-mail address:** personnel@cctexas.com. **World Wide Web address:** http://www.cctexasjobs.com. **Description:** The main offices for the city's government and administrative activities. **NOTE:** A completed application is required for any position. The application can be downloaded at the website or interested jobseekers may apply online.

EL PASO, CITY OF
2 Civic Center Plaza, El Paso TX 79901-1196. 915/541-4504. **Fax:** 915/541-4220. **Recorded jobline:** 915/541-4094. **Contact:** Human Resources. **World Wide Web address:** http: www.elpasotexas.gov. **Description:** Administrative offices for the city of El Paso. **NOTE:** Applications must be received by Human Resources no later than 5:00 p.m. on the last day of the job's filing period. **Positions advertised include:** Geographic Information Systems Technician; Police Chief; Assistant Director of Facilities Management; Legal File Clerk; Water Conservation Technician; Library Branch Manager. **Office hours:** Monday – Friday; 8:00 a.m. – 5:00 p.m.

LOWER COLORADO RIVER AUTHORITY
CORPORATE HEADQUARTERS
3700 Lake Austin Boulevard, Austin TX 78703. 512/473-3200. **Recorded jobline:** 800/776-5272x3333. **Contact:** Human Resources. **E-mail address:** jobline@lcra.org. **World Wide Web address:** http://www.lcra.org. **Description:** A low-cost electricity supplier to rural customers in the Central Texas region. Manages water utilities and public recreation locations. **NOTE:** Full-time and part-time positions available. Resumes and applications may be mailed, e-mailed or hand-delivered. An application can be downloaded online at the website. **Positions advertised include:** Administrative Associate; Construction Worker/Helper; Senior Accountant; System Reliability Analyst. **Special programs:** Internships; Volunteer.

OFFICE OF THE SECRETARY OF THE STATE OF TEXAS
1019 Brazo, Room 405, P.O. Box 12887, Austin TX 78711-2887. 512/463-5701. **Contact:** Human Resources. **World Wide Web address:** http://www.sos.state.tx.us. **Description:** A constitutional officer of the executive branch appointed by the governor with the consent of the senate. This agency is organized into five functional divisions: Executive, Elections, Information Services, Statutory Filings, and Administrative Services. **NOTE:** An application must be submitted with a resume. The application can be downloaded at the website.

SAN ANTONIO, CITY OF
111 Plaza De Armas, San Antonio TX 78207. **Recorded jobline:** 210/207-7280. **Contact:** Human Resources. **World Wide Web address:** http://www.sanantonio.gov. **Description:** Administrative offices for the City of San Antonio, including its Fire and Police Departments. **NOTE:** Part-time and temporary jobs available. See website for job listings and application information. **Positions advertised include:** Parking Supervisor; Events Attendant; Management Analyst; Senior Engineer; Contracts Services Manager; Assistant Marketing Manager; Special Projects Coordinator; Community Center Coordinator; Equipment Operator; Enrichment Specialist.

TEXAS DEPARTMENT OF CRIMINAL DEFENSE
P.O. Box 13084, Capitol Station, Austin TX 78711-3084. 936/437-4141. **Physical Address:** 209 West 14th Street, Austin TX 78701. **Contact:** Human Resources. **E-mail address:** human.res@tdcj.state.tx.us. **World Wide Web address:** http://www.tdcj.state.tx.us. **Description:** Manages the state's extensive prison system. **NOTE:** Part-time positions are available. A completed application is required for any position. Applications can be downloaded online at the website. The website provides job listings for all the Texas correctional facilities. See website for all locations and their job openings. Apply online. **Special programs:** Correctional Training; Internships. **Positions advertised include:** Correctional Officer; Parole Officer; Parole Caseworker; Clerk, Food Service Manager; Laundry Manager.

TEXAS DEPARTMENT OF HEALTH
1100 West 49th Street, Austin TX 78756-3199. 512/458-7111. **Toll-free phone:** 888/963-7111. **Contact:** Human Resources. **E-mail address:** HHSJobs@tdh.state.tx.us. **World Wide Web address:** http://www.tdh.state.tx.us. **Description:** Employing 6,300 people statewide, the Texas Department of Health is a government department offering health services across the state. **NOTE:** Apply online at this organization's website. **Positions advertised include:** Environmental Specialist; Program Specialist; Network Specialist; Medical Technologist; Administrative Assistant. **Special programs:** Internships. **Corporate headquarters location:** This location. **Operations at this facility include:** Administration.

TEXAS DEPARTMENT OF HUMAN SERVICES
P.O. Box 149030, 701 West 55th Street, Austin TX 78751. **Toll-free phone:** 888/834-7406. **Contact:** Human Resources. **World Wide Web address:** http://www.dhs.state.tx.us. **Description:** This location houses the welfare office, which provides food stamps and oversees Medicaid services. **NOTE:** See this organization's website for job listings, application requirements and contact information. **Positions advertised include:** Program Consultant; Attorney; Accountant; Nurse; Pharmacist

TEXAS DEPARTMENT OF MENTAL HEALTH AND MENTAL RETARDATION, CENTRAL OFFICE
909 West 45th Street, Austin TX 78751. 512/454-3761. **Contact:** Human Resources. **World Wide Web address:** http://www.mhmr.state.tx.us. **Description:** Administrative offices for mental health and retardation services and facilities statewide. **NOTE:** Part-time positions are available. This website provides job listings for all the Texas mental health and retardation facilities, including schools and hospitals. An application is required for any position. Apply online. **Positions advertised include:** Reimbursement Officer; Clerk; Interpreter; Aquatics Instructor; Services Aide; Therapist Technician; Food Service Worker; Cook; LVN; RN; Pharmacist; Physician; Psychiatrist; Psychologist; Social Worker; Therapist.

TEXAS DEPARTMENT OF PUBLIC SAFETY
P.O. Box 4087, Austin TX 78773-0001. 512/424-2000. **Physical address:** 5805 North Lamar Boulevard, Austin TX 78752-4422. **Contact:** Human Resources. **World Wide Web address:** http://www.txdps.state.tx.us. **Description:** Administrative offices for motor vehicles, including safety and drivers licenses. This location is also the state office for crime investigations and the central office for Texas state patrol officers. **NOTE:** See website for job listings and applications. Mail all resumes and completed applications to the P.O. Box address, Attention: Human Resources, unless a job posting states otherwise. **Positions advertised include:** Administrative Assistant; Inspector; Research Specialist; Crime Lab Evidence Technician; Program Specialist; Security Worker; Data Entry Operator; Trooper Trainee. Special Programs: State Trooper Training.

TEXAS DEPARTMENT OF TRANSPORTATION

P.O. Drawer 15426, Austin TX 78761.512/416-2994. **Toll-free phone:** 800/893-6817. **Recorded jobline:** 800/893-6848. **Contact:** Human Resources. **World Wide Web address:** http://www.dot.state.tx.us. **Description:** Designs, builds, and maintains roads and highways throughout the state of Texas. **NOTE:** This organization provides job listings for its locations throughout Texas. See website for job listings and apply online.

TEXAS HIGHER EDUCATION COORDINATING BOARD

P.O. Box 12788, Austin TX 78711-2788. 512/427-6101. **Recorded jobline:** 512/427-6574. **Contact:** Betty Sharp, Personnel Director. **World Wide Web address:** http://www.thecb.state.tx.us. **Description:** A governmental board that regulates educational issues in Texas. **NOTE:** A completed application is required for any position. See the organization's website for application information and job listings. **Office hours:** Monday – Friday, 8:00 a.m. – 5:00 p.m.

TEXAS PARKS & WILDLIFE

4200 Smith School Road, Austin TX 78744. 512/389-4800. **Toll-free phone:** 800/792-1112. **Recorded jobline:** 512/389-4954. **Contact:** Human Resources. **World Wide Web address:** http://www.tpwd.state.tx.us. **Description:** Dedicated to preserving the nature and wildlife of Austin and the surrounding Texas area. **NOTE:** This organization's website provides job listings for its locations throughout Texas. Apply online for open positions.

TEXAS STATE AUDITOR'S OFFICE

P.O. Box 12067, Austin TX 78711. 512/936-9500. **Fax:** 512/936-9400. **Contact:** Dennis Wilson, Human Resources Officer. **World Wide Web address:** http://www.sao.state.tx.us. **Description:** The independent auditor for the Texas state government. Texas State Auditor's Office provides legislators, agency management, and the citizens of Texas with information about the operations of state-run agencies and universities. Additional duties include the management of control audits, statewide financial and compliance audits, special investigations, classification compliance audits, briefing reports, legislative requests, and special issue areas. **NOTE:** An application is required. See the office's website for job listings and application. **Positions advertised include:** Senior Auditor; Senior Information Systems Audit Analyst; Staff Auditor; Texas State Auditor. **Special programs:** Internships; Training.

HEALTH CARE SERVICES, EQUIPMENT, AND PRODUCTS

You can expect to find the following types of companies in this section:
Dental Labs and Equipment • Home Health Care Agencies • Hospitals and Medical Centers • Medical Equipment Manufacturers and Wholesalers • Offices and Clinics of Health Practitioners • Residential Treatment Centers/Nursing Homes • Veterinary Services

ABBOTT LABORATORIES
3900 Howard Lane, Austin TX 78728. 512/255-2000. **Contact:** Human Resources. **World Wide Web address:** http://www.abbott.com. **Description:** This location manufactures intravenous bags for the medical industry. Overall, Abbott Laboratories manufactures a wide range of health care products including pharmaceuticals, hospital products, diagnostic products, chemical products, and nutritional products. **NOTE:** Please visit website to search for jobs and apply online. **Positions advertised include:** Quality Assurance and Regulatory Affairs Specialist; Sales and Marketing Specialist. **Special programs:** Internships; Co-ops; Summer programs. **Corporate headquarters location:** Abbott Park IL. **Other U.S. locations:** Nationwide. **International locations:** Worldwide. **Parent company:** Abbott Laboratories is an international manufacturer of a wide range of health care products including pharmaceuticals, hospital products, diagnostic products, chemical products, and nutritional products. **Listed on:** New York Stock Exchange. **Stock exchange symbol:** ABT. **Number of employees worldwide:** 70,000.

THE AUSTIN DIAGNOSTIC CENTER
12221 North Mopac Expressway, Austin TX 78758. 512/901-1111. **Toll-free phone:** 800/925-8899. **Recorded jobline:** 512/901-4050. **Contact:** Human Resources. **E-mail address:** jobs@adclinic.com. **World Wide Web address:** http://www.adclinic.com. **Description:** A physician-owned clinic with approximately 120 doctors in various specialties., such audiology, cosmetic laser surgery, diabetes management, menopause management, and optometry. Founded in 1995. **NOTE:** The center has several health facilities throughout Texas. The website lists jobs for all locations. All resumes must accompany an application which can be downloaded at the website or picked up at this location. **Positions advertised include**: LVN; Orthopedic Cast Technician; Business Associate Coordinator; IMX Data Entry; Cardiologist; Adult and Child Psychiatrist; Endocrinologist; Internal Medicine Physician.

AUSTIN REGIONAL CLINIC
6633 Highway 290 East, Suite 300, Austin TX, Austin TX 78723. 512/407-6463. **Fax:** 512/407-6464. **Contact:** Human Resources. **E-mail address:** jobs@covenantmso.com. **World Wide Web address:**

http://www.austinregionalclinic.com. **Description:** An acute care, outpatient, multispecialty facility that offers primary care for adults and children, OB/GYN, occupational medicine, mental health services, dermatology, surgery, optometry, allergy treatment, and immunology. **Positions advertised include:** Accounts Payable Technician; Coding Specialist; Patient Registration Representative; Accounts Receivable Clerk; Medical Lab Technician; LVN; Medical Assistant; Patient Services Representative; HIM Technician; Patient Services Representative; RN Team Leader.

AUSTIN STATE HOSPITAL
4110 Guadalupe Street, Austin TX 78751. 512/452-0381. **Fax:** 512/419-2306. **Contact:** Human Resources. **World Wide Web address:** http://www.mhmr.state.tx.us/hospitals/austinsh/austinsh.html.
Description: A 350-bed, acute psychiatric hospital. Austin State Hospital has many services to offer including a Deaf Unit, Children's Unit, and the Trinity Treatment Center, which aids people with mental retardation. **NOTE:** Please visit website to search for jobs and to download application forms. You may subscribe to have job postings e-mailed to you: Send an e-mail to hiring.services@mhmr.state.tx.us with the word "Subscribe" in the subject; do not send resumes or applications to this e-mail address. **Positions advertised include:** Psychiatrist; Clerk; MHMR Services Assistant; Custodian; Clinical Social Worker; Interpreter; Nurse; Nurse RN; LVN.

BAPTIST MEDICAL CENTER
111 Dallas Street, San Antonio TX 78205-1230. 210/297-7000. **Fax:** 210/297-0951. **Contact:** Annette Dunlap, Recruiter. **E-mail address:** amdunlap@baptisthealthsystem.com. **World Wide Web address:** http://www.baptisthealthsystem.org/bmc.asp. **Description:** A 689-bed, nonprofit, acute care hospital offering complete medical facilities for cardiac care, intensive care, emergency services, maternity, surgery, and other specialized services. **NOTE:** Please visit website to view job listings, apply online, or download application form. You may submit your resume or application directly to the hospital, or you can contact the Human Resources Center at 417 Camden, San Antonio TX 78215, fax is 210/297-0093. Volunteer positions are also available. **Positions advertised include:** Certified Occupational Therapy Assistant; LVN; Physical Therapist; RN. . **Parent company:** Baptist Memorial Hospital System is a health care system that is comprised of five acute care, nonprofit hospitals: Baptist Medical Center, Northeast Baptist Hospital, Southeast Baptist Hospital, North Center Baptist Hospital, and St. Luke's Baptist Hospital. In total, these hospitals contain 1,700 beds.

BAPTIST ST. ANTHONY HEALTH SYSTEM
1600 Wallace Boulevard, Amarillo TX 79106. 806/212-2000. **Contact:** Human Resources Manager. **World Wide Web address:** http://www.bsahs.com. **Description:** A 255-bed general hospital. Baptist St. Anthony Health System also offers home health services, a hospice program, a rehabilitation/skilled nursing facility, a senior health center and a sports and occupational health center. **NOTE:** Please visit website

to search for jobs and apply online. **Positions advertised include:** Area Technician; Administrative Assistant; Facility Technician; Billing Clerk; Cook; Office Clerk; RN; Nursing Technician; CNA; Paramedic; Biomedical Technician; Radiology Equipment Specialist; Nurse Practitioner; Physical Therapist; Respiratory Therapist; Speech Therapist.

BIG SPRING STATE HOSPITAL
1901 North Highway 87, Big Spring TX 79720. 432/268-7244. **Fax:** 432/268-7285. **Contact:** Dennis Warrington, Director of Human Resources. **E-mail address:** dennis.warrington@mhmr.state.tx.us. **World Wide Web address:** http://www.mhmr.state.tx.us/hospitals/bigspringsh/bigspringsh.html. **Description:** A nonprofit, state-governed facility that specializes in the treatment of patients with mental illness. **NOTE:** Entry-level positions and second and third shifts are offered. **Special programs:** Internships. **Corporate headquarters location:** Austin TX. **Parent company:** Texas Department of Mental Health and Mental Retardation. **Operations at this facility include:** Administration. **Number of employees at this location:** 650.

BLOOD AND TISSUE CENTER OF CENTRAL TEXAS
P.O. Box 4679, Austin TX 78765-4679. 512/206-1266. **Physical address:** 4300 North Lamar Boulevard, Austin TX 78756. **Fax:** 512/206-1261. **Recorded jobline:** 512/467-53416. **Contact:** Human Resources. **E-mail address:** resumes@tcms.com. **World Wide Web address:** http://www.bloodandtissue.org. **Description:** The blood bank for 100 Central Texas-area hospitals. It also provides human tissue and organs for 66 area hospitals. **NOTE:** Part-time positions offered. Resumes may be faxed, e-mailed or mailed. Interested jobseekers may also apply in person at the Human Resources office. **Positions advertised include:** Apheresis Technician; Technical Services Director; Donor Coordinator; Medical History Interviewer; Mobile Staff Training Coordinator. **Office hours:** Monday – Friday, 9:00 a.m. – 4:00 p.m.

CARBOMEDICS, INC.
1300 East Anderson Lane, Austin TX 78752-1799. 512/435-3200. **Fax:** 512/435-3350. **Recorded jobline:** 512/435-3413. **Contact:** Human Resources. **E-mail address:** employment@carbomedics.com. **World Wide Web address:** http://www.carbomedics.com. **Description:** A manufacturer of heart valve replacement products. **Parent company:** Sorin Group.

CARDINAL HEALTH
One Butterfield Trail, El Paso TX 79906. 915/779-3681. **Fax:** 915/775-9125. **Contact:** Human Resources. **World Wide Web address:** http://www.cardinal.net. **Description:** Cardinal Health is a producer, developer, and distributor of medical products and technologies for use in hospitals and other health care settings. **NOTE:** Please visit website to register, search for jobs, and apply online. **Positions advertised include:** Distribution Expeditor; Inventory Cycle Counter; Technical

Associate; Maintenance Supervisor; Sterilization Superintendent; Human Resources Manager; Raw Material Wholesale Supervisor; Group Plant Controller; Drafter; Production Supervisor; Programmer Analyst. **Corporate headquarters location:** Dublin OH. **Operations at this facility include:** This location manufactures disposable hospital gowns and drapes. **Listed on:** New York Stock Exchange. **Stock exchange symbol:** CAH. **Number of employees worldwide:** 55,000.

CHRISTUS SANTA ROSA HOSPITAL
333 North Santa Rosa Street, San Antonio TX 78207. 210/704-2011. **Contact:** Human Resources. **World Wide Web address:** http://www.christussantarosa.org. **Description:** Santa Rosa Hospital is an acute care hospital with 500 beds. **NOTE:** Contact Human Resources at 210/704-2067. Visit http://heavenlycareers.com to search for jobs. **Positions advertised include:** Registered Nurse; Pre Access Nurse; Licensed Vocational Nurse; Nurse Liaison; Respiratory Therapist; Medical Technologist; Physical Therapist; Registered Nuclear Medicine Technologist; Histology Technician; Medical Lab Technician; Radiology Technician; Laboratory Section Supervisor; OR Technician; Physical Therapy Assistant; Pharmacist; Case Manager; Social Worker; Enterstomal Therapy Nurse; PAL Supervisor; Speech Pathologist; Recreation Therapist; Occupational Therapist; Radiology Director; Senior Financial Analyst; Clerk Phlebotomist. **Parent company:** CHRISTUS Health.

CHRISTUS SPOHN HOSPITAL SHORELINE
600 Elizabeth Street, Corpus Christi TX 78404. 361/881-3000. **Contact:** Human Resources. **World Wide Web address:** http://www.christusspohn.org. **Description:** A 432-bed acute care medical facility. **NOTE:** Please visit website to search for jobs and apply online. **Positions advertised include:** Vice President of Strategic Planning and Business Development; Clinical Dietitian; CRT; LVN; OR Technician; Radiology Technologist; RN – Various Departments; Registered Respiratory Therapist; Ultrasound Technician. **Corporate headquarters location:** San Antonio TX. **Parent company:** CHRISTUS Health. **Operations at this facility include:** Service.

CITIZENS MEDICAL CENTER
P.O. Box 2024, Victoria TX 77902. 361/573-9181. **Physical address:** 2701 Hospital Drive, Victoria TX 77901. **Fax:** 361/573-0611. **Contact:** Shelley Frank, Employment Specialist. **E-mail address:** sfrank@cmcvtx.org. **World Wide Web address:** http://www.citizensmedicalcenter.com. **Description:** A 368-bed acute care medical center. Citizens Medical Center provides many services including a Women's Pavilion and a cancer treatment floor. Founded in 1956. **NOTE:** Contact Employment directly at 361/572-5066. **Positions advertised include:** Fitness Specialist; Physical Therapist; Physical Therapy Assistant; RN – Various Departments. **Number of employees at this location:** 1,300.

EDINBURG REGIONAL MEDICAL CENTER

1102 West Trenton Road, P.O. Box 2000, Edinburg TX 78539. 956/388-6000. **Contact:** Human Resources. **World Wide Web address:** http://www.edinburgregional.com. **Description:** A 130-bed medical center offering a wide variety of medical and diagnostic services. **NOTE:** Job listings found on UHS website: uhsinc.com. **Corporate headquarters location:** King of Prussia PA. **Parent company:** Universal Health Services, Inc. **Listed on:** New York Stock Exchange. **Stock exchange symbol:** UHS.

ETHICON, INC.

3348 Pulliam Street, San Angelo TX 76905-4430. 915/482-5200. **Contact:** Human Resources. **World Wide Web address:** http://www.ethicon.com. **Description:** Manufactures products for precise wound closure including sutures, ligatures, mechanical wound closure instruments, and related products. The company makes its own surgical needles and provides thousands of needle-suture combinations to surgeons. Ethicon also provides women's health products under the trade name Gynecare. **Parent company:** Johnson & Johnson (New Brunswick NJ). **Listed on:** New York Stock Exchange. **Stock exchange symbol:** JNJ.

HARBOR VIEW CARE CENTER

1314 Third Street, Corpus Christi TX 78404. 361/888-5511. **Contact:** Jill Doire, Divisional Recruiter. **World Wide Web address:** http://www.tricare.com. **Description:** A 116-bed hospital. Founded in 1993. **Parent company:** Trans Healthcare.

HARRINGTON CANCER CENTER

1500 Wallace Boulevard, Amarillo TX 79106. 806/359-4673. **Toll-free phone:** 800/274-HOPE. **Fax:** 806/354-5881. **Contact:** Lynda McCarty, Human Resources Manager. **World Wide Web address:** http://www.harringtoncc.org. **Description:** Provides various services to cancer patients who formerly had to travel hundreds of miles for treatment. Medical specialties include radiation services, medical oncology, blood diseases and hematology, supportive care, a women's center, and cancer prevention and education. Volunteer opportunities are available. **NOTE:** All interested jobseekers must fill out a job application to be considered for employment. Applications can be picked up in the Human Resources Department or obtained online.

HENDRICK HEALTH SYSTEM

1242 North 19th Street, Abilene TX 79601-2316. 915/670-2000. **Fax:** 325/670-4417. **Recorded jobline:** 325/670-3300. **Contact:** Human Resources. **E-mail address:** hrdept@ehendrick.org. **World Wide Web address:** http://www.hendrickhealth.org. **Description:** Operates a 525-bed, general hospital. Founded in 1924. **Positions advertised include:** Admitting Representative; Attendant; Audiologist; Cafeteria Aide; Certified Surgical Technician; Clinical Coordinator/Educator; Construction Technician; Cook; Customer Service Representative; Environmental Services Technician; File Technician; Financial Analyst;

General Supervisor; Home Health Aide; LVN; Medical Office Specialist; Medical Technologist; Nurse Aide; Nurse Practitioner; Physical Therapist; Registered Nurse; Security Officer; Specialty Technician; Storage/Retrieval Technician; Trayline Aide. **Parent company:** Baptist General Convention of Texas.

HILL COUNTRY MEMORIAL HOSPITAL
P.O. Box 835, Fredericksburg TX 78624-0835. 830/997-4353. **Physical address:** 1020 South State Highway 16, Fredericksburg TX 78624. **Contact:** Human Resources. **World Wide Web address:** http://www.hillcountrymemorial.com. **E-mail address:** hr@hillcountrymemorial.com. **Description:** A 77-bed, acute care hospital. Hill County Memorial Hospital offers a skilled nursing unit, medical surgery, OB/GYN, urology, and orthopedics. The hospital also has a Wellness Center that offers preventative care. Founded in 1971. **NOTE:** Applications for positions can be found at the company's website. **Positions advertised include:** RN; LVN; Physical Therapist; Nurse Aide; Thrift Shop Helper; Computer Technician; Staffing Clerk; Staffing Clerk.

INTERNATIONAL BIOMEDICAL, INC.
8508 Cross Park Drive, Austin TX 78754. 512/873-0033. **Contact:** Human Resources. **World Wide Web address:** http://www.int-bio.com. **Description:** A manufacturer of high-technology medical instruments including infant incubators and radiation gloves. International Biomedical also manufactures electronic equipment used in research, testing, and teaching. **Corporate headquarters location:** Cleburne TX. **Operations at this facility include:** Manufacturing.

KCI (KINECTIC CONCEPTS, INC.)
14th Floor, KCI Tower, 8023 Vantage Drive, San Antonio TX 78265-9508. 210/524-9000. **Toll-free phone:** 210/275-4524. **Fax:** 210/255-6998. **Contact:** Human Resources. **World Wide Web address:** http://www.kci1.com. **Description:** Manufactures, sells, services, and rents hospital beds for the critically ill. **NOTE:** This company provides job listings and specific contact information on its website. **Corporate headquarters location:** This location. **Listed on:** New York Stock Exchange. **Stock exchange symbol:** KCI.

KERRVILLE STATE HOSPITAL
721 Thompson Drive, Kerrville TX 78028. 830/896-2211. **Contact:** Human Resources. **Description:** A psychiatric hospital with 200 inpatient beds and 33 medical unit beds. Founded in 1951. **World Wide Web address:** http://www.mhmr.state.tx.us/hospitals/kerrvillesh. **NOTE:** A completed application must be submitted with each resume. The application can be found on the website. **Positions advertised include:** RN; LVN. **Corporate headquarters location:** Austin TX.

KIMBERLY-CLARK TECNOL INC.
14 Finnegan Drive, Del Rio TX 78840. 830/774-7482. **Contact:** Human Resources. **World Wide Web address:** http://www.kchealthcare.com.

Description: A warehouse that distributes medical products. **Parent company:** Kimberly-Clark Corporation. **Listed on:** New York Stock Exchange. **Stock exchange symbol:** KMB.

LUMINEX CORPORATION
12212 Technology Boulevard, Austin TX. 78727-6115. 512/219-8020. **Toll-free phone:** 888/219-8020. **Fax:** 512/219-5195. **Contact:** Human Resources. **World Wide Web address:** http://www.luminexcorp.com. **Description:** Manufacturer of sensor and measurement equipment for biotechnology companies. **NOTE:** Apply online. **Positions advertised include:** Software Quality Assurance Engineer. **Listed on:** NASDAQ. **Stock exchange symbol:** LMNX.

MCALLEN MEDICAL CENTER
301 West Expressway 83, McAllen TX 78503. 956/632-4000. **Contact:** Human Resources. **World Wide Web address:** http://www.mcallenmedicalcenter.com. **Description:** Part of the South Texas Health System, a full-service acute care hospital. The medical center has a well-known heart hospital, too. **NOTE:** Apply online for open positions. **Parent company:** Universal Health Network.

McKENNA MEMORIAL HOSPITAL
600 North Union Avenue, New Braunfels TX 78130. 830/606-9111. **Recorded jobline:** 830/606-2151. **Contact:** Human Resources Coordinator. **E-mail address:** hr@mckenna.org. **World Wide Web address:** http://www.mckenna.org. **Description:** A 116-bed, short-term care hospital. McKenna Memorial Hospital also offers an occupational health department. **NOTE:** An application must submitted for any position. The application can be obtained at the company's website. **Positions advertised include:** Coder; Care Coordinator; Parenting Instructor; Medical Technologist; Clinical Recruiter; Occupational Therapist; Monitor Technician; RN; LVN; Ultrasound Technician; Radiology Technician; Respiratory Therapist.

MEDICAL CENTER HOSPITAL/ODESSA
500 West Fourth Street, Odessa TX 79761. 915/640-4000. **Fax:** 915/640-1245. **Contact:** Candy Powell RN, Recruitment/Retention Coordinator.. **E-mail address:** lmelson@echd.org. **World Wide Web address:** http://www.odessamch.org. **Description:** A 396-bed, acute care hospital. Medical Center Hospital provides various services including a neonatal care nursery, skilled nursing facility, Intensive Care Unit, Critical Care Unit, and 24-hour emergency care. **NOTE:** An application must be submitted for any position. See company's website for application **Positions advertised include:** Charge RN; Unit Clerk; Divisional Director; Paramedic.

MESA HILLS SPECIALTY HOSPITAL
2311 North Oregon Street, Fifth Floor, El Paso TX 79902. 915/545-1823. **Contact:** Jill Doire, Divisional Recruiter. **World Wide Web address:** http://www.tricare.com. **Description:** A 181-bed long-term, acute care hospital. Parent company: Trans Healthcare.

METHODIST SPECIALTY AND TRANSPLANT HOSPITAL
8026 Floyd Curl Drive, San Antonio TX 78229. 210/575-8110. **Recorded jobline:** 210/575-4562. **Contact:** Human Resources. **World Wide Web address:** http://www.mhshealth.com. **Description:** A 382-bed, licensed medical facility specializing in organ and tissue transplants, impotency treatments, incontinence treatments, gastroenteric procedures, and laparoscopic surgery. **NOTE:** Interested jobseekers may apply online at the company's website. **Positions advertised include:** Activity Therapist; Ancillary Support Technician; Diet Clerk; Echo Technician; LVN; RN: Physical Therapist.

METROPOLITAN METHODIST HOSPITAL
1310 McCullough Avenue, San Antonio TX 78212. 210/208-2200. **Fax:** 210/208-2924. **Recorded jobline:** 210/575-4562. **Contact:** Human Resources. **World Wide Web address:** http://www.metro.sahealth.com. **Description:** A 263-bed hospital that offers both long-term and short-term care. This hospital is part of the Methodist Healthcare System. **NOTE:** Interested jobseekers must complete an application which can be found on the company's website. **Positions advertised include:** Coding/Compliance Manager; Data Entry Clerk; Decentralized Pediatric Pharmacist; Histology Technician; Radiologist.

MIDLAND MEMORIAL HOSPITAL
2200 West Illinois Avenue, Midland TX 79701. 432/685-1111. **Contact:** Maria McAllister, Human Resources Director. **World Wide Web address:** http://www.midland-memorial.com. **Description:** A full-service, 300-bed health facility. Midland Memorial is part of a group of three hospitals serving the Midland area. The other hospitals are Memorial West and Memorial Rehabilitation **NOTE:** Interested jobseekers must complete an application for all positions. The application can be found on the company's website. **Positions advertised include:** RN; Respiratory Care Technician; Human Resources Assistant; Paramedic; Nuclear Medicine Technician; Physical Therapist.

MISSION HOSPITAL, INC.
900 South Bryan Road, Mission TX 78572. 956/580-9188. **Contact:** Marissa Aldrete, Hospital Recruiter at 956/584-4683. . **E-mail address:** maldrete@missionhospital.org. **World Wide Web address:** http://www.missionhospital.org. **Description:** A 138-bed acute care facility. **Positions advertised include:** Respiratory Therapist; Registered Nurse; Radiology Technician; Registration Representative. **Operations at this facility include:** Health Care; Service.

NIX HEALTH CARE SYSTEM
414 Navarro Street, San Antonio TX 78205. 210/271-1800. **Fax:** 210/271-2167. **Contact:** Human Resources. **World Wide Web address:** http://www.nixhealth.com. **Description:** Operates a 150-bed hospital. Nix Health Care offers such services as prenatal care, a geriatric psychiatry unit, and a skilled nursing unit. **Positions advertised include:** Financial Analyst; Needs Assessment Clinician; Community

Education Coordinator; Commercial/Managed Care Collector; Medicare Collector; Patient Access Specialist; RN; LVN; Food Service Aide; Food Service Supervisor.

NORTHEAST BAPTIST MRI CENTER
8815 Village Drive, San Antonio TX 78217. 210/297-2870. **Contact:** Human Resources. **World Wide Web address:** http://www.baptisthealth.org. **Description:** A medical center that performs MRIs. The center is part of Baptist Hospital.

NORTHWEST TEXAS HEALTHCARE SYSTEM
1506 Coulter Street, Amarillo TX 79106. 806/354-1000. **Recorded jobline:** 806/354-1905. **Contact:** Human Resources. **World Wide Web address:** http://www.nwtexashealthcare.com. **Description:** Operates Northwest Texas Hospital and The Pavilion. Northwest Texas Hospital offers more than 35 medical specialties and subspecialties. The Pavilion is a full-service mental health facility that provides a comprehensive range of services to people of all ages. **NOTE:** Applications are only accepted in the office for current positions. Application is available online. **Positions advertised include:** RN; LVN. **Parent company:** Universal Health Services. **Office hours:** Monday – Friday, 7:00 a.m. – 5:00 p.m.

ODESSA REGIONAL HOSPITAL
520 East Sixth Street, Odessa TX 79760. 915/334-8397. **Contact:** Human Resources. **World Wide Web address:** http://www.odessaregionalhospital.com. **Description:** A hospital offering specialized labor/delivery services, pediatrics, family care, and surgical services. **NOTE:** An application is required for any position. The application can be found online at the hospital's website. **Positions advertised include:** RN; Respiratory Therapist; Medical Auditor.. **Parent company:** IASIS Healthcare. **Listed on:** Privately held..

SID PETERSON MEMORIAL HOSPITAL
710 Water Street, Kerrville TX 78028. 830/258-7440. **Recorded jobline:** 830/258-7562. **Contact:** Human Resources. **E-mail address:** jobs@spmh.com. **World Wide Web address:** http://www.spmh.com. **Description:** A long-term care general hospital offering centers for cardiac rehabilitation, osteoporosis, and cancer treatment. **NOTE:** This hospital requires interested jobseekers to complete an application. Applications can be downloaded at the website. Full-time and part-time positions are available. **Positions advertised include:** Floor Technician; Housekeeper; Clinical Coordinator; LVN; RN; Administrative Assistant; Speech Language Pathologist; Rehabilitation Aide; Case Manager; Coder; Communications Operator.

PRIME MEDICAL SERVICES, INC.
1301 Capital of Texas Highway South, Suite C-300, Austin TX 78746. 512/328-2892. **Contact:** Human Resources. **World Wide Web address:** http://www.primemedical.com. **Description:** Through its subsidiaries, Prime Medical Services provides non-medical management services to

lithotripsy and cardiac rehabilitation centers. Prime Medical Services operates 67 lithotripters.. **Listed on:** NASDAQ. **Stock exchange symbol:** PMSI.

RIO VISTA REHABILITATION HOSPITAL
1740 Curie Drive, El Paso TX 79902. 915/544-3399. **Contact:** Human Resources. **World Wide Web address:** http://www.sphn.com. **Description:** An inpatient and outpatient rehabilitation facility that assists patients experiencing orthopedic problems, joint replacement, trauma, arthritis, or amputation. **NOTE:** Apply online at this hospital's website. **Positions advertised include:** RN; LVN; Endoscopy Technician; Case Manager; Surgery Coordinator; Laboratory Assistant; Administrative Director. **Parent company:** Tenet Health System.

ROUND ROCK MEDICAL CENTER
2400 Round Rock Avenue, Round Rock TX 78681. 512/341-1000. **Contact:** Human Resources. **World Wide Web address:** http://www.roundrockhospital.com. **Description:** A 109-bed general hospital. Services include a 24-hour emergency room, Family Birthing Center, medical/surgical unit, six-bed intensive care unit, and a nine-bed skilled nursing unit. Founded in 1983. This hospital is part of the HealthCare Partnership with three other hospitals in Austin TX. **NOTE:** Submit resume online for open positions. **Positions advertised include:** Clinical Dietitian; RN; Supervisor; Pharmacy Technician; Food Services Associate; Security Guard; Mammographer; Speech Language Pathologist.

ST. DAVID'S MEDICAL CENTER
98 San Jacinto Boulevard, Suite 1800, Austin TX, 78701. 512/708-9700. **Contact:** Human Resources. **World Wide Web address:** http://www.stdavids.com. **Description:** A 400-bed hospital specializing in all types of adult medical care. **Positions advertised include:** Patient Care Technician; Phlebotomist; Pharmacy Technician; RN; Physical Therapist; Radiology Technician; Physical Therapist; Diet Clerk.

SAN MARCOS TREATMENT CENTER
120 Bert Brown Road, San Marcos TX 78666. 512/396-8500. **Fax:** 512/754-3883. **Contact:** Human Resources.. **World Wide Web address:** http://www.psysolutions.com. **Description:** A 186-bed neuropsychiatric hospital that specializes in treating adolescents and young adults who have not had success in other settings. The center's patients are primarily those who experience emotional disturbances, severe impulses, aggressive behavior patterns, unprovoked mood swings, known neurological or organic disorders, seizure disorders, language problems, or severe learning complications due to substance abuse and sexual trauma. Founded in 1940. **NOTE:** Jobseekers should visit the center to complete an application. **Office hours:** Monday – Friday, 7:00 a.m. – 11:00 p.m. **Parent company:** Psychiatric Solutions, Inc.

SETON HEALTHCARE NETWORK

1201 West 38th Street, Austin TX 78705. 512/324-4000. **Toll-free phone:** 800/880-0038. **Fax:** 512/324-1672. **Recorded jobline:** 512/324-1679. **Contact:** Human Resources Recruiters. **World Wide Web address:** http://www.seton.net. **Description:** A nonprofit, multi-facility health care network. Facilities include four acute care hospitals, community clinics, home care providers, outreach programs, and physicians' offices. **NOTE:** Entry-level positions and second and third shifts are offered. See the company's website for application information and job listings or visit the Human Resources office. **Company slogan:** Health.Care.Made Simpler. **Office hours:** Monday – Friday, 8:00 a.m. – 4:30 p.m. **Corporate headquarters location:** St. Louis MO. **Parent company:** Daughters of Charity.

SHANNON CLINIC

120 East Beauregard, San Angelo TX 76903. 325/658-1511x3159. **Fax:** 325/481-2181. **Contact:** Human Resources. **World Wide Web address:** http://www.shannonhealth.com. **Description:** Part Of The Shannon Health System, this clinic is composed of specialty physicians in Cardiology, Vision, OB/GYN, and Pediatrics. **NOTE:** See website for job listings and applications. **Other area locations:** Del Angelo TX; Big Lake TX.

SHANNON MEDICAL CENTER

120 East Harris, San Angelo TX 76903. 325/657-5243. **Fax:** 325/481-8521. **Recorded jobline:** 325/657-5298. **Contact:** Human Resources. **E-mail address:** jobs@shannonhealthorg. **World Wide Web address:** http://www.shannonhealth.com. **Description:** A 400-bed, non-profit hospital offering surgery, intensive care, orthopedic, oncology, telemetry, skilled nursing, and cardiac services. Shannon Medical Center also operates a Level III trauma and sleep disorder center. Founded in 1932. This medical center is affiliated with three other healthcare facilities. **NOTE:** Entry-level positions and second and third shifts are offered. **Positions advertised include:** Cashier; Surgery Assistant; Registration Assistant; Dietitian; Medical Technologist; Occupational Therapist; Recreational Therapist; RN; Food Service Worker; Monitor Technician. **Special programs:** Training. **Office hours:** Monday - Friday, 8:00 a.m. - 5:00 p.m. **Corporate headquarters location:** This location.

SIERRA PROVIDENCE HEALTH NETWORK

1625 Medical Center Drive, El Paso, TX 79902. 915/577-6000. **Contact:** Human Resources. **World Wide Web address:** http://www.sphn.com. **Description:** The network consists of three hospitals in the area: The Sierra Medical Center, Providence Memorial Hospital, and Rio Vista, a rehab hospital. Combined the network has nearly 900 beds and provides comprehensive acute care medical services. Rio Vista provides services to those patients with brain injuries. **NOTE:** A completed application is required for any position at any of the three hospitals. The website provides job listings for all three facilities. Apply online. **Positions advertised include:** EKG Technician; ECHO Technician; Assistant Security Director; Medical Transcriptionist; RN (Various); LVN (Various);

Plant Maintenance; Insurance Verifier; Secretary; Admitting Representative; Speech Therapist; Ultrasound Technician; Pharmacist; Medical Records Coder. **Parent company:** Tenet Healthcare.

SOUTH AUSTIN HOSPITAL
901 West Ben White Boulevard, Austin TX 78704. 512/448-7110. **Toll-free phone:** 800/568-3297. **Contact:** Human Resources. **World Wide Web address:** http://www.southaustinhospital.com. **Description:** An acute care, 162-bed hospital that provides basic care for the region. **NOTE:** Apply online at this hospital's website. **Positions advertised include:** Health Information Management Director; Food Service Supervisor; Pharmacy Technician; Medical Technician; Patient Care Technician; Anesthesia Technician; RN; Food Services Associate.

SOUTHWEST GENERAL HOSPITAL
7400 Barlite Boulevard, San Antonio TX 78224. 210/921-3439. **Fax:** 210/921-3450. **Recorded jobline:** 210/921-3439. **Contact:** Recruiter. **World Wide Web address:** http://www.swgeneralhospital.com. **Description:** A 319-bed, acute care hospital. Southwest General Hospital offers multiple diagnostic treatment and services in the following medical specialties: general and orthopedic surgery; physical therapy and rehabilitation, the treatment of strokes and complications resulting from diabetes; plastic and oral surgery; pediatrics; cardiac and pulmonary services; treatment of infectious diseases; and diabetes treatment. Southwest General Hospital offers a full range of psychi services including adult inpatient, adolescent inpatient, and partial hospitalization for adults. Founded in 1979. Southwest General has three sister facilities in Texas: Mid-Jefferson Hospital (Nederland TX); Odessa Regional Hospital (Odessa TX); and, Park Place Medical Center (Port Arthur TX). **NOTE:** Apply online at this hospital's website. **Positions advertised include:** RN; Biomedical Technician; Case Manager; LVN; Medical Technologist; Coder; Dietician. **Corporate headquarters location:** Franklin TN. **Other U.S. locations:** Nationwide. **Parent company:** IASIS Healthcare. **Operations at this facility include:** Administration; Service.

SOUTHWEST TEXAS METHODIST HOSPITAL
METHODIST WOMEN'S & CHILDREN'S HOSPITAL
7700 Floyd Curl Drive, San Antonio TX 78229. 210/575-4000. **Recorded jobline:** 210/57-4562. **Contact:** Human Resources. **World Wide Web address:** http://www.sahealth.com. **Description:** A 626-bed hospital that offers both short- and long-term care. Methodist Women's & Children's Hospital is a 150-bed hospital that specializes in labor, delivery, and pediatrics. **NOTE:** Apply online at the hospital's website for open positions.

SPECIALTY HOSPITAL OF SAN ANTONIO
7310 Oak Manor Drive, San Antonio 78229. 210/308-0261. **Contact:** Jill Doire, Divisional Recruiter. **World Wide Web address:** http://www.tricare.com. **Description:** A long-Term, acute Care hospital.

Note: Entry-level positions and part-time jobs are offered. **Positions advertised include:** Administrator. **Parent company:** Trans Healthcare.

STARLITE RECOVERY CENTER
Elm Pass Road, Center Point TX 78010-0317. 830/634-2212. **Contact:** Human Resources. **World Wide Web address:** http://www.starliterecovery.com. **Description:** A residential treatment center for adults and adolescents, offering specialized care for substance abusers. **Parent company:** CRC Health Corporation.

TEXAS CENTER FOR INFECTIOUS DISEASE
2303 SE Military Drive, San Antonio TX 78223. 210/534-8857x2255. **Fax:** 210/531-4504. **Contact:** Human Resources Director. **World Wide Web address:** http://www.tdh.state.tx.us/tcid. **Description:** A hospital that provides acute and chronic care to all patients referred for evaluation. **NOTE:** Texas Center for Infectious Disease offers career opportunities in the following areas: Chronic Respiratory Disease Services, which allows individuals to work with inpatient respiratory disease patients with a concentration on physical rehabilitation, patient education, and lifestyle adaptations; Diabetic Services, in which care includes medical evaluation and patient teaching; Chest Disease Services, through which the hospital treats diseases such as lung cancer, fungal disease, and tuberculosis; and Ambulatory Services, which offers an opportunity to work in a variety of clinics to include chest, Hansen's Disease, diabetes, and infectious diseases. The Texas Center for Infectious Disease also has a Tuberculosis Education Center. **NOTE:** Apply online at this organization's website. **Special programs:** Internships. **Corporate headquarters location:** Austin TX. **Operations at this facility include:** Administration; Research and Development; Service.

TRANS HEALTHCARE, INC.
7310 Oak Manor Drive, San Antonio TX 78229. 210/308-0261. **Contact:** Jill Doire, Divisional Recruiter. **E-mail address:** jill.doire@his-inc.com. **World Wide Web address:** http://www.thicare.com. **Description:** A 138-bed acute care hospital offering a wide range of long- and short-term care services. **NOTE:** This company operates several hospitals in Dallas, Corpus Christi and El Paso TX. See company's website for information and job listings for these locations. Jill Doire is the contact for all the hospitals.

UMC HEALTH SYSTEM
602 Indiana Avenue, Lubbock TX 79415. 806/775-9222. **Recorded jobline:** 806/775-9215. **Contact:** Human Resources Manager. **World Wide Web address:** http://www.teamumc.org. **Description:** A 354-bed facility that includes The Children's Hospital, The Southwest Cancer and Research Center, Level I Trauma Center, a Pre-Hospital Emergency Service, a Burn Intensive Care Unit, and Community Outreach Programs. **NOTE:** For nursing opportunities, call 806/775-8912. A complete application is required for any position. Visit the website to print an application or apply online. **Positions advertised include:**

Accountant; Cafeteria Aide; Cardiac Sonographer; Health Unit Coordinator; RN, LVN, Patient/Staff Educator; Renovation Technician. **Special programs:** Volunteer.

U.S. DEPARTMENT OF VETERANS AFFAIRS
AMARILLO VA HEALTH CARE SYSTEM
6010 West Amarillo Boulevard, Amarillo TX 79106. 806/355-9703. **Fax:** 806/354-7860. **Recorded jobline:** 806/354-7828. **Contact:** Human Resources. **World Wide Web address:** http://www.va.gov. **Description:** Part of the U.S. Veterans Administration, this organization is composed of healthcare facilities that include 200 beds for acute, geriatric and extended care. Serves the Childress, Lubbock, Stratford TX communities, Clovis NM, and Liberal KS. This location is also a teaching facility. **NOTE:** Apply in person at this facility's Human Resources office. Monday – Friday, 7:30 a.m. – 4:30 p.m.

U.S. DEPARTMENT OF VETERANS AFFAIRS
EL PASO VA HEALTH CARE SYSTEM
5001 North Pledras Street, El Paso TX 79930-4211. 915/564-6100. **Fax:** 915/564-7920. **Contact:** Human Resources. **World Wide Web address:** http://www.va.gov. **Description:** This system provides acute medical care for military personnel. It is also a teaching facility with residences in internal medicine and psychiatry. **NOTE:** Apply in person at the Human Resources Office.

U.S. DEPARTMENT OF VETERANS AFFAIRS
SOUTH TEXAS VETERANS HEALTH CARE SYSTEM
740 Merton Minter Boulevard, San Antonio TX 78229. 210/617-5300. **Contact:** Human Resources. **World Wide Web address:** http://www.vasthcs.med.va.gov. **Description:** A medical center with nearly 1,500 beds for medical, psychiatric and rehabilitative services. Affiliated with the Veterans Administration and the Texas Health Science Center. It has a number of outpatient clients and community-based clinics, including homeless programs, throughout surrounding Texas locations. **NOTE:** apply online. **Other area locations:** Kerrville TX (Medical Center).

U.S. DEPARTMENT OF VETERANS AFFAIRS
WEST TEXAS VA HEALTH CARE SYSTEM
300 Veterans Boulevard, Big Spring, TX 79720. 325/263-7361. **Fax:** 325/264-4834. **Contact:** Human Resources. **World Wide Web address:** http://www.va.gov. **Description:** A medical center consisting of about 100 beds and serves nearly 50 West Texas and New Mexico communities. Ophthalmology is a specialty. A teaching facility.

VALLEY BAPTIST MEDICAL CENTER
P.O. Drawer 2588, Harlingen TX 78550. 956/389-4703. **Physical address:** 2101 Pease Street, Harlingen TX 78550. **Toll-free phone:** 800/828-8262. **Recorded jobline:** 956/389-2330. **Contact:** Human Resources. **E-mail address:** humanresources@valleybaptist.net. **World Wide Web address:** http://www.vbmc.org. **Description:** A 588-bed,

nonprofit, acute care, medical center. **NOTE:** Part-time, second and third shifts are offered. A completed application is required for any position. Apply online or fax or mail application. Walk-in applicants are also accepted in Human Resources during regular office hours. **Positions advertised include:** Accounting; Speech Language Pathologist; Electro-Physiology Technologist; Corporate Communications Coordinator; Licensed Physical Therapist; Bereavement Coordinator; Nurse Recruiter; RN; LVN; Medication Aide; Buyer—Project Coordinator. **Special programs:** Internships; Co-ops; Summer Jobs. **Corporate headquarters location:** This location.

VALLEY REGIONAL MEDICAL CENTER
100A Alton Gloor Boulevard, Brownsville TX 78526. 956/350-7000. **Contact:** Human Resources. **World Wide Web address:** http://www.valleyregionalmedicalcenter.com. **Description:** This 171-bed, acute care medical center offers services such as skilled nursing, rehabilitation, and various medical specialties. **NOTE:** Part-time, weekend, flex-time positions offered. Apply online at the center's website. **Positions advertised include:** Director of Imaging; Case Manager; RN; Director of Therapeutic Services; Speech Therapist. **Special programs:** Volunteers.

ZIMMER, INC.
9900 Spectrum Drive, Austin TX 78717. 512/432-9900. **Fax:** 512/432-9200. **Recorded jobline:** 512/432-9283. **Contact:** Human Resources. **World Wide Web address:** http://www.centerpulsorthropedics.com. **Description:** A worldwide leader in the manufacture and distribution of orthopedic implants for knees, hips, and shoulders. **NOTE:** Apply online at this company's website or in person at the Human Resources Office. **Positions advertised include:** Associate Scientist; Internal System Auditor; Temporary Machinist; Sales Support Representative.

HOTELS AND RESTAURANTS

You can expect to find the following types of companies in this section:
Casinos • Dinner Theaters • Hotel/Motel Operators • Resorts • Restaurants

---

ALAMO CAFE
P.O. BOX 790721, San Antonio TX 78279-0721. 210/341-1336. **Fax:** 210/341-3036. **Contact:** Human Resources. **World Wide Web address:** http://www.alamocafe.com. **Description:** A family-style restaurant that serves both American and Mexican foods. **Corporate headquarters location:** This location. **Parent company:** Alamo Restaurants Inc.

BEST VALUE INN & SUITES
6911 North Interstate Highway 35, Austin TX 78752. 512/459-4251. **Contact:** Human Resources. **World Wide Web address:** http://www.bestvalueinn.com. **Description:** One location of the nationwide hotel chain. **Other area locations:** Buda TX.

DOUBLETREE GUEST SUITES HOTEL
303 West 15th Street, Austin TX 78701. 512/478-7000. **Fax:** 512/478-3562. **Contact:** Monica D'Richards, Human Resources Director. **NOTE:** Applications only on Mondays and Tuesdays from 9:00 a.m.-noon. **World Wide Web address:** http://www.doubletree.com. **Description:** A 189-room hotel. **Parent company:** Hilton.

EMBASSY SUITES HOTEL
300 South Congress Avenue, Austin TX 78704. 512/469-9000. **Contact:** Human Resources Department. **World Wide Web address:** http://www.embassy-suites.com. **Description:** A 262-room hotel.

EMBASSY SUITES HOTEL
4250 Ridgemont Drive, Abilene TX 79606. 915/698-1234. **Contact:** Human Resources Department. **World Wide Web address:** http://www.embassy-suites.com. **Description:** A 176-room hotel.

FRONTIER ENTERPRISES
8520 Crownhill Boulevard, San Antonio TX 78209-1199. 210/828-1493. **Contact:** Ms. Pat Gomez, Human Resources Director.. **World Wide Web address:** http://www.jimsrestaurants.com. **Description:** Owns and operates Jim's Family Restaurants, Magic Time Machine Restaurants, and Towers of America Restaurants. Magic Time Machine Restaurants are seafood and steak dining establishments and the Towers of America Restaurants are family-style restaurants set approximately 6,000 feet in the air. **NOTE:** Online applications available at company's website for all Texas locations. **Positions advertised include:** Manager; Assistant Manager; Waitstaff; Cook; Busperson; Cashier. **Corporate**

headquarters location: This location. **Other area locations**: Austin TX; San Antonio TX; Waco TX.

HYATT REGENCY HILL COUNTRY RESORT AND SPA
9800 Hyatt Resort Drive, San Antonio TX 78251. 210/647-1234. **Contact:** Penny Nichols Bowden, Human Resources Director. **World Wide Web address:** http://www.hyatt.com. **Description:** Operates as a unit of the nationwide chain of hotels. Hyatt Regency Hill Country Resort has six locations throughout Texas. **Positions advertised include:** Banquet Server; Bartender; Bell Attendant; Cocktail Server; Food Runner; Deli Attendant; Massage Therapist; Nail Technician; Spa Attendant; Retail Clerk; Sales Manager; Room Service Server; Valet Attendant; Yoga Instructor. **Parent company:** Hyatt Hotels Corporation.

LDB CORPORATION
444 Sidney Baker Street South, Kerrville TX 78028. 830/257-2000. **Contact:** Barbara Fisher, Human Resources Manager. **Description:** Operates the Mr. Gatti's national pizza chain. **Corporate headquarters location:** This location.

LA QUINTA INNS, INC.
909 Hidden Ridge, Suite 600, Irving TX 75038. 210/302-6000. **Contact:** Human Resources. **World Wide Web address:** http://www.lq.com. **Description:** Develops, owns, and operates a nationwide chain of lodging inns. La Quinta Inns has more than 330 locations in 32 states. Founded in 1964. **NOTE:** To apply for hotel positions, see company's website for job listings. **Positions advertised include:** PeopleSoft Administrator. **Corporate headquarters location:** This location. **Parent company:** Meditrust. **Listed on:** New York Stock Exchange. **Stock exchange symbol:** LQI. **Number of employees nationwide:** More than 7,000.

LABATT FOOD SERVICE
P.O. Box 2140, San Antonio TX 78297-2140. 210/661-4216. **Physical address:** 4500 Industry Park, San Antonio TX 78218. **Fax:** 210/661-0973. **Contact:** Human Resources Department. **World Wide Web address:** http://www.labattfood.com. **Description:** A food distributor for restaurants, hospitals, military bases, schools, and other institutions. **NOTE:** Jobseekers interested in positions at this location can fax or mail their resumes. See website for other locations, positions and mailing addresses. **Other area locations:** Corpus Christi TX; Austin TX; Harlingen TX; Houston TX. **Operations at this facility include:** Office; Warehouse.

LUBY'S CAFETERIAS
P.O. Box 33069, San Antonio TX 78265. 210/654-9000. **Fax:** 210/225-5750. **Physical address:** 2211 NE Loop 410, San Antonio TX 78217. **Contact:** Human Resources. **E-mail address:** careers@lubys.com. **World Wide Web address:** http://www.lubys.com. **Description:** A national chain restaurant that serves cafeteria-style food. **NOTE:** Hourly positions available. **Positions advertised include:** Restaurant Manager.

Special programs: Management Training. **Corporate headquarters location:** This location. **Listed on:** New York Stock Exchange. **Stock exchange symbol:** LUB. **Number of employees nationwide:** 11,000.

TACO CABANA, INC.
8918 Tesoro Drive, Suite 200, San Antonio TX 78217. 210/804-0990. **Fax:** 210/804-2425. **Recorded jobline:** 800/357-9924x326. **Contact:** Human Resources. **E-mail address:** recruiting@tacocabana.com. **World Wide Web address:** http://www.tacocabana.com. **Description:** Taco Cabana operates a chain of Mexican restaurants. Founded in 1978. **NOTE:** Jobseekers may also apply at the nearest Taco Cabana restaurant. See the company's website for locations. **Corporate headquarters location:** This location. **Parent company:** Carrols Corporation.

WHATABURGER, INC.
4600 Parkdale Drive, Corpus Christi TX 78411. 361/878-0650. **Contact:** Director of Human Resources. **World Wide Web address:** http://www.whataburger.com. **Description:** Operates 500 restaurants in the Sunbelt area. Founded in 1950. **NOTE:** This website has job listings for all of its locations. Apply online. **Positions advertised include:** General Manager; Manager; Help Desk Support; Purchasing Manager. **Corporate headquarters location:** This location. **Other U.S. locations:** AZ.

INSURANCE

You can expect to find the following types of companies in this section:
Commercial and Industrial Property/Casualty Insurers • Health Maintenance Organizations (HMO's) • Medical/Life Insurance Companies

---

CITIZENS, INC.
P.O. Box 149151, Austin TX 78714. 512/837-7100. 400 East Anderson Lane, Austin TX 78752. **Fax:** 512/836-9785. **Contact:** Human Resources. **World Wide Web address:** http://www.citizensinc.com. **Description:** A life insurance holding company. **NOTE:** Please visit website to view job listings and apply online. **Positions advertised include:** Executive Assistant; Accounting Manager; Commissions Technician; Actuarial Manager; Operations Manager; Claims Processor; Customer Relations Manager; Assistant Counselor; Training Director. **Corporate headquarters location:** This location. **Listed on:** New York Stock Exchange. **Stock exchange symbol:** CIA.

FIC INSURANCE GROUP
6500 River Place Boulevard, Building 1, Austin, TX 78730. 512/404-5000. **Contact:** Human Resources. **World Wide Web address:** http://www.ficgroup.com. **Description:** An insurance company that specializes in life insurance. **NOTE:**
Resumes can be sent via company's website. **Corporate headquarters location:** This location. **Other U.S. locations:** Seattle WA.

FARMERS INSURANCE GROUP
P.O. Box 149044, Austin TX 78714-9044. 512/238-4400. **Contact:** Human Resources. **World Wide Web address:** http://www.farmersinsurance.com. **Description:** Operates as the center for applications and payments for processing auto, home, boat, and life insurance.

PRINCIPAL FINANCIAL GROUP
7330 San Pedro Street, Suite 700, San Antonio TX 78216. 210/349-5454. **Contact:** Human Resources. **World Wide Web address:** http://www.principal.com. **Description:** Provides financial services including real estate, annuities, home mortgages, mutual funds, and retirement plans. The Principal Financial Group also offers dental, disability, health, life, and vision insurance policies. **NOTE:** This company has offices throughout Texas. See the website for job listings and contact information. **Other U.S. locations:** Nationwide. **Corporate headquarters location:** Des Moines IA.

PROGRESSIVE COUNTY MUTUAL INSURANCE COMPANY
1124 South IH 35, Austin TX 78704. 512/441-2000. **Fax:** 512/464-1136. **Recorded jobline:** 512/464-1164. **Contact:** Human Resources. **World Wide Web address:** http://www.progressive.com. **Description:** An automobile insurance company. **NOTE:** Progressive has many locations throughout Texas. See website for additional locations. **Positions advertised include:** Direct Sales Representative; Customer Service Trainee; Claims Representative Trainee; National Claims Processor. **Other U.S. locations:** Nationwide. **Listed on:** New York Stock Exchange. **Stock exchange symbol:** PGR.

LEGAL SERVICES

**You can expect to find the following types of companies
in this section:**
Law Firms • Legal Service Agencies

ARMBRUST & BROWN L.L.P.
100 Congress Avenue, Suite 1300, Austin TX 78701-2744. 512/435-2300. **Fax:** 512/435-2360. **Contact:** Human Resources Department. **World Wide Web address:** http://www.abaustin.com. **Description:** A law firm specializing in real estate and product liability law.

BOBBIT, HALTER & WATSON
8700 Crownhill Boulevard, Suite 300, San Antonio TX 78209. 210/824-1555. **Fax:** 210/820-3441. **Contact:** Richard Halter, Managing Partner. **Description:** A law firm involved in many different areas including real estate, litigation, wills, and probates.

CLARK, THOMAS & WINTERS
P.O. Box 1148, Austin TX 78767. 512/472-8800. **Physical address:** 300 West 6th Street, 15th Floor, Austin TX 78701. **Fax:** 512/474-1129. **Contact:** Jean Atkisslin, Assistant to the President. **World Wide Web address:** http://www.ctw.com. **Description:** A law firm specializing in a variety of areas including antitrust, environmental, and product liability law. **NOTE:** Please visit website to view job listings. **Corporate headquarters location:** This location. **Other area locations:** San Antonio TX.

PLUNKETT & GIBSON, INC.
70 Northeast Loop 410, Suite 1100, San Antonio TX 782161. 210/734-7092. **Fax:** 210/734-0379.. **Contact:** Human Resources. **World Wide Web address:** http://www.plunkett-gibson.com. **Description:** A defense law firm specializing in a variety of areas including insurance, medical malpractice, bankruptcy, and litigation.

WEBB, STOKES & SPARKS, L.L.P.
P.O. Box 1271, San Angelo TX 76902. 915/653-6866. **Physical address:** 314 West Harris Avenue, San Angelo TX 76903. **Toll-free phone:** 800/727-4529. **Fax:** 915/655-1250. **Contact:** Human Resources Department. **World Wide Web address:** http://www.webbstokessparks.com. **Description:** A law office specializing in personal injury cases.

MANUFACTURING: MISCELLANEOUS CONSUMER

You can expect to find the following types of companies in this section:
Art Supplies • Batteries • Cosmetics and Related Products • Household Appliances and Audio/Video Equipment • Jewelry, Silverware, and Plated Ware • Miscellaneous Household Furniture and Fixtures • Musical Instruments • Tools • Toys and Sporting Goods

COMMEMORATIVE BRANDS
P.O. Box 149107, Austin TX 78714-9207. 512/444-0571. **Physical address:** 7211 Circle S. Road, Austin TX 78745. **Contact:** Human Resources. **World Wide Web address:** http://www.artcarved.com. **Description:** Manufactures custom jewelry for schools, sports, and businesses. Other areas of activity include service award programs and the printing of announcements. **Corporate headquarters location:** This location. **Operations at this facility include:** Administration; Divisional Headquarters; Manufacturing; Sales; Service.

GOLFSMITH INTERNATIONAL INC.
11000 North Interstate Highway 35, Austin TX 78753. 512/837-8810. **Fax:** 512/821-4191. **Contact:** Human Resources. **E-mail address:** hr@golfsmith.com. **World Wide Web address:** http://www. golfsmith.com. **Description:** Designs, assembles, and distributes golf equipment. **Positions advertised include:** Floor Supervisor; Sales Associate; Retail Advertising Coordinator; Accounts Receivable Clerk. **Operations at this facility include:** Administration; Manufacturing.

HELEN OF TROY LTD.
One Helen of Troy Plaza, El Paso TX 79912. 915/225-8000. **Fax:** 915/225-8010. **Contact:** Human Resources. **World Wide Web address:** http://www.hotus.com. **Description:** Helen of Troy markets hair care appliances through major retail outlets worldwide. The company manufactures products under brand names including Vidal Sassoon, Revlon, Sable, and Helen of Troy. The company also services the professional retail market with an extensive collection of professional hair care appliances for salon use. **Corporate headquarters location:** This location. **Operations at this facility include:** This division serves as one of the primary development arenas for all corporate product lines. **Listed on:** NASDAQ. **Stock exchange symbol:** HELE.

KOHLER COMPANY
P.O. Box 1709, Brownwood TX 76804. 915/643-2661. **Contact:** Human Resources. **World Wide Web address:** http://www.kohler.com. **Description:** A large manufacturer of vitreous china. Kohler also has a plastics division that produces showers and baths. **Special programs:** Internships. **Corporate headquarters location:** Kohler WI. **Operations at this facility:** Manufactures plumbing parts and accessories.

MANUFACTURING: MISCELLANEOUS INDUSTRIAL

You can expect to find the following types of companies in this section:
Ball and Roller Bearings • Commercial Furniture and Fixtures • Fans, Blowers, and Purification Equipment • Industrial Machinery and Equipment • Motors and Generators/Compressors and Engine Parts • Vending Machines

ALAMO GROUP, INC.

P.O. Box 549, Seguin TX 78156-0549. 830/379-1480. **Physical address:** 1502 East Walnut, Seguin TX 78155. **Toll-free phone:** 800/882-5762. **Fax:** 830/379-4363. **Contact:** Gabrielle Garcia, Personnel Manager. **E-mail address:** info@alamo-group.com. **World Wide Web address:** http://www.alamo-group.com. **Description:** A manufacturer of agricultural and industrial machinery. Founded 1969. **NOTE:** Please visit website to search for jobs and apply online. Online applications are preferred. Positions advertised include: Manufacturing Engineer. **Corporate headquarters location:** This location. **Other U.S. locations:** Sioux Falls SD; Holton KS; Indianola IA; Gibson City IL; Huntsville AL. **International locations:** England; France; the Netherlands; Canada; Australia. **Listed on:** New York Stock Exchange. **Stock exchange symbol:** ALG. **President/CEO:** Ronald A. Robinson.

CORRECTIONS PRODUCTS COMPANY
10700 Sentinel Street, San Antonio TX 78217. 210/829-7951. **Fax:** 210/824-3119. **Contact:** Personnel. **Description:** Manufactures locks and sliding devices for security within prison and jail systems.

HART & COOLEY
12504 Weaver Road, El Paso TX 79928. 915/852-9111. **Fax:** 915/852-1309. **Contact:** Human Resources. **World Wide Web address:** http://www.hartandcooley.com. **Description:** Manufactures registers and grills for heating and cooling systems. **Parent company:** Tomkins PLC.

KASPER WIRE WORKS INC.
P.O. Box 667, Shiner TX 77984-0667. 361/594-3327. **Toll-free phone:** 800/337-0610. **Fax:** 361/594-3311. **Contact:** Human Resources. **World Wide Web address:** http://www.kasperwireworks. com. **Description:** Manufactures wire and metal products used in restaurants, hospitals, and other industries.

KEWAUNEE SCIENTIFIC CORPORATION
1300 SM 20 East, Lockhart TX 78644. 512/398-5292. **Contact:** Human Resources. **E-mail address:** humanresources@kewaunee.com. **World Wide Web address:** http://www.kewaunee.com. **Description:** Manufactures laboratory and technical workstations, furniture, and related accessories for industrial and commercial markets. **NOTE:**

Interested jobseekers may mail their resumes to Human Resources Department, Kewaunee Scientific Corporation; P.O. Box 182, Statesville NC 28687-1842. **Corporate headquarters location:** Statesville NC. **Listed on:** NASDAQ. **Stock exchange symbol:** KEQU.

LANCER CORPORATION
6655 Lancer Boulevard, San Antonio TX 78219. 210/310-7000. **Contact:** Human Resources. **World Wide Web address:** http://www.lancercorp.com. **Description:** A manufacturer of soft drink and related food service equipment. **Positions advertised include** Project Cost Analyst; Tester; Mechanical Assembler; Manufacturing Engineer. **Corporate headquarters location:** This location. **International locations:** Mexico; Australia; Belgium; New Zealand; Russia; Brazil. **Listed on:** American Stock Exchange. **Stock exchange symbol:** LAN. **Number of employees nationwide:** 1,500.

LINCO-ELECTROMATIC, INC.
4580 West Wall Street, Midland TX 79703. 432/694-9644. **Fax:** 432/694-0921. **Contact:** Human Resources. **World Wide Web address:** http://www.lmc.comm. **Description:** Founded in 1967, this company manufactures and distributes calibration and measurement equipment. Primary markets are the oil and related industries. **NOTE:** Mail resumes to: P.O. Box 4096, Midland TX 797704; Attention: Fabrication West. Jobseekers may e-mail resumes to dbaumbach@lemc.com. **Positions advertised include:** Service/Meter Technician. **Other area locations:** Kilgore TX; Houston TX; Corpus Christi TX; Wichita Falls TX. **Other U.S. locations:** OK.

MENSOR CORPORATION
201 Barnes Drive, San Marcos TX 78666-5917. 512/396-4200. **Fax:** 512/396-1820. **Contact:** Human Resources. **World Wide Web address:** http://www.mensor.com. **Description:** Manufactures precision instruments and pressure systems.

NOBLE CONSTRUCTION EQUIPMENT, INC.
1802 East 50th Street, Lubbock TX 79404. 806/747-4663. **Contact:** Human Resources. **World Wide Web address:** http://www.noblecei.com. **Description:** Manufactures and distributes industrial machinery and other industrial equipment. **International locations:** Mexico.

REYNOLDS INTERNATIONAL INC.
P.O. Box 550, McAllen TX 78505-0550. 956/687-7500. **Contact:** Human Resources. **World Wide Web address:** http://www.reynoldsinternational.com. **Description:** Manufactures tractor equipment. **Corporate headquarters location:** This location.

THERMON MANUFACTURING COMPANY
P.O. Box 609, San Marcos TX 78667-0609. 512/396-5801. **Physical address:** 100 Thermon Drive, San Marcos TX 78666. **Contact:** Human Resources. **E-mail address:** human.resources@thermon.com. **World**

Wide Web address: http://www.thermon.com. **Description:** A manufacturer of heat tracings. **Corporate headquarters location:** This location. **Other U.S. locations:** CA; DE; LA; NC. **International locations:** Worldwide.

3M
6801 River Place Boulevard, Austin TX 787726-9000. 512/984-1800. Fax: 512/984-1800. **Recorded jobline:** 512/984-6908. **Contact:** Human Resources. **World Wide Web address:** http://www.3m.com. **Description:** 3M manufactures products in three sectors: Industrial and Consumer; Information, Imaging, and Electronic; and Life Sciences. The Industrial and Consumer Sector manufactures a variety of products under brand names including 3M, Scotch, Post-it, Scotch-Brite, and Scotchgard. The Information, Imaging, and Electronic Sector is a leader in several high-growth global industries including telecommunications, electronics, electrical, imaging, and memory media. The Life Science Sector serves two broad market categories: health care, and traffic and personal safety. In the health care market, 3M is a leading provider of medical and surgical supplies, drug-delivery systems, and dental products; in traffic and personal safety, 3M is a leader in products for worker protection, vehicle and sign graphics, and out-of-home advertising. **NOTE:** Apply online at this company's website. **Positions advertised include:** Sales Representative; Financial Analyst. **Corporate headquarters location:** St. Paul MN. **Other area locations:** Brownswood TX (Manufacturing). **Operations at this facility include:** Regional office. **Listed on:** New York Stock Exchange. **Stock exchange symbol:** MMM.

XEROX CORPORATION
6836 Austin Center Boulevard, Suite 300, Austin TX 78731. 512/343-5600. **Contact:** Human Resources Center. **World Wide Web address:** http://www.xerox.com. **Description:** Xerox is a leader in the global document market providing document solutions that enhance business productivity. Xerox develops, manufactures, markets, sells, and services a full range of document processing products and solutions. **NOTE:** Apply online. **Positions advertised include:** Sales Manager. **Corporate headquarters location:** Stamford CT. **Operations at this facility include:** This location is a regional sales and service office. **Listed on:** New York Stock Exchange. **Stock exchange symbol:** XRX.

MINING, GAS, PETROLEUM, ENERGY RELATED

You can expect to find the following types of companies in this section:
Anthracite, Coal, and Ore Mining • Mining Machinery and Equipment • Oil and Gas Field Services • Petroleum and Natural Gas

---

ABRAXAS PETROLEUM CORPORATION
P.O. Box 701007, San Antonio TX 78270-1007. 210/490-4788. **Physical address:** 500 North Loop 1604 East, Suite 100, San Antonio TX 78232. **Fax:** 210/490-8816. **Contact:** Carol O'Brien, Human Resources. **E-mail address:** cobrienabraxaspetroleum.com. **World Wide Web address:** http://www.abraxaspetroleum.com. **Description:** An independent crude oil and natural gas exploration and production company with operations concentrated in western Canada, Texas, and Wyoming. The company has participated in the drilling of over 500 wells in 17 states. Abraxas Petroleum Corporation owns interests in over 450 oil wells, 120 gas wells, and 170 service wells. The company operates the following three centralized production facilities in Texas: Abraxas Production Corporation (Midland TX), Abraxas Production Corporation (Ira TX), and Portilla Gas Plant (Sinton TX). Founded in 1977. **Corporate headquarters location:** This location. **International locations:** Calgary, Alberta Canada. **Listed on:** American Stock Exchange. **Stock exchange symbol:** ABP. **President/CEO:** Robert L.G. Watson.

AERIFORM CORPORATION
3813 County Road West, Odessa TX 79764. 432/362-0384. **Fax:** 432/362-3512. **Contact:** Human Resources. **E-mail address:** humanresources@aeriform.com. **World Wide Web address:** http://www.aeriform.com. **Description:** Aeriform ranks among the nation's largest independent suppliers of specialty gases, medical gases, welding equipment, and cryogenic products. **Positions advertised include:** Driver; Inside/Counter Sales Representative; Branch Manager; Customer Service Manager. **Corporate headquarters location:** Houston TX. **Other area locations:** Statewide. **Other U.S. locations:** KS; OK; AK; LA.

CITGO
CORPUS CHRISTI REFINERY
1802 Nueces Bay Boulevard Corpus Christi TX 78408. 361/844-4000. **Contact:** Human Resources. **World Wide Web address:** http://www.citigroup.com. **Description:** One of the world's largest oil producers. It produces about 1 million gallons a day. It has 13,000 gas stations nationwide. **Positions advertised include:** Environmental Advisor; Manager Machinery Maintenance & Reliability, Project Engineers; Project Manager. **NOTE:** Apply online. Other U.S. locations include: LA; IL.

ENERGY TRANSFER
800 East Sonterra Boulevard, Suite 400, San Antonio TX 78258.
210/403-7300. **Fax:** 210/403-7500. **Contact:** Human Resources. **World Wide Web address:** http://www.energytransfer.com. **Description:** Purchases, gathers, transports, processes, and markets natural gas and natural gas liquids. **Other area locations:** Dallas TX. **Other U.S. locations:** Tulsa OK. **Listed on:** New York Stock Exchange. **Stock exchange symbol:** ETP.

THE EXPLORATION COMPANY
500 North Loop 1604 East, Suite 250, San Antonio TX 78232. 210/496-5300. **Fax:** 210/496-3232. **Contact:** Human Resources. **World Wide Web address:** http://www.txco.com. **Description:** Acquires, explores, and develops oil and gas properties. The Exploration Company operates through three divisions: Oil and Gas Operations, ExproFuels Operations, and Mineral Properties. The company also converts vehicle engines that use gasoline for combustion to propane or natural gas, supplies alternative fuels to customers, and constructs alternative fuels refueling facilities. **Listed on:** NASDAQ. **Stock exchange symbol:** TXCO.

GULF MARINE FABRICATORS
P.O. Box 3000, Aransas Pass TX 78335. 361/776-7551. **Fax:** 361/776-8102.. **Contact:** Human Resources. **World Wide Web address:** http://technip.com. **Description:** Manufactures offshore rigs. **Corporate headquarters location:** Paris. **Other area locations:** Houston TX. **Other U.S. locations:** AL; LA; CA; NJ; FL. **International locations:** Worldwide. **Parent company:** Technip. **Listed on:** New York Stock Exchange. **Stock exchange symbol:** TKP.

PATTERSON-UTI ENERGY, INC.
P.O. Drawer 1416, Snyder TX 79550. 915/573-1831. **Physical address:** 4510 Lamesa Highway, Snyder TX 79549. **Contact:** Human Resources. **World Wide Web address:** http://www.patenergy.com. **Description:** Engaged in onshore drilling for oil and gas; and the exploration, development, and production of oil and gas. The company's operations are conducted in Texas, New Mexico, Oklahoma, Louisiana, Mississippi, Colorado, Utah, and Wyoming. **Corporate headquarters location:** This location. **Other area locations:** Midland TX. **Listed on:** NASDQ. **Stock exchange symbol:** PTEN.

POOL COMPANY
P.O. Box 1117, Crane TX 79731. 915/558-2561. **Fax:** 915/558-2402. **Contact:** Human Resources. **Description:** Engaged in pulling wells and hauling water. **Corporate headquarters location:** This location.

SOUTHERN CLAY PRODUCTS INC.
1212 Church Street, Gonzales TX 78629. 830/672-2891. **Fax:** 830/672-1908. **Contact:** Human Resources. **World Wide Web address:** http://www.scprod.com. **Description:** Mines and processes clay minerals for use in a variety of products including paint. **Corporate headquarters location:** This location.

SOUTHWEST ROYALTIES, INC.

P.O. Box 11390, Midland TX 79702. 915/686-9927. **Contact:** Patty Hollums, Personnel Manager. **World Wide Web address:** http://www.swrinc.com. **Description:** Engaged in oil exploration and development. This company also manages Cyberbasin, an Internet service provider (Midland TX). **Corporate headquarters location:** This location. **Other U.S. locations:** NM. **Listed on:** Privately held.

TESORO PETROLEUM CORPORATION

300 Concord Plaza Drive, San Antonio TX 78216. 210/828-8484. **Toll-free phone:** 800/837-6762. **Recorded jobline:** 210/283-2600. **Contact:** J. Lopez, Human Resources. **World Wide Web address:** http://www.tesoropetroleum.com. **Description:** Engaged in the refining, transportation, and marketing of natural gas, crude oil, and related products. Other operations include exploration and oil field services such as supplying lubricants, fuels, and specialty products to the U.S. drilling industry. Tesoro Petroleum has refining facilities in Alaska, exploration and production facilities in Texas, and sells its products to customers primarily in Alaska, the Far East, and the Rocky Mountain region. **NOTE:** This company only accepts resumes and applications for open positions. See its website for job listings. **Positions advertised include:** Solutions Delivery Analyst Family; Commercial Analyst; Card and Loyalty Programs Coordinator; Internal Auditor; Lease Crude Accountant; Programs Specialist; Services Coordinator. **Corporate headquarters location:** This location. **Listed on:** New York Stock Exchange. **Stock exchange symbol:** TSO.

UTI DRILLING, LP

1950 Avenue S, Levelland TX 79336. 806/894-5479. **Fax:** 806/785-8400. **Contact:** Human Resources. **Description:** Operates oil and gas drilling rigs and provides contract drilling services to the oil and gas industry. **Parent company:** Patterson Energy.

VALERO ENERGY CORPORATION

P.O. Box 500, San Antonio TX 78292. 210/370-2000. **Physical address:** One Valero Place, San Antonio TX 78212. **Toll-free phone:** 800/531-7911. **Fax:** 210/370-2646. **Contact:** Human Resources. **World Wide Web address:** http://www.valero.com. **Description:** Valero Energy Corporation has an extensive refining system with a throughput capacity of nearly 2 million barrels per day. The company's geographically diverse refining network stretches from Canada to the U.S. Gulf Coast, and West Coast. Valero has almost 5,000 retail sites in the United States and Canada, branded as Valero, Diamond Shamrock, Ultramar, Beacon, and Total. Valero is a leading producer of premium environmentally clean products, such as reformulated gasoline, (CARB) Phase II gasoline, low-sulfur diesel and oxygenates. The company also operates a credit card program with over 500,000 active accounts. **NOTE:** Part-time positions offered. Apply on this company's website for all positions. **Positions advertised include:** Pipeline Integrity Engineer; Human Resources Analyst; Optimization and Performance Analysis Manager; Systems

Specialist; Control Systems Engineer; Chief Refining Inspector; Engineering Associate; Customer Account Representative; Store Manager; Assistant Store Manager. **Corporate headquarters location:** This location. **Other area locations:** Corpus Christi TX; Houston TX; Krotz Springs, TX; McKee TX; Three Rivers TX; Sunray TX. **Listed on:** New York Stock Exchange. **Stock exchange symbol:** VLO. **Number of employees worldwide:** 20,000.

PAPER AND WOOD PRODUCTS

You can expect to find the following types of companies in this section:
Forest and Wood Products and Services • Lumber and Wood Wholesalers • Millwork, Plywood, and Structural Members • Paper and Wood Mills

---

CAPITAL CITY CONTAINER CORP.
P.O. Box 870, Buda TX 78610-0870. 512/312-1222. **Physical address:** 150 Precision Drive, Buda TX. **Fax:** 512/295-4375. **Contact:** Human Resources. **World Wide Web address:** http://www.capitalcitycontainer.com. **Description:** Manufactures corrugated containers and provides die cut, direct print, and four-color process services.

ROCK-TENN COMPANY
1385 Northwestern Drive, El Paso TX 79912. 915/581-5492. **Contact:** Human Resources. **World Wide Web address:** http://www.rocktenn.com. **Description:** Manufactures recycled paperboard and paperboard products. Over two-thirds of paperboard production is used by the company's own converting plants to produce folding cartons, book and notebook covers, components for the furniture industry, and solid fiber partitions used in shipping glass and plastic containers. **Positions advertised include:** Mill Superintendent. **Corporate headquarters location:** Norcross GA. **Other U.S. locations:** Nationwide. **Listed on:** New York Stock Exchange. **Stock exchange symbol:** RKT.

TEMPLE-INLAND, INC.
P.O. Box 40, Austin TX 78767. 512/434-5800. **Contact:** Human Resources. **World Wide Web address:** http://www.templeinland.com. **Description:** A holding company offering corrugated packaging, bleached paperboard, building products, and financial services. **Other area locations:** Diboll TX; Houston TX; Dallas TX; Bellville TX; McKinney TX; San Antonio TX. **Positions advertised include:** Account Executive; Advertising Manager; Banking Center Manager; Business Analyst. **Corporate headquarters location:** This location. **Listed on:** New York Stock Exchange. **Stock exchange symbol:** TIN.

PRINTING AND PUBLISHING

You can expect to find the following types of companies in this section:
Book, Newspaper, and Periodical Publishers • Commercial Photographers • Commercial Printing Services • Graphic Designers

---

AMARILLO GLOBE -NEWS
P.O. Box 2091, Amarillo TX 79166. 806/376-4488. **Fax:** 806/345-3370. **Contact:** Human Resources. **World Wide Web address:** http://www.amarillonet.com. **Description:** Publishes morning and afternoon daily papers. The Sunday edition has a circulation of approximately 74,000. **NOTE:** Human Resources phone is 806/345-3333.

AUSTIN AMERICAN-STATESMAN
P.O. Box 670, Austin TX 78767. **Physical address:** 305 South Congress Avenue, Austin TX 78704. 512/445-3500. **Fax:** 512/445-3883. **Recorded jobline:** 512/416-5700 Ext. 5621. **Contact:** Personnel Director. **E-mail address:** aa-sjobs@statesman.com. **World Wide Web address:** http://www.statesman.com. **Description:** Publishes the *Austin American-Statesman*, a daily newspaper. **NOTE:** Call Human Resources at 512/445-3709. Please visit http://jobs.statesman.com to search for jobs and apply online. You may also visit the office to fill out an application in person. **Positions advertised include:** Telemarketing Representative; Research Analyst; New Business Development Sales Representative; National Advertising Sales Representative. **Office hours:** Monday – Friday, 8:30 a.m. – 5:00 p.m.

CORPUS CHRISTI CALLER-TIMES
P.O. Box 9136, Corpus Christi TX 78469-9136. 361/884-2011. **Physical address:** 820 North Lower Broadway, Corpus Christi TX 78401. **Toll-free phone:** 800/827-2011. **Fax:** 361/884-5357. **Contact:** Veronica Rodriguez, Human Resources. **World Wide Web address:** http://www.caller.com. **Description:** A daily newspaper delivered throughout southwestern Texas. Founded in 1883. **Parent company:** Scripps Howard.

CLARKE AMERICAN CHECKS, INC.
10931 Laureate Drive, San Antonio TX 78249. 210/697-8888. **Recorded jobline:** 210/690-6500. **Contact:** Human Resources. **World Wide Web address:** http://www.clarkeamerican.com. **Description:** A leading printer of checks and share drafts for the financial industry. Founded in 1874. **NOTE:** Please visit http://www.monster.com to search for jobs and apply online. **Positions advertised include:** Director of e-Commerce; Vice President of Information Technology Service Delivery; Human Resources Generalist. **Special programs:** Internships. **Corporate headquarters location:** This location. **Other U.S. locations:**

Nationwide. **Parent company:** Novar plc. **Operations at this facility include:** Regional Headquarters. **Listed on:** Privately held. **Number of employees nationwide:** 3,500.

CONSTRUCTION DATA CORPORATION
11940 Jollyville Road, Suite 305-S, Austin TX 78759. 512/219-5150. **Toll-free phone:** 800/872-7878. **Fax:** 772/299-0818. **Contact:** Human Resources. **E-mail address:** jobs@cdcnews.com. **World Wide Web address:** http://www.cdcnews.com. **Description:** A construction trade publication that provides planning news and bidding opportunities. CDC produces 29 editions from Maine to California. Founded in 1977. **NOTE:** Entry-level positions and part-time jobs are offered. **Positions advertised include:** Reporter/Editor; Inside Sales Representative. **Special programs:** Internships. **Corporate headquarters location:** Vero Beach FL. **Listed on:** Privately held.

EL PASO TIMES INC.
P.O. Box 20, El Paso TX 79999. 915/546-6100. **Contact:** Malena Field, Human Resources Director. **World Wide Web address:** http://www.elpasotimes.com. **Description:** Writes, publishes, prints, and distributes a daily newspaper throughout Texas and New Mexico. The newspaper reaches250,000 people daily. The company also publishes and distributes the *El Paso Herald Post*. **Office hours:** Monday – Friday, 8:00 a.m. – 5:00 p.m.

GREAT WESTERN DIRECTORIES
2400 Lakeview Drive, Suite 109, Amarillo TX 79109. 806/353-5155. **Contact:** Human Resources. **World Wide Web address:** http://www.worldpages.com. **Description:** A publisher of telephone directories. **NOTE:** Job listings for all locations available on the company's website. **Parent company:** Transwestern Publishing Company. **Corporate headquarters location:** San Diego CA.

HOLLAND PHOTO IMAGING
1221 South Lamar Boulevard, Austin TX 78704. 512/442-4274. **Toll-free phone:** 800/477-4024. **Fax:** 512/442-5898. **Contact:** Human Resources. **World Wide Web address:** http://www.hollandphoto.com. **Description:** A film and digital photo processing company. This company offers scanning, restoration, shipping, duplicating and mounting services. Founded in 1982.

LUBBOCK AVALANCHE-JOURNAL
P.O. Box 491, Lubbock TX 79408. 806/762-8844. **Contact:** Shelby Caballero, Human Resources Manager. **E-mail address:** Shelby.caballero@lubbockonline.com. **World Wide Web address:** http://www.lubbockonline.com. **Description:** A daily newspaper. The *Lubbock Avalanche-Journal* has a circulation of approximately 67,000 daily and 74,000 on Sundays.

NORWOOD PROMOTIONAL PRODUCTS, INC.
106 East Sixth Street, Suite 300, Austin TX 78701. 512/476-7100.
Contact: Human Resources. **World Wide Web address:**
http://www.norwood.com. **Description:** Through its subsidiaries and
divisions, Norwood Promotional Products imprints and distributes over
1,000 promotional items to over 6,500 distributors nationwide. Product
lines include badges, business gifts, buttons, headwear, Koozie insulator
products, mugs and glassware, paper products, packet specialties,
recognition and award items, and writing instruments. The company
markets its products under trade names including The Action Line,
Barlow, Econ-O-Line, Koozie, RCC, and Salam. **Positions advertised
include:** Credit Analyst; Manufacturing Engineer; Paralegal; Territory
Sales Representative. **Subsidiaries include:** ArtMold; Barlow; Key;
RCC. **International locations:** Canada; Hong Kong. **Number of
employees worldwide:** 3,500.

SAN ANTONIO EXPRESS NEWS
P.O. Box 2171, San Antonio TX 78297-2171. **Physical address:** 309
North Alamo, San Antonio TX 78297-2171. 210/225-7411. **Contact:**
Human Resources. **E-mail address:** employment@express-news.net.
World Wide Web address: http://www.mysanantonio.com. **Description:**
A newspaper with a circulation of approximately 250,000 daily and
365,000 on Sundays. **Positions advertised include:** Classified Account
Executive; Sales Assistant; New Business Development Sales
Representative; Quality Service Representative; Customer Service
Representative.

TEXAS MONTHLY
P.O. Box 1569, Austin TX 78767. 512/320-6900. **Fax:** 512/476-9007.
Contact: Angela Hollinsworth, Human Resources. **E-mail address:**
humanresources@texasmonthly.com. **World Wide Web address:**
http://www.texasmonthly.com. **Description:** *Texas Monthly* is a regional,
general interest magazine. Articles range from health and travel to true
crime. The magazine has a circulation of approximately 300,000.
Founded in 1972. **Positions advertised include:** National Account
Manager; Advertising Sales Manager.. **Special programs:** Internships.
Corporate headquarters location: This location. **Parent company:**
Emmis Communications (Indianapolis IN).

TRANSWESTERN PUBLISHING
9211 Waterford Centre Boulevard Street, Austin TX 78758. 512/451-
2121. **Fax:** 512/451-7595. **Contact:** Human Resources. **World Wide
Web address:** http://www.twpsite.com. Founded in 1980. **Description:**
creates and distributes directories in more than 20 states. **Positions
advertised include:** Account Executive. **NOTE:** Apply online.
Corporate headquarters location: San Diego CA. **Operations at this
facility include:** This is primarily a sales location. **Listed on:** Privately
held. **Number Of employees nationwide:** 2,000.

REAL ESTATE

You can expect to find the following types of companies in this section:
Land Subdividers and Developers • Real Estate Agents, Managers, and Operators • Real Estate Investment Trusts

---

BRADFIELD PROPERTIES INC.
11306 Sir Winston, San Antonio TX 78216. 210/340-6500. **Fax:** 210/340-7130. **Contact:** Betty Dickens, Director of Training and Career Development. **E-mail address:** betdickens@satx.rr.com **World Wide Web address:** http://www.bradfieldproperties.com. **Description:** A real estate company specializing in residential, commercial, and multifamily property management. Founded 1982. **NOTE:** There are seven locations in San Antonio in addition to the corporate office. **Corporate headquarters location:** This location. **Other area locations:** Boerne TX; Bulverde TX; New Braunfels TX.

CAPSTONE REAL ESTATE SERVICES
210 Baron Springs Road, Suite 300, Austin TX 78704. 512/646-6700. **Fax:** 512/646-6798. **Contact:** Human Resources. **E-mail address:** info@capstonemanagement.com. **World Wide Web address:** http://www.capstonerealestate.com. **Description:** Sells, rents, and leases apartments and commercial properties. **Corporate headquarters location:** This location. **Other area locations:** Houston TX; Dallas/Fort Worth TX; San Antonio TX. **Other U.S. locations:** FL. **President:** James W. Berkey. **Number of employees nationwide:** 550.

COLDWELL BANKER
3100 Padre Boulevard, South Padre Island TX 78597-3469. 956/761-7802. **Fax:** 956/761-4855. **Contact:** Personnel. **World Wide Web address:** http://www.coldwellbanker.com. **Description:** Coldwell Banker is one of the largest residential real estate companies in the United States and Canada in terms of total home sales transactions. Coldwell Banker is also a leader in corporate relocation services. **NOTE:** Please visit website to search for jobs. **Corporate headquarters location:** Parsippany NJ. **Other U.S. locations:** Nationwide. **Parent company:** Cendant Corporation. **Listed on:** New York Stock Exchange. **Stock exchange symbol:** CD. **Number of employees worldwide:** 112,000.

KUPER REALTY CORPORATION
6606 North New Braunfels Avenue, San Antonio TX 78209. 210/822-8602. **Toll-free phone:** 800/584-5400. **Fax:** 210/822-6646. **Contact:** Human Resources. **World Wide Web address:** http://www.kuperrealty.com. **Description:** A real estate agency engaged in the sale of residential and commercial properties as well as ranches and land. Kuper Realty has additional locations throughout San Antonio.

USAA REAL ESTATE COMPANY
9800 Fredersicksburg Road, San Antonio TX 78288. 210/498-1289. **Toll-free phone:** 800/531-8022. **Fax:** 210/498-8986. **Contact:** Human Resources. **World Wide Web address:** http://www. usaa.com. **Description:** Engaged in commercial real estate services for corporate, institutional, and private investors. **NOTE:** On its website, this company provides job listings, addresses, and contact information for its other locations. **Positions advertised include:** Senior Financial Advisor; Financial Analyst; Commercial Strategy Advisor; Managing Editor; Marketing Director; Teller; Shipper; Consumer Loan Processing; Legal Secretary; Employee Communications Writer; Credit Card Specialist. **Other U.S. locations:** AZ; VA; CO; FL; CA. **International locations:** London; Frankfurt.

WILDWOOD MANAGEMENT GROUP
18585 Sigimi, Suite 101, San Antonio TX 78258. 210/403-9785. **Contact:** Human Resources. **Description:** Engaged in property management for apartments and condominiums.

RETAIL

You can expect to find the following types of companies in this section:
Catalog Retailers • Department Stores, Specialty Stores • Retail Bakeries • Supermarkets

---

ANCIRA ENTERPRISES INC.
6111 Bandera Road, San Antonio TX 78238-1643. 210/681-4900. **Contact:** Human Resources. **World Wide Web address:** http://www.ancira.com. **Description:** Sells new and used automobiles including Chevrolet, Subaru, and Volkswagen. This location also has a service, parts, and body shop. **Corporate headquarters location:** This location.

BRIDGESTONE AMERICAS HOLDING, INC. /FIRESTONE, INC.
6050 South Padre Island A, Corpus Christi TX 78412. 361/993-1375. **Contact:** Sandy Scarbro, Human Resources. **World Wide Web address:** http://www.bridgestone-firestone.com. **Description:** An automotive services and manufacturing company. **Corporate headquarters location:** Nashville TN. **Operations at this facility include:** This location is a district office for south Texas.

FAMILY CHRISTIAN STORES
5303 Walzem Road, San Antonio TX 78218. 210/656-3403. **Contact:** Human Resources. **World Wide Web address:** http://www.familychristian.com. **Description:** A location of the national chain of retail stores selling inspirational books, videos, and other items. Family Christian stores has three locations in San Antonio and more than 300 locations nationwide. **NOTE:** Apply online or at the nearest store location. **Positions advertised include:** Store Manager. **Corporate headquarters location:** Grand Rapids, MI. **Listed on:** Privately held.

FERGUSON ENTERPRISES, INC.
19 Burwood Lane, San Antonio TX 78216. 210/344-4950. **Fax:** 210/344-1253. **Contact:** **Human Resources.** **E-mail address:** resumes@ferguson.com. **World Wide Web address:** http://www.ferguson.com. **Description:** A retail and wholesale distributor of plumbing supplies. **Positions advertised include:** Sales/Management Trainee; Controller Trainee. **Corporate headquarters location:** This location. **Other U.S. locations:** Nationwide.

FOOD BASKET IGA
4202 South Bryant Boulevard, San Angelo TX 76903. 325/658-5602. **Contact:** Human Resources. **Description:** A grocery store chain with locations throughout Texas. **Corporate headquarters location:** This location.

HEB GROCERY COMPANY

P.O. Box 839999, San Antonio TX 78283. 210/938-8000. **Recorded jobline:** 210/938-5222. **Contact:** Human Resources. **E-mail address:** careers@heb.com. **World Wide Web address:** http://www.heb.com. **Description:** Operates a chain of retail grocery stores. Founded in 1905. **NOTE:** Interested jobseekers should contact the jobline before sending a resume. **Office hours:** Monday - Friday, 8:00 a.m. - 5:00 p.m. **Corporate headquarters location:** This location. **Listed on:** Privately held. **President:** Charles Butt.

ANTHONY NAK FINE JEWELRY

800 Brazos Street, Suite 300, Austin TX 78701. 512/454-7029. Fax: 512/454-7031. **Contact:** Human Resources. **E-mail address:** retail@anthonynak.com. **World Wide Web address:** http://www.anthonynak.com. **Description:** A specialty art jewelry store known for its appeal to movie stars and other high-profile people. **NOTE:** Apply during store hours or mail resume. **Office hours:** Tuesday, Thursday, Saturday, 10:00 a.m. to 6:00 p.m.

OFFICE DEPOT, INC.

2209 Rutland Drive, Suite A100, Austin TX 78758. 512/837-8999. **Fax:** 512/837-1221. **Contact:** Human Resources. **World Wide Web address:** http://www.officedepot.com. **Description:** One of the nation's leading office products dealers. The company offers over 11,000 business products including furniture; desk accessories; office essentials; computer products; business machines; visual communications; safety and maintenance supplies; personalized organizers and dated goods; writing instruments; business cases and binders; filing and storage; paper, envelopes, and business forms; and labels and mailing supplies. This company has locations throughout Texas and the United States. **NOTE:** This location is part of Office Depot's Business Services division, which focuses primarily on sales and service to the business market. There is another location in Houston. Job listings for the Business Services Division, as well other divisions, including retail, can be found on the company's website. **Corporate headquarters location:** Delray Beach FL. **Subsidiaries include:** Viking Office Products is a direct mail marketer. **Listed on:** New York Stock Exchange. **Stock exchange symbol:** ODP.

STRAUS-FRANK COMPANY/CAR QUEST

P.O. Box 600, San Antonio TX 78292-0600. 210/226-0101. **Contact:** Peggy Mamirez, Human Resources Manager. **Description:** A wholesaler of automobile parts. Straus-Frank Company is a partner with GPI who owns the retail chain automotive parts store Car Quest. **NOTE:** Car Quest has locations throughout Texas and the United States. Apply in person at the nearest location. See website for locations and addresses. **Corporate headquarters location:** This location.

SUPER S FOODS

401 Isom Road, Building 100, San Antonio TX 78216. 210/344-1960. **Fax:** 210/341-6326. **Contact:** Human Resources. **Description:** A corporate division of the retail grocery store chain Super S Foods. Super S Foods has stores throughout Texas. **NOTE:** A completed application must be mailed or faxed to the company. The application can be found on the company's website. **Positions advertised include:** Store Manager; Assistant Store Manager; Market Manager; Produce Manager. **Corporate headquarters location:** This location. **Parent company:** Mass Marketing, Inc.

UNITED SUPERMARKETS

7830 Orlando Avenue, Lubbock TX 79423. 806/792-0220. **Contact:** Human Resources. **E-mail address:** info@unitedtexas.com. **World Wide Web address:** http://www.unitedtexas.com. **Description:** This chain of supermarkets has more than 40 stores in Texas. **NOTE:** This company provides a list of all its locations on its website. For retail positions, apply at the nearest location. **Special programs:** Manager Training. **Corporate headquarters location:** This location.

WHOLE FOODS MARKET INC.

601 North Lamar Boulevard, Suite 300, Austin TX 78703. 512/477-4455. **Contact:** Human Resources. **World Wide Web address:** http://www.wholefoods.com. **Description:** Owns and operates a chain of natural foods supermarkets. **NOTE:** This company has other Texas locations. See its website for job listings for all its locations. Apply online. **Positions advertised include:** Business Systems Analyst; National Replenishment Coordinator; Purchasing Systems Team Lead; Senior Buyer/Product Developer. **Other U.S. locations:** CA; LA; MA; NC; RI. **Operations at this facility include:** Regional Headquarters. **Listed on:** NASDAQ. **Stock exchange symbol:** WFMI.

STONE, CLAY, GLASS, AND CONCRETE PRODUCTS

You can expect to find the following types of companies in this section:
Cement, Tile, Sand, and Gravel • Crushed and Broken Stone • Glass and Glass Products • Mineral Products

AMERICAN FLAT GLASS DISTRIBUTORS, INC. (AFGD)
3822 Airport Boulevard, Austin TX 78722. 512/474-2375. **Fax:** 512/474-5821. **Contact:** Human Resources. **World Wide Web address:** http://www.afgd.com. **Description:** Specializes in architectural insulated glass units and custom tempering. AFGD manufactures a complete line of insulated glass units for commercial and residential applications. The product line includes clear, tint, and reflective glass; wire glass; and equipment for the handling, storage, and transportation of glass. There are 50 AFGD locations throughout North America. **Corporate headquarters location:** Atlanta GA. **Other area locations:** Austin TX; Houston TX; San Antonio TX. **Other U.S. locations:** Nationwide. **International locations:** Canada. **Subsidiaries include:** AFGD Canada. **Parent company:** AFG Industries, Inc. **Operations at this facility include:** Manufacturing; Sales. **Listed on:** Privately held. **President:** John Stilwell.

AMERICAN FLAT GLASS DISTRIBUTORS, INC. (AFGD)
10750 Sentinel Drive, San Antonio TX 78217. 210/653-7790. **Toll-free phone:** 800/727-7790. **Fax:** 210/655-3945. **Contact:** Human Resources. **World Wide Web address:** http://www.afgd.com. **Description:** Specializes in architectural insulated glass units and custom tempering. AFGD manufactures a complete line of insulated glass units for commercial and residential applications. The product line includes clear, tint, and reflective glass; wire glass; and equipment for the handling, storage, and transportation of glass. There are 50 AFGD locations throughout North America. **Corporate headquarters location:** Atlanta GA. **Other area locations:** Austin TX; Houston TX; San Antonio TX. **Other U.S. locations:** Nationwide. **International locations:** Canada. **Subsidiaries include:** AFGD Canada. **Parent company:** AFG Industries, Inc. **Operations at this facility include:** Manufacturing; Sales. **Listed on:** Privately held. **President:** John Stilwell.

FORDYCE COMPANY
P.O. Box 1417, Victoria TX 77902. 361/573-4309. **Physical address:** 120 South Main Place, Suite 500, Victoria TX 77901. **Contact:** Human Resources. **Description:** Produces sand and gravel. **Corporate headquarters location:** This location. **Number of employees at this location:** 120.

JOBE CONCRETE PRODUCTS INC.
One McKelligon Canyon Road, El Paso TX 79930. 915/565-4681. **Fax:** 915/562-6218. **Contact:** Linda Armendariz, Human Resources Manager at 915/564-8405.. **World Wide Web address:** http://www.jobeconcrete.com. **Description:** Manufactures concrete and related products. Jobe Concrete Products also provides landscaping services. **Other area locations:** El Paso TX. **Other U.S. locations:** NM.

MARTIN MARIETTA MATERIALS
4243 North FM 1604 West, San Antonio TX 78257. 210/696-8500. **Contact:** Human Resources. **World Wide Web address:** http://www.martinmarietta.com. **Description:** Martin Marietta Materials produces a wide variety of construction aggregates and related materials. **Corporate headquarters location:** Raleigh NC. **Operations at this facility include:** This location is a surface mining company that manufactures products including limestone, base materials, and asphalt. **Listed on:** New York Stock Exchange. **Stock exchange symbol:** MLM.

MUR-TEX FIBERGLASS
P.O. Box 31240, Amarillo TX 79120. 806/373-7418. **Toll-free phone:** 800/299-7418. **Fax:** 806/373-9448. **Contact:** Human Resources. **World Wide Web address:** http://www.mur-tex. com. **Description:** Manufactures fiberglass tanks for industrial usage. **Corporate headquarters location:** This location.

VULCAN MATERIALS
4303 North FM 1604 East, San Antonio TX 78247. 210/494-9555. **Contact:** Human Resources. **World Wide Web address:** http://www.vulcanmaterials.com. **Description:** Fabricators of concrete, asphalt, and other stone products. **NOTE:** Vulcan has many manufacturing plants and sales locations throughout Texas. See its website for job listings and addresses. **Corporate headquarters location:** Birmingham AL. **Listed on:** New York Stock Exchange. **Stock exchange symbol:** VMC.

TRANSPORTATION AND TRAVEL

You can expect to find the following types of companies in this section:
Air, Railroad, and Water Transportation Services • Courier Services • Local and Interurban Passenger Transit • Ship Building and Repair • Transportation Equipment • Travel Agencies • Trucking • Warehousing and Storage

ABILENE AERO INC.
2850 Airport Boulevard, Abilene TX 79602. 325/677-2601. **Fax:** 325/671-8018. **Contact:** Mr. Joe Crawford, General Manager. **E-mail address:** jcrawford@abileneaero.com. **World Wide Web address:** http://www.abileneaero.com. **Description:** Operates a small airport offering flight instruction, charter and pilot service, aircraft fueling, parts, and maintenance. Founded in 1968. **Corporate headquarters location:** This location.

BALDWIN DISTRIBUTION SERVICES
P.O. Box 51618, Amarillo YX 79159. **Physical address:** 7702 Broadway, Amarillo TX 79108. 806/383-7650. **Toll-free phone:** 800/692-1333. **Contact:** Recruiting. **World Wide Web address:** http://www.baldwin-dist.com. **Description:** Provides long-haul trucking services. Baldwin Distribution Services operates in 48 states, Canada, and Mexico. **NOTE:** Contact Recruiting office at 866/4-BALDWIN. Recruiting office is located at I 40 & Loop 335, Amarillo TX. **Positions advertised include:** Long Haul Driver; Lease Purchase Operator. **Corporate headquarters location:** This location. **President/CEO:** Dudley Baldwin.

BLUE WHALE MOVING COMPANY
8291 Springdale Road, Suite 100, Austin TX 78724. 512/328-6688. **Fax:** 512/454-1463. **Contact:** Human Resources. **E-mail address:** bluewhale@bluewhale.com. **World Wide Web address:** http://www.bluewhale.com. **Description:** Provides both furniture storage and moving services throughout Texas. Founded in 1985.

CAPITAL METRO
2910 East Fifth Street, Austin TX 78702. 512/389-7400. **Fax:** 512/369-6010. **Recorded jobline:** 512/389-7450. **Contact:** Human Resources. **E-mail address:** application@capmetro.org. **World Wide Web address:** http://www.capmetro.austin.tx.us. **Description:** Operates the public bus system for the metropolitan Austin area. **NOTE:** Contact Human Resources directly at 512/389-7445. Please visit website for a listing of jobs and download application form. Resumes are accepted for additional information, but you must complete an application. **Positions advertised include:** Fleet Mechanic; Marketing Coordinator; Data

Analyst; Budget Analyst. **Office hours:** Monday – Friday, 8:00 a.m. – 5:00 p.m. **Corporate headquarters location:** This location.

CITY MACHINE & WELDING, INC.
P.O. Box 51018, Amarillo TX 79159-1018. 806/358-7293. **Physical address:** 9701 Interchange 552, Amarillo TX 79124. **Fax:** 806/358-7906. **Contact:** Human Resources. **World Wide Web address:** http://www.cmwelding.com. **Description:** Manufactures transport trailers and performs welding services. **President:** L.A. Oeschger.

RAILAMERICA, INC

4040 Broadway, Suite 200, San Antonio TX 78209. 210/841-7600. **Fax:** 561/226-1627. **Contact:** Human Resources. **E-mail address:** employment@railamerica.com. **World Wide Web address:** http://www.railamerica.com. **Description:** A leading operator of short line railroads nationwide. **Positions advertised include:** Electrician. **NOTE:** Send resumes to: RailAmerica, Inc., Employment, 5300 Broken Sound Boulevard Northwest, Boca Raton FL 33487.

VIA METROPOLITAN TRANSIT
1021 San Pedro, San Antonio TX 78212. 210/362-2240. **Contact:** Human Resources. **E-mail address:** hr.emp@viainfo.net. **World Wide Web address:** http://www.viainfo.net. **Description:** A bus line for the city of San Antonio. **NOTE:** Apply at Human Resources office. **Positions advertised include:** Strategic Planning Coordinator; Shop Attendant; Bus Operator; Paratransit Operator; Substitute Teacher; Temporary Clerical Pool. **Office hours:** Monday – Friday, 7:30 a.m. – 5:00 p.m. **Corporate headquarters location:** This location.

UTILITIES: ELECTRIC, GAS, AND WATER

You can expect to find the following types of companies in this section:
Gas, Electric, and Fuel Companies • Other Energy-Producing Companies • Public Utility Holding Companies • Water Utilities

---

EL PASO ELECTRIC COMPANY
P.O. Box 982, Location – 245, El Paso TX 79960. 915/543-2027. Fax: 915/521-4787. Recorded jobline: 915/543-2233. **Contact:** Human Resources. **E-mail address:** Human_Resources@epelectric.com. **World Wide Web address:** http://www.epelectric.com. **Description:** El Paso Electric generates and distributes electricity through an interconnected system to approximately 314,000 customers in El Paso and an area of the Rio Grande Valley in west Texas and southern New Mexico. The company's service area extends about 110 miles northwest from El Paso to the Caballo Dam in New Mexico and about 120 miles southeast from El Paso to Van Horn TX. Founded in 1901. **Listed on:** New York Stock Exchange. **Stock exchange symbol:** EE.

EL PASO NATURAL GAS COMPANY
100 North Stanton, El Paso TX 79901. 915/496-2600. **Contact:** Human Resources. **World Wide Web address:** http://www.epenergy.com. **Description:** Owns and operates one of the nation's largest field and mainline natural gas transmission systems. The company has over 17,000 miles of pipeline connecting natural gas supply regions in New Mexico, Texas, Oklahoma, and Colorado to markets in California, Nevada, Arizona, New Mexico, Texas, and Mexico. **NOTE:** This company only accepts resumes for open positions. Check website for current list of openings. **Internship information:** For information, e-mail this company at internships@elpaso.com. **Parent company:** El Paso Energy Corporation.

EL PASO WATER UTILITIES
P.O. Box 511, El Paso TX 79961. 915/594-5519. **Physical address:** 1154 Hawkins Boulevard, El Paso TX 79925. **Fax:** 915/594-5679. **Contact:** Human Resources. **NOTE:** Job listings and resumes are accepted for this company by the City of El Paso on its website, http://www.elpasotexas.gov. **World Wide Web address:** http://www.epwu.org. **Description:** A nonprofit provider of water and wastewater services for the city of El Paso and the surrounding region.

SOUTHERN UNION COMPANY
221 West Sixth Street, Austin TX 78701. 512/370-8321. **Fax:** 512/370-8380. **Contact:** Human Resources. **World Wide Web address:** http://www.southernunionco.com. **Description:** A natural gas distribution and utility company with subsidiaries serving several U.S. states. This website has job listings for corporate jobs and utility jobs in Wilkes Barre

PA. Each subsidiary features its job listings on its own websites. See the corporate site for links. **Special programs:** Internships. **Corporate headquarters location:** Wilkes Barre PA. **Other U.S. locations:** FL; MA; MO; PA; OK; RI. **Subsidiaries include:** Panhandle Energy (Houston TX) operates major pipelines to distribute natural gas throughout the country. Missouri Gas Energy, (Kansas City MO) serves approximately500,000 customers in central and western Missouri. PG Energy (Wilkes Barre PA) serves nearly 160,000 customers in central PA. New England Gas Co. (Providence RI) provides natural gas to about 290,000 customers in Rhode Island and Massachusetts. **Operations at this facility include:** Administration; Sales. **Listed on:** New York Stock Exchange. **Stock exchange symbol:** SUG.

XCEL ENERGY
P.O. Box 1261, Amarillo TX 79170-0001. 806/378-2121. **Contact:** Doris Brasille, Employee Services Manager. **World Wide Web address:** http://www.xcelenergy.com. **Description:** Provides electric service to the Amarillo area. **NOTE:** Entry-level positions offered. Apply online for all positions. **Special programs:** Internships. **Corporate headquarters location:** Minneapolis MN. **Listed on:** New York Stock Exchange. **Stock exchange symbol:** XEL.

MISCELLANEOUS WHOLESALING

**You can expect to find the following types of companies
in this section:**
Exporters and Importers • General Wholesale Distribution Companies

AMC INDUSTRIES
P.O. Box 171290 San Antonio TX, 78217. 210/545-2566. **Physical address:** 3535 Metro Parkway, San Antonio TX 78247. **Fax:** 210/545-2977. **Contact:** Human Resources. **Description:** A wholesale distributor of water well parts. **Corporate headquarters location:** This location. **Other U.S. locations:** Austin TX; Houston TX; Pharr TX; Buda TX.

W.W. GRAINGER
430 Sun Belt Drive, Corpus Christi TX 78408. 361/289-9201. **Fax:** 361/289-7943. **Contact:** Human Resources. **World Wide Web address:** http://www.grainger.com. **Description:** W.W. Grainger is a national supplier of industrial equipment such as motors, pumps, and safety maintenance equipment. The company distributes a variety of equipment and components to the industrial, commercial, contracting, and institutional markets. Products are sold through local branches and include equipment and components for motors, air tools, hydraulic products, refrigeration items, power and hand tools, office equipment, computer supplies, replacement parts, industrial products, safety items, cold weather clothing, and storage equipment. Founded in 1927. **Operations at this facility include:** This location sells industrial supplies. **Other area locations:** Statewide. **Other U.S. locations:** Nationwide.

IKON OFFICE SOLUTIONS
7401 East Ben White Boulevard, Building 2, Austin TX 78741-7418. 512/385-5100. **Contact:** Human Resources. **E-mail address:** resumes@ikon.com. **World Wide Web address:** http://www.ikon.com. **Description:** IKON Office Solutions is one of the largest independent copier distribution networks in North America. **Positions advertised include:** Recruiter/Trainer; Strategic Account Sales Analyst; Major Account Executive. **Operations at this facility include:** This location is a sales and service center.

PASSAGE SUPPLY COMPANY
P.O. Box 971395, El Paso TX 79997-1395. 915/778-9377. **Fax:** 915/772-9602. **Contact:** Ron Passage, General Manager. **Description:** A heating and cooling systems distributor. **Corporate headquarters location:** This location.

INDUSTRY ASSOCIATIONS

ACCOUNTING AND MANAGEMENT CONSULTING

AMERICAN ACCOUNTING ASSOCIATION
5717 Bessie Drive, Sarasota FL 34233-2399. 941/921-7747. **Fax:** 943/923-4093. **E-mail address:** Office@aaahq.org. **World Wide Web address:** http://aaahq.org. **Description:** A voluntary organization founded in 1916 to promote excellence in accounting education, research and practice.

AMERICAN INSTITUTE OF CERTIFIED PUBLIC ACCOUNTANTS
1211 Avenue of the Americas, New York NY 10036. 212/596-6200. **Toll-free phone:** 888/777-7077. **Fax:** 212/596-6213. **World Wide Web address:** http://www.aicpa.org. **Description:** A non-profit organization providing resources, information, and leadership to its members.

AMERICAN MANAGEMENT ASSOCIATION
1601 Broadway, New York NY 10019. 212/586-8100. **Fax:** 212/903-8168. **Toll-free phone:** 800/262-9699. **E-mail address:** info@amanet.org. **World Wide Web address:** http://www.amanet.org. **Description:** A non-profit association providing its members with management development and educational services.

ASSOCIATION OF GOVERNMENT ACCOUNTANTS
2208 Mount Vernon Avenue, Alexandria VA 22301. 703/684-6931. **Toll-free phone:** 800/AGA-7211. **Fax:** 703/548-9367. **World Wide Web address:** http://www.agacgfm.com. **Description:** A public financial management organization catering to the professional interests of financial managers at the local, state and federal governments and public accounting firms.

ASSOCIATION OF MANAGEMENT CONSULTING FIRMS
380 Lexington Avenue, Suite 1700, New York NY 10168. 212/551-7887. **Fax:** 212/551-7934. **E-mail address:** info@amcf.org. **World Wide Web address:** http://www.amcf.org. **Description:** Founded in 1929 to provide a forum for confronting common challenges; increasing the collective knowledge of members and their clients; and establishing a professional code conduct.

CONNECTICUT SOCIETY OF CERTIFIED PUBLIC ACCOUNTANTS
845 Brook Street, Building Two, Rocky Hill CT 06067-3405. 860/258-4800. **Fax:** 860/258-4859. **E-mail address:** info@cs-cpa.org. **World Wide Web address:** http://www.cs-cpa.org. **Description:** A statewide professional membership organization catering to CPAs.

INSTITUTE OF INTERNAL AUDITORS
247 Maitland Avenue, Altamonte Springs FL 32701-4201. 407-937-1100. **Fax:** 407-937-1101. **E-mail address:** iia@theiia.org. **World Wide Web address:** http://www.theiia.org. **Description:** Founded in 1941 to serves

members in internal auditing, governance and internal control, IT audit, education, and security worldwide.

INSTITUTE OF MANAGEMENT ACCOUNTANTS
10 Paragon Drive, Montvale NJ 07645-1718. 201/573-9000. **Fax:** 201/474-1600. **Toll-free phone:** 800/638-4427. **E-mail address**: ima@imanet.org. **World Wide Web address:** http://www.imanet.org. **Description:** Provides members personal and professional development opportunities in management accounting, financial management and information management through education and association with business professionals and certification in management accounting and financial management.

INSTITUTE OF MANAGEMENT CONSULTANTS
2025 M Street, NW, Suite 800, Washington DC 20036-3309. 202/367-1134. **Toll-free phone:** 800/221-2557. **Fax:** 202/367-2134. **E-mail address:** office@imcusa.org. **World Wide Web address:** http://www.imcusa.org. **Description** Founded in 1968 as the national professional association representing management consultants and awarding the CMC (Certified Management Consultant) certification mark.

NATIONAL ASSOCIATION OF TAX PROFESSIONALS
720 Association Drive, PO Box 8002, Appleton WI 54912-8002. 800/558/3402. **Fax:** 800/747-0001. **E-Mail address:** natp@natptax.com. **World Wide Web address:** http://www.natptax.com. **Description:** Founded in 1979 as a nonprofit professional association dedicated to excellence in taxation with a mission to serve professionals who work in all areas of tax practice.

NATIONAL SOCIETY OF PUBLIC ACCOUNTANTS
1010 North Fairfax Street, Alexandria VA 22314. 703/549-6400. **Toll-free phone:** 800/966-6679. **Fax:** 703/549-2984. **Email address:** members@nsacct.org. **World Wide Web address:** http://www.nsacct.org. **Description:** For more than 50 years, NSA has supported its members with resources and representation to protect their right to practice, build credibility and grow the profession. NSA protects the public by requiring its members to adhere to a strict Code of Ethics.

ADVERTISING, MARKETING, AND PUBLIC RELATIONS

ADVERTISING RESEARCH FOUNDATION
641 Lexington Avenue, New York NY 10022. 212/751-5656. **World Wide Web address:** http://www.thearf.com. **Description:** Founded in 1936 by the Association of National Advertisers and the American Association of Advertising Agencies, the Advertising Research Foundation (ARF) is a nonprofit corporate-membership association, which is today the preeminent professional organization in the field of advertising, marketing and media research. Its combined membership represents more than 400 advertisers, advertising agencies, research firms, media companies, educational institutions and international organizations.

AMERICAN ASSOCIATION OF ADVERTISING AGENCIES
405 Lexington Avenue, 18th Floor, New York NY 10174-1801. 212/682-2500. **Fax:** 212/682-8391. **World Wide Web address:** http://www.aaaa.org. **Description:** Founded in 1917 as the national trade association representing the advertising agency business in the United States.

AMERICAN MARKETING ASSOCIATION
311 South Wacker Drive, Suite 5800, Chicago IL 60606. 312/542-9000. **Fax:** 312/542-9001. **Toll-free phone:** 800/AMA-1150. **E-mail address:** info@ama.org. **World Wide Web address:** http://www.marketingpower.com. **Description:** A professional associations for marketers providing relevant marketing information that experienced marketers turn to everyday.

DIRECT MARKETING ASSOCIATION
1120 Avenue of the Americas, New York NY 10036-6700. 212/768-7277. **Fax:** 212/302-6714. **E-mail address:** info@the-dma.org. **World Wide Web address:** http://www.the-dma.org. **Description:** Founded in 1917 as a non-profit organization representing professionals working in all areas of direct marketing.

INTERNATIONAL ADVERTISING ASSOCIATION
521 Fifth Avenue, Suite 1807, New York NY 10175. 212/557-1133. **Fax:** 212/983-0455. **E-mail address:** iaa@iaaglobal.org. **World Wide Web address:** http://www.iaaglobla.org. **Description:** A strategic partnership that addresses the common interests of all the marketing communications disciplines ranging from advertisers to media companies to agencies to direct marketing firms to individual practitioners.

MARKETING RESEARCH ASSOCIATION
1344 Silas Deane Highway, Suite 306, PO Box 230, Rocky Hill CT 06067-0230. 860/257-4008. **Fax:** 860/257-3990. **E-mail address:** email@mra-net.org. **World Wide Web address:** http://www.mra-net.org. **Description:** MRA promotes excellence in the opinion and marketing

research industry by providing members with a variety of opportunities for advancing and expanding their marketing research and related business skills. To protect the marketing research environment, we will act as an advocate with appropriate government entities, other associations, and the public.

PUBLIC RELATIONS SOCIETY OF AMERICA
33 Maiden Lane, 11th Floor, New York NY 10038-5150. 212/460-1400. **Fax:** 212/995-0757. **E-mail address:** info@prsa.org. **World Wide Web address:** http://www.prsa.org. **Description:** A professional organization for public relations practitioners. Comprised of nearly 20,000 members organized into 116 Chapters represent business and industry, counseling firms, government, associations, hospitals, schools, professional services firms and nonprofit organizations.

AEROSPACE

AMERICAN INSTITUTE OF AERONAUTICS AND ASTRONAUTICS
1801 Alexander Bell Drive, Suite 500, Reston VA 20191-4344. 703/264-7500. **Toll-free phone:** 800/639-AIAA. **Fax:** 703/264-7551. **E-mail address:** info@aiaa.org. **World Wide Web address:** http://www.aiaa.org. **Description:** The principal society of the aerospace engineer and scientist.

NATIONAL AERONAUTIC ASSOCIATION OF USA
1815 N. Fort Myer Drive, Suite 500, Arlington VA 22209. 703/527-0226. **Fax:** 703/527-0229. **E-mail address:** naa@naa-usa.org. **World Wide Web address:** http://www.naa-usa.org. **Description:** A non-parochial, charitable organization serving all segments of American aviation whose membership encompass all areas of flight including skydiving, models, commercial airlines, and military fighters.

PROFESSIONAL AVIATION MAINTENANCE ASSOCIATION
717 Princess Street, Alexandria VA 22314. 703/683-3171. **Toll-free phone:** 866/865-PAMA. **Fax:** 703/683-0018. **E-mail address:** hq@pama.org. **World Wide Web address:** http://www.pama.org. **Description:** A non-profit organization concerned with promoting professionalism among aviation maintenance personnel; fostering and improving methods, skills, learning, and achievement in aviation maintenance. The association also conducts regular industry meetings and seminars.

APPAREL, FASHION, AND TEXTILES

AMERICAN APPAREL AND FOOTWEAR ASSOCIATION
1601 North Kent Street, Suite 1200, Arlington VA 22209. 703/524-1864. **Fax:** 703/522-6741. **World Wide Web address:** http://apparelandfootwear.org. **Description:** The national trade association representing apparel, footwear and other sewn products companies, and their suppliers. Promotes and enhances its members' competitiveness, productivity and profitability in the global market.

AMERICAN TEXTILE MANUFACTURERS INSTITUTE
1130 Connecticut Avenue, NW, Suite 1200, Washington DC 20036-3954. 202/862-0500. **Fax:** 202/862-0537. **ATMI FactsLine:** 202/862-0572. **World Wide Web address:** http://www.atmi.org. **Description:** The national trade association for the domestic textile industry with members operating in more than 30 states and the industry employs approximately 450,000 people.

THE FASHION GROUP
8 West 40th Street, 7th Floor, New York NY 10018. 212/301-5511. **Fax:** 212/302-5533. **E-mail address:** info@fgi.org. **World Wide Web address:** http://www.fgi.org. **Description:** A non-profit association representing all areas of the fashion, apparel, accessories, beauty and home industries.

INTERNATIONAL ASSOCIATION OF CLOTHING DESIGNERS AND EXECUTIVES
34 Thorton Ferry Road #1, Amherst NH 03031. 603/672-4065. **Fax:** 603/672-4064. **World Wide Web address:** http://www.iacde.com. **Description:** Founded in 1911, with the mission to serve as a global network for the sharing of information by its members on design direction and developments, fashion and fiber trends, and technical innovations affecting tailored apparel, designers, their suppliers, retailers, manufacturing executives and educational institutions for the purpose of enhancing their professional standing and interests.

ARCHITECTURE, CONSTRUCTION, AND ENGINEERING

AACE INTERNATIONAL: THE ASSOCIATION FOR TOTAL COST MANAGEMENT
209 Prairie Avenue, Suite 100, Morgantown WV 26501. 304/296-8444. **Fax:** 304/291-5728. **E-mail address:** info@aacei.org. **World Wide Web address:** http://www.aacei.org. **Description:** Founded 1956 to provide its approximately 5,500 worldwide members with the resources to enhance their performance and ensure continued growth and success. Members include cost management professionals: cost managers and engineers, project managers, planners and schedulers, estimators and bidders, and value engineers.

AMERICAN ASSOCIATION OF ENGINEERING SOCIETIES
1828 L Street, NW, Suite 906, Washington DC 20036. 202/296-2237. **Fax:** 202/296-1151. **World Wide Web address:** http://www.aaes.org. **Description:** A multidisciplinary organization of engineering societies dedicated to advancing the knowledge, understanding, and practice of engineering.

AMERICAN CONSULTING ENGINEERS COMPANIES
1015 15th Street, 8th Floor, NW, Washington DC, 20005-2605. 202/347-7474. **Fax:** 202/898-0068. **E-mail address:** acec@acec.org. **World Wide Web address:** http://www.acec.org. **Description:** Engaged in a wide range of engineering works that propel the nation's economy, and enhance and safeguard America's quality of life. These works allow Americans to drink clean water, enjoy a healthy life, take advantage of new technologies, and travel safely and efficiently. The Council's mission is to contribute to America's prosperity and welfare by advancing the business interests of member firms.

AMERICAN INSTITUTE OF ARCHITECTS
1735 New York Avenue, NW, Washington DC 20006. 202/626-7300. **Fax:** 202/626-7547. **Toll-free phone:** 800/AIA-3837. **E-mail address:** infocentral@aia.org. **World Wide Web address:** http://www.aia.org. **Description:** A non-profit organization for the architecture profession dedicated to: Serving its members, advancing their value, improving the quality of the built environment. Vision Statement: Through a culture of innovation, The American Institute of Architects empowers its members and inspires creation of a better-built environment.

AMERICAN INSTITUTE OF CONSTRUCTORS
466 94th Avenue North, St. Petersburg FL 33702. 727/578-0317. **Fax:** 727/578-9982. **E-mail address:** admin@aicenet.org. **World Wide Web address:** http://www.aicnet.org. **Description:** Founded to help individual construction practitioners achieve the professional status they deserve and serves as the national qualifying body of professional constructor. The Institute AIC membership identifies the individual as a true

professional. The Institute is the constructor's counterpart of professional organizations found in architecture, engineering, law and other fields.

AMERICAN SOCIETY FOR ENGINEERING EDUCATION
1818 N Street, NW, Suite 600, Washington DC, 20036-2479. 202/331-3500. **Fax:** 202/265-8504. **World Wide Web address:** http://www.asee.org. **Description:** A nonprofit member association, founded in 1893, dedicated to promoting and improving engineering and technology education.

AMERICAN SOCIETY OF CIVIL ENGINEERS
1801 Alexander Bell Drive, Reston VA 20191-4400. 703/295-6300. **Fax:** 703/295-6222. **Toll-free phone:** 800/548-2723. **World Wide Web address:** http://www.asce.org. **Description:** Founded to provide essential value to its members, their careers, partners and the public by developing leadership, advancing technology, advocating lifelong learning and promoting the profession.

AMERICAN SOCIETY OF HEATING, REFRIGERATION, AND AIR CONDITIONING ENGINEERS
1791 Tullie Circle, NE, Atlanta GA 30329. 404/636-8400. **Fax:** 404/321-5478. **Toll-free phone:** 800/527-4723. **E-mail address:** ashrae@ashrae.org. **World Wide Web address:** http://www.ashrae.org. **Description:** Founded with a mission to advance the arts and sciences of heating, ventilation, air conditioning, refrigeration and related human factors and to serve the evolving needs of the public and ASHRAE members.

AMERICAN SOCIETY OF MECHANICAL ENGINEERS
Three Park Avenue, New York, NY 10016-5990. 973-882-1167. **Toll-free phone:** 800/843-2763. **E-mail address:** infocentral@asme.org. **World Wide Web address:** http://www.asme.org. **Description:** Founded in 1880 as the American Society of Mechanical Engineers, today ASME International is a nonprofit educational and technical organization serving a worldwide membership of 125,000.

AMERICAN SOCIETY OF NAVAL ENGINEERS
1452 Duke Street, Alexandria VA 22314-3458. 703/836-6727. **Fax:** 703/836-7491. **E-mail address:** asnehq@navalengineers.org. **World Wide Web address:** http://www.navalengineers.org. **Description:** Mission is to advance the knowledge and practice of naval engineering in public and private applications and operations, to enhance the professionalism and well being of members, and to promote naval engineering as a career field.

AMERICAN SOCIETY OF PLUMBING ENGINEERS
8614 Catalpa Avenue, Suite 1007, Chicago IL 60656-1116. 773/693-2773. **Fax:** 773/695-9007. **E-mail address:** info@aspe.org. **World Wide Web address:** http://www.aspe.org. **Description:** The international organization for professionals skilled in the design, specification and inspection of plumbing systems. ASPE is dedicated to the advancement

of the science of plumbing engineering, to the professional growth and advancement of its members and the health, welfare and safety of the public.

AMERICAN SOCIETY OF SAFETY ENGINEERS
1800 E Oakton Street, Des Plaines IL 60018. 847/699-2929. **Fax:** 847/768-3434. **E-mail address:** customerservice@asse.org. **World Wide Web address:** http://www.asse.org. **Description:** A non-profit organization promoting the concerns of safety engineers.

ASSOCIATED BUILDERS AND CONTRACTORS
4250 N. Fairfax Drive, 9th Floor, Arlington VA 22203-1607. 703/812-2000. **E-mail address:** gotquestions@abc.org. **World Wide Web address:** http://www.abc.org. **Description:** A national trade association representing more than 23,000 merit shop contractors, subcontractors, material suppliers and related firms in 80 chapters across the United States. Membership represents all specialties within the U.S. construction industry and is comprised primarily of firms that perform work in the industrial and commercial sectors of the industry.

ASSOCIATED GENERAL CONTRACTORS OF AMERICA, INC.
333 John Carlyle Street, Suite 200, Alexandria VA 22314. 703/548-3118. **Fax:** 703/548-3119. **E-mail address:** info@agc.org. **World Wide Web address:** http://www.agc.org. **Description:** A construction trade association, founded in 1918 on a request by President Woodrow Wilson.

THE ENGINEERING CENTER (TEC)
One Walnut Street, Boston MA 02108-3616. 617/227-5551. **Fax:** 617/227-6783. **E-mail address:** tec@engineers.org. **World Wide Web address:** http://www.engineers.org. **Description:** Founded with a mission to increase public awareness of the value of the engineering profession; to provide current information affecting the profession; to offer administrative facilities and services to engineering organizations in New England; and to provide a forum for discussion and resolution of professional issues.

ILLUMINATING ENGINEERING SOCIETY OF NORTH AMERICA
120 Wall Street, Floor 17, New York NY 10005. 212/248-5000. **Fax:** 212/248-5017(18). **E-mail address:** iesna@iesna.org. **World Wide Web address:** http://www.iesna.org. **Description:** To advance knowledge and to disseminate information for the improvement of the lighted environment to the benefit of society.

JUNIOR ENGINEERING TECHNICAL SOCIETY
1420 King Street, Suite 405, Alexandria VA 22314. 703/548-5387. **Fax:** 703/548-0769. **E-mail address:** info@jets.org. **World Wide Web address:** http://www.jets.org. **Description:** JETS is a national non-profit education organization that has served the pre-college engineering community for over 50 years. Through competitions and programs, JETS

serves over 30,000 students and 2,000 teachers, and holds programs on 150 college campuses each year.

NATIONAL ACTION COUNCIL FOR MINORITIES IN ENGINEERING
440 Hamilton Avenue, Suite 302, White Plains NY 10601-1813. 914/539-4010. **Fax:** 914/539-4032. **E-mail address:** webmaster@nacme.org. **World Wide Web address:** http://www.nacme.org. **Description:** Founded in 1974 to provide leadership and support for the national effort to increase the representation of successful African American, American Indian and Latino women and men in engineering and technology, math- and science-based careers.

NATIONAL ASSOCIATION OF HOME BUILDERS
1201 15th Street, NW, Washington DC 20005. 202/266-8200. **Toll-free phone:** 800/368-5242. **World Wide Web address:** http://www.nahb.org. **Description:** Founded in 1942, NAHB has been serving its members, the housing industry, and the public at large. A trade association that promotes the policies that make housing a national priority.

NATIONAL ASSOCIATION OF MINORITY ENGINEERING PROGRAM ADMINISTRATORS
1133 West Morse Boulevard, Suite 201, Winter Park FL 32789. 407/647-8839. **Fax:** 407/629-2502. **E-mail address:** namepa@namepa.org **World Wide Web address:** http://www.namepa.org. **Description:** Provides services, information, and tools to produce a diverse group of engineers and scientists, and achieve equity and parity in the nation's workforce.

NATIONAL ELECTRICAL CONTRACTORS ASSOCIATION
3 Bethesda Metro Center, Suite 1100, Bethesda MD 20814. 301/657-3110. **Fax:** 301/215-4500. **World Wide Web address:** http://www.necanet.org. **Description:** Founded in 1901 as representative segment of the construction market comprised of over 70,000 electrical contracting firms.

NATIONAL ASSOCIATION OF BLACK ENGINEERS
1454 Duke Street, Alexandria VA 22314. 703/549-2207. **Fax:** 703/683-5312. **E-mail address:** info@nsbe.org. **World Wide Web address:** http://www.nsbe.org. **Description:** A non-profit organization dedicated to increasing the number of culturally responsible Black engineers who excel academically, succeed professionally and positively impact the community.

NATIONAL SOCIETY OF PROFESSIONAL ENGINEERS
1420 King Street, Alexandria VA 22314-2794. 703/684-2800. **Fax:** 703/836-4875. **World Wide Web address:** http://www.nspe.org. **Description:** An engineering society that represents engineering professionals and licensed engineers (PEs) across all disciplines. Founded in 1934 to promote engineering licensure and ethics, enhance the engineer image, advocate and protect legal rights, publish industry news, and provide continuing education.

SOCIETY OF FIRE PROTECTION ENGINEERS
7315 Wisconsin Avenue, Suite 620E, Bethesda MD 20814. 301/718-2910. **Fax:** 301/718-2242. **E-mail address:** sfpehqtrs@sfpe.org. **World Wide Web address:** http://www.sfpe.org. **Description:** Founded in 1950 and incorporated as in independent organization in 1971, the professional society represents professionals in the field of fire protection engineering. The Society has approximately 3500 members in the United States and abroad, and 51 regional chapters, 10 of which are outside the US.

ARTS, ENTERTAINMENT, SPORTS, AND RECREATION

AMERICAN ASSOCIATION OF MUSEUMS
1575 Eye Street NW, Suite 400, Washington DC 20005. 202/289-1818. **Fax:** 202/289-6578. **World Wide Web address:** http://www.aam-us.org. **Description:** Founded in 1906, the association promotes excellence within the museum community. Services include advocacy, professional education, information exchange, accreditation, and guidance on current professional standards of performance.

AMERICAN FEDERATION OF MUSICIANS
1501 Broadway, Suite 600, New York NY 10036. 212/869-1330. **Fax:** 212/764-6134. **World Wide Web address:** http://www.afm.org. **Description:** Represents the interests of professional musicians. Services include negotiating agreements, protecting ownership of recorded music, securing benefits such as health care and pension, or lobbying our legislators. The AFM is committed to raising industry standards and placing the professional musician in the foreground of the cultural landscape.

AMERICAN MUSIC CENTER
30 West 26th Street, Suite 1001, New York NY 10010. 212/366-5260. **Fax:** 212/366-5265. **World Wide Web address:** http://www.amc.net. **Description:** Dedicated to fostering and composition, production, publication, and distribution of contemporary (American) music.

AMERICAN SOCIETY OF COMPOSERS, AUTHORS, AND PUBLISHERS (ASCAP)
One Lincoln Plaza, New York NY 10023. 212/621-6000. **Fax:** 212/724-9064. **E-mail address:** info@ascap.com. **World Wide Web address:** http://www.ascap.com. **Description:** A membership based association comprised of composers, songwriters, lyricists, and music publishers across all genres of music.

AMERICAN SYMPHONY ORCHESTRA LEAGUE
33 West 60th Street, 5th Floor, New York NY 10023-7905. 212/262-5161. **Fax:** 212/262-5198. **E-mail address:** league@symphony.org. **World Wide Web address:** http://www.symphony.org. **Description:** Founded in 1942 to exchange information and ideas with other orchestra leaders. The league also publishes the bimonthly magazine.

AMERICAN ZOO AND AQUARIUM ASSOCIATION
8403 Colesville Road, Suite 710, Silver Spring MD 20910-3314. 301/562-0777. **Fax:** 301/562-0888. **World Wide Web address:** http://www.aza.org. **Description:** Dedicated to establishing and maintaining excellent professional standards in all AZA Institutions through its accreditation program; establishing and promoting high standards of animal care and welfare; promoting and facilitating collaborative conservation and research programs; advocating effective

governmental policies for our members; strengthening and promoting conservation education programs for our public and professional development for our members, and; raising awareness of the collective impact of its members and their programs.

ASSOCIATION OF INDEPENDENT VIDEO AND FILMMAKERS
304 Hudson Street, 6th floor, New York NY 10013. 212/807-1400. **Fax:** 212/463-8519. **E-mail address:** info@aivf.org. **World Wide Web address:** http://www.aivf.org. **Description:** A membership organization serving local and international film and videomakers including documentarians, experimental artists, and makers of narrative features.

NATIONAL ENDOWMENT FOR THE ARTS
1100 Pennsylvania Avenue, NW, Washington DC 20506. 202/682-5400. **E-mail address:** webmgr@arts.endow.com. **World Wide Web address:** http://www.nea.gov. **Description:** Founded in 1965 to foster, preserve, and promote excellence in the arts, to bring art to all Americans, and to provide leadership in arts education.

NATIONAL RECREATION AND PARK ASSOCIATION
22377 Belmont Ridge Road, Ashburn VA 20148-4150. 703/858-0784. **Fax:** 703/858-0794. **E-mail address:** info@nrpa.org. **World Wide Web address:** http://www.nrpa.org. **Description:** Works "to advance parks, recreation and environmental conservation efforts that enhance the quality of life for all people."

WOMEN'S CAUCUS FOR ART
P.O. Box 1498, Canal Street Station, New York NY 10013. 212/634-0007. **E-mail address:** info@nationalwca.com. **World Wide Web address:** http://www.nationalwca.com. **Description:** Founded in 1972 in connection with the College Art Association (CAA), as a national organization unique in its multi-disciplinary, multicultural membership of artists, art historians, students /educators, museum professionals and galleries in the visual arts.

AUTOMOTIVE

NATIONAL AUTOMOBILE DEALERS ASSOCIATION
8400 Westpark Drive, McLean VA 22102. 703/821-7000. **Toll-free phone:** 800/252-6232. **E-mail address:** nadainfo@nada.org. **World Wide Web address:** http://www.nada.org. **Description:** NADA represents America's franchised new-car and -truck dealers. Today there are more than 19,700 franchised new-car and -truck dealer members holding nearly 49,300 separate new-car and light-, medium-, and heavy-duty truck franchises, domestic and import. Founded in 1917.

NATIONAL INSTITUTE FOR AUTOMOTIVE SERVICE EXCELLENCE
101 Blue Seal Drive, SE, Suite 101, Leesburg VA 20175. 703/669-6600. **Toll-free phone:** 877/ASE-TECH. **World Wide Web address:** http://www.ase.com. **Description:** An independent, non-profit organization established in 1972 to improve the quality of vehicle repair and service through the testing and certification of repair and service professionals. More than 420,000 professionals hold current ASE credentials.

SOCIETY OF AUTOMOTIVE ENGINEERS
400 Commonwealth Drive, Warrendale PA 15096-0001. 724/776-4841. **E-mail address:** customerservice@sae.org. **World Wide Web address:** http://www.sae.org. **Description:** An organization with more than 84,000 members from 97 countries who share information and exchange ideas for advancing the engineering of mobility systems.

BANKING

AMERICA'S COMMUNITY BANKERS
900 Nineteenth Street, NW, Suite 400, Washington DC 20006. 202/857-3100. **Fax:** 202/296-8716. **World Wide Web address:** http://www.acbankers.org. **Description:** Represents the nation's community banks of all charter types and sizes providing a broad range of advocacy and service strategies to enhance their members' presence and contribution to the marketplace.

AMERICAN BANKERS ASSOCIATION
1120 Connecticut Avenue, NW, Washington DC 20036. 800/BANKERS. **World Wide Web address:** http://www.aba.com. **Description:** Founded in 1875 and represents banks on issues of national importance for financial institutions and their customers. Members include all categories of banking institutions, including community, regional and money center banks and holding companies, as well as savings associations, trust companies and savings banks.

BIOTECHNOLOGY, PHARMACEUTICALS, AND SCIENTIFIC R&D

AMERICAN ASSOCIATION FOR CLINICAL CHEMISTRY
2101 L Street, NW, Suite 202, Washington DC 20037-1558. 202/857-0717. **Fax:** 202/887-5093. **Toll-free phone:** 800/892-1400. **World Wide Web address:** http://www.aacc.org. **Description:** Founded in 1948 as an international scientific/medical society of clinical laboratory professionals, physicians, research scientists and other individuals involved with clinical chemistry and other clinical laboratory science-related disciplines. The society has 10,000 members.

AMERICAN ASSOCIATION OF COLLEGES OF PHARMACY
1426 Prince Street, Alexandria VA 22314. 703/739-2330. **Fax:** 703/836-8982. **E-mail address:** mail@aacp.org. **World Wide Web address:** http://www.aacp.org. **Description:** Founded in 1900 as the national organization representing the interests of pharmaceutical education and educators. Comprising all 89 U.S. pharmacy colleges and schools including more than 4,000 faculty, 36,000 students enrolled in professional programs, and 3,600 individuals pursuing graduate study, AACP is committed to excellence in pharmaceutical education.

AMERICAN ASSOCIATION OF PHARMACEUTICAL SCIENTISTS
2107 Wilson Boulevard, Suite 700, Arlington VA 22201-3042. 703/243-2800. **Fax:** 703/243-9650. **E-mail address:** aaps@aaps.org. **World Wide Web address:** http://www.aaps.org. **Description:** Founded in 1986 as professional, scientific society of more than 10,000 members employed in academia, industry, government and other research institutes worldwide. The association advances science through the open exchange of scientific knowledge; serves as an information resource; and contributes to human health through pharmaceutical research and development.

AMERICAN COLLEGE OF CLINICAL PHARMACY (ACCP)
3101 Broadway, Suite 650, Kansas City MO 64111. 816/531-2177. **Fax:** 816/531-4990. **E-mail address:** accp@accp.com **World Wide Web address:** http://www.accp.com. **Description:** A professional and scientific society providing leadership, education, advocacy, and resources enabling clinical pharmacists to achieve excellence in practice and research.

AMERICAN PHARMACISTS ASSOCIATION
2215 Constitution Avenue, NW, Washington DC 20037-2985. 202/628-4410. **Fax:** 202/783-2351. **E-mail address:** info@aphanet.org. **World Wide Web address:** http://www.aphanet.org. **Description:** Founded in 1852 as the national professional society of pharmacists. Members include practicing pharmacists, pharmaceutical scientists, pharmacy students, pharmacy technicians, and others interested in advancing the profession.

AMERICAN SOCIETY FOR BIOCHEMISTRY AND MOLECULAR BIOLOGY
9650 Rockville Pike, Bethesda MD 20814-3996. 301/634-7145. **Fax:** 301/634-7126. **E-mail address:** asbmb@asbmb.faseb.org. **World Wide Web address:** http://www.asbmb.org. **Description:** A nonprofit scientific and educational organization with over 11,900 members. Most members teach and conduct research at colleges and universities. Others conduct research in various government laboratories, nonprofit research institutions and industry. The Society's student members attend undergraduate or graduate institutions.

AMERICAN SOCIETY OF HEALTH-SYSTEM PHARMACISTS
7272 Wisconsin Avenue, Bethesda MD 20814. 301/657-3000. **Toll-free phone:** 866/279-0681. **World Wide Web address:** http://www.ashp.org. **Description:** A national professional association representing pharmacists who practice in hospitals, health maintenance organizations, long-term care facilities, home care, and other components of health care systems.

NATIONAL SPACE BIOMEDICAL RESEARCH INSTITUTE
One Baylor Plaza, NA-425, Houston TX 77030. 713/798-7412. **Fax:** 713/798-7413. **E-mail address:** info@www.nsbri.org. **World Wide Web address:** http://www.nsbri.org. **Description:** Conducts research into health concerns facing astronauts on long missions.

NATIONAL PHARMACEUTICAL COUNCIL
1894 Preston White Drive, Reston VA 20191-5433. 703/620-6390. **Fax:** 703/476-0904. **E-mail address:** main@npcnow.com. **World Wide Web address:** http://www.npcnow.org. **Description:** Conducts research and education programs geared towards demonstrating that the appropriate use of pharmaceuticals improves both patient treatment outcomes and the cost effective delivery of overall health care services.

BUSINESS SERVICES & NON-SCIENTIFIC RESEARCH

AMERICAN SOCIETY OF APPRAISERS
555 Herndon Parkway, Suite 125, Herndon VA 20170. 703/478-2228. **Fax:** 703/742-8471. **E-mail address:** asainfo@appraisers.org. **World Wide Web address:** http://www.appraisers.org. **Description:** Fosters professional excellence through education, accreditation, publication and other services. Its goal is to contribute to the growth of its membership and to the appraisal profession.

EQUIPMENT LEASING ASSOCIATION OF AMERICA
4301 North Fairfax Drive, Suite 550, Arlington VA 22203-1627. 703/527-8655. **Fax:** 703/527-2649. **World Wide Web address:** http://www.elaonline.com. **Description:** Promotes and serves the general interests of the equipment leasing and finance industry.

NATIONAL ASSOCIATION OF PERSONNEL SERVICES
The Village at Banner Elk, Suite 108, P.O. Box 2128, Banner Elk NC 28604. 828/898-4929. **Fax:** 828/898-8098. **World Wide Web address:** http://www.napsweb.org. **Description**: Serves, protects, informs, and represents all facets of the personnel services industry regarding federal legislation and regulatory issues by providing education, certification, and member services which enhance the ability to conduct business with integrity and competence.

174 /The Austin/San Antonio JobBank

CHARITIES AND SOCIAL SERVICES

AMERICAN COUNCIL FOR THE BLIND
1155 15th Street, NW, Suite 1004, Washington DC 20005. 202/467-5081. **Fax:** 202/467-5085. **Toll-free phone:** 800/424-8666. **World Wide Web address:** http://www.acb.org. **Description:** The nation's leading membership organization of blind and visually impaired people. It was founded in 1961.

CATHOLIC CHARITIES USA
1731 King Street, Alexandria VA 22314. 703/549-1390. **Fax:** 703/549-1656. **World Wide Web address:** http://www.catholiccharitiesusa.org. **Description:** A membership association of social service networks providing social services to people in need.

NATIONAL ASSOCIATION OF SOCIAL WORKERS
750 First Street, NE, Suite 700, Washington DC 20002-4241. 202/408-8600. **E-mail address:** membership@naswdc.org. **World Wide Web address:** http://www.naswdc.org. **Description:** A membership organization comprised of professional social workers working to enhance the professional growth and development of its members, to create and maintain professional standards, and to advance sound social policies.

NATIONAL COUNCIL ON FAMILY RELATIONS
3989 Central Avenue, NE, #550, Minneapolis MN 55421. 763/781-9331. **Fax:** 763/781-9348. **Toll-free phone:** 888/781-9331. **E-mail address:** info@ncfr.org. **World Wide Web address:** http://www.ncfr.org. **Description:** Provides a forum for family researchers, educators, and practitioners to share in the development and dissemination of knowledge about families and family relationships, establishes professional standards, and works to promote family well-being.

NATIONAL FEDERATION OF THE BLIND
1800 Johnson Street, Baltimore MD 21230-4998. 410/659-9314. **Fax:** 410/685-5653. **World Wide Web address:** http://www.nfb.org. **Description:** Founded in 1940, the National Federation of the Blind (NFB) is the nation's largest membership organization of blind persons. With fifty thousand members, the NFB has affiliates in all fifty states plus Washington D.C. and Puerto Rico, and over seven hundred local chapters. As a consumer and advocacy organization, the NFB is a leading force in the blindness field today.

NATIONAL MULTIPLE SCLEROSIS SOCIETY
733 Third Avenue, New York NY 10017. **Toll-free phone:** 800/344-4867. **World Wide Web address:** http://www.nmss.org. **Description:** Provides accurate, up-to-date information to individuals with MS, their families, and healthcare providers is central to our mission.

CHEMICALS, RUBBER, AND PLASTICS

AMERICAN CHEMICAL SOCIETY
1155 Sixteenth Street, NW, Washington DC 20036. 202/872-4600. **Fax:** 202/872-6067. **Toll-free phone:** 800/227-5558. **E-mail address:** help@acs.org. **World Wide Web address:** http://www.acs.org. **Description:** A self-governed individual membership organization consisting of more than 159,000 members at all degree levels and in all fields of chemistry. The organization provides a broad range of opportunities for peer interaction and career development, regardless of professional or scientific interests. The Society was founded in 1876.

AMERICAN INSTITUTE OF CHEMICAL ENGINEERS
3 Park Avenue, New York NY 10016-5991. 212/591-8100. **Toll-free phone:** 800/242-4363. **Fax:** 212/591-8888. **E-mail address:** xpress@aiche.org. **World Wide Web address:** http://www.aiche.org. **Description:** Founded in 1908 and provides leadership in advancing the chemical engineering profession; fosters and disseminates chemical engineering knowledge, supports the professional and personal growth of its members, and applies the expertise of its members to address societal needs throughout the world.

THE ELECTROCHEMICAL SOCIETY
65 South Main Street, Building D, Pennington NJ 08534-2839. 609/737-1902. **Fax:** 609/737-2743. **World Wide Web address:** http://www.electrochem.org. **Description:** Founded in 1902, The Electrochemical Society has become the leading society for solid-state and electrochemical science and technology. ECS has 8,000 scientists and engineers in over 75 countries worldwide who hold individual membership, as well as roughly 100 corporate members.

SOCIETY OF PLASTICS ENGINEERS
14 Fairfield Drive, PO Box 403, Brookfield CT 06804-0403. 203/775-0471. **Fax:** 203/775-8490. **E-mail address:** info@4spe.org. **World Wide Web address:** http://www.4spe.org. **Description:** A 25,000-member organization promoting scientific and engineering knowledge relating to plastics. Founded in 1942.

THE SOCIETY OF THE PLASTICS INDUSTRY, INC.
1801 K Street, NW, Suite 600, Washington DC 20006. 202/974-5200. **Fax:** 202/296-7005. **World Wide Web address:** http://www.socplas.org. **Description:** Founded in 1937, The Society of the Plastics Industry, Inc., is the trade association representing one of the largest manufacturing industries in the United States. SPI's members represent the entire plastics industry supply chain, including processors, machinery and equipment manufacturers and raw materials suppliers. The U.S. plastics industry employs 1.4 million workers and provides more than $310 billion in annual shipments.

COMMUNICATIONS:TELECOMMUNICATIONS AND BROADCASTING

ACADEMY OF TELEVISION ARTS & SCIENCES
5220 Lankershim Boulevard, North Hollywood CA 91601-3109. 818/754-2800. **Fax:** 818/761-2827. **World Wide Web address:** http://www.emmys.com. **Description:** Promotes creativity, diversity, innovation and excellence though recognition, education and leadership in the advancement of the telecommunications arts and sciences.

AMERICAN DISC JOCKEY ASSOCIATION
2000 Corporate Drive, #408, Ladera Ranch CA 92694. 888/723-5776. **World Wide Web address:** http://www.adja.org. **Description:** Promotes ethical behavior, industry standards and continuing education for its members.

AMERICAN WOMEN IN RADIO AND TELEVISION, INC.
8405 Greensboro Drive, Suite 800, McLean VA 22102. 703/506-3290. **Fax:** 703/506-3266. **E-mail address:** info@awrt.org. **World Wide Web address:** http://www.awrt.org. **Description:** A non-profit, professional organization of women and men who work in the electronic media and allied fields.

COMPTEL/ASCENT
1900 M Street, NW, Suite 800, Washington DC 20036. 202/296-6650. **Fax:** 202/296-7585. **World Wide Web address:** http://www.comptelascent.org. **Description:** An association representing competitive telecommunications companies in virtually every sector of the marketplace: competitive local exchange carriers, long-distance carriers of every size, wireless service providers, Internet service providers, equipment manufacturers, and software suppliers.

MEDIA COMMUNICATIONS ASSOCIATION-INTERNATIONAL
7600 Terrace Avenue, Suite 203, Middleton WI 53562. 608/827-5034. **Fax:** 608/831-5122. **E-mail address:** info@mca-i.org. **World Wide Web address:** http://www.itva.org. **Description:** A not-for-profit, member-driven organization that provides opportunities for networking, forums for education and the resources for information to media communications professionals.

NATIONAL ASSOCIATION OF BROADCASTERS
1771 N Street, NW, Washington DC 20036. 202/429-5300. **Fax:** 202/429-4199. **E-mail address:** nab@nab.org. **World Wide Web address:** http://www.nab.org. **Description:** A trade association that represents the interests of free, over-the-air radio and television broadcasters.

NATIONAL CABLE & TELECOMMUNICATIONS ASSOCIATION
1724 Massachusetts Avenue, NW, Washington DC 20036. 202/775-3550. **E-mail address:** webmaster@ncta.com. **World Wide Web**

address: http://www.ncta.com. **Description:** The National Cable and Telecommunications Association is the principal trade association of the cable and telecommunications industry. Founded in 1952, NCTA's primary mission is to provide its members with a strong national presence by providing a single, unified voice on issues affecting the cable and telecommunications industry.

PROMAX & BDA
9000 West Sunset Boulevard, Suite 900, Los Angeles CA 90069. 310/788-7600. **Fax:** 310/788-7616. **World Wide Web address:** http://www.promax.org. **Description:** A non-profit association dedicated to advancing the role and effectiveness of promotion, marketing, and broadcast design professionals in the electronic media.

U.S. TELECOM ASSOCIATION
1401 H Street, NW, Suite 600, Washington DC 20005-2164. 202/326-7300. **Fax:** 202/326-7333. **E-mail address:** membership@usta.org. **World Wide Web address:** http://www.usta.org. **Description:** A trade association representing service providers and suppliers for the telecom industry. Member companies offer a wide range of services, including local exchange, long distance, wireless, Internet and cable television service.

COMPUTER HARDWARE, SOFTWARE, AND SERVICES

ASSOCIATION FOR COMPUTING MACHINERY
1515 Broadway, New York NY, 10036. 212/626-0500. 212/626-0500. **Toll-free phone:** 800/342-6626. **World Wide Web address:** http://www.acm.org. **Description:** A 75-000-member organization founded in 1947 to advance the skills of information technology professionals and students worldwide.

ASSOCIATION FOR MULTIMEDIA COMMUNICATIONS
PO Box 10645, Chicago IL 60610. 773/276-9320. **E-mail address:** info@amcomm.org. **World Wide Web address:** http://www.amcomm.org. **Description:** A networking and professional organization for people who create New Media, including the Web, CD-ROMs and DVDs, interactive kiosks, streaming media, and other digital forms. The association promotes understanding of technology, e-learning, and e-business.

ASSOCIATION FOR WOMEN IN COMPUTING
41 Sutter Street, Suite 1006, San Francisco CA 94104. 415/905-4663. **Fax:** 415/358-4667. **E-mail address:** info@awc-hq.org. **World Wide Web address:** http://www.awc-hq.org. **Description:** A not-for-profit, professional organization for individuals with an interest in information technology. The association is dedicated to the advancement of women in the computing fields, in business, industry, science, education, government, and the military.

BLACK DATA PROCESSING ASSOCIATES
6301 Ivy Lane, Suite 700, Greenbelt MD 20770. 301/220-2180. **Fax:** 301/220-2185. **Toll-free phone:** 800/727-BDPA. **World Wide Web address:** http://www.bdpa.org. **Description:** A member-focused organization that positions its members at the forefront of the IT industry. BDPA is committed to delivering IT excellence to our members, strategic partners, and community.

INFORMATION TECHNOLOGY ASSOCIATION OF AMERICA
1401 Wilson Boulevard, Suite 1100, Arlington VA 22209. 703/522-5055. **Fax:** 703/525-2279. **Wide Web address:** http://www.itaa.org. **Description:** A trade association representing the U.S. IT industry and providing information about its issues, association programs, publications, meetings, and seminars.

INTERNATIONAL WEBMASTER'S ASSOCIATION- HTML WRITERS GUILD
119 E. Union Street, Suite F, Pasadena CA 91030. **World Wide Web address:** http://www.hwg.org. **Description:** Provides online web design training to individuals interested in web design and development.

NETWORK PROFESSIONAL ASSOCIATION
17 South High Street, Suite 200, Columbus OH 43215. 614/221-1900. **Fax:** 614/221-1989. **E-mail address:** npa@npa.org. **World Wide Web address:** http://www.npa.org. **Description:** A non-profit association for professionals in Network Computing.

SOCIETY FOR INFORMATION MANAGEMENT
401 North Michigan Avenue, Chicago IL 60611. 312/527-6734. **E-mail address:** sim@simnet.org **World Wide Web address:** http://www.simnet.org. **Description:** With 3,000 members, SIM is a network for IT leaders including CIOs, senior IT executives, prominent academicians, consultants, and others. SIM is a community of thought leaders who share experiences and knowledge, and who explore future IT direction. Founded in 1968.

SOCIETY FOR TECHNICAL COMMUNICATION
901 North Stuart Street, Suite 904, Arlington VA 22203-1822. Fax: 703/522-2075. **World Wide Web address:** http://www.stc.org. **Description:** A 25-000 member organization dedicated to advancing the arts and sciences of technical communication

SOFTWARE & INFORMATION INDUSTRY ASSOCIATION
1090 Vermont Avenue, NW, Sixth Floor, Washington DC 20005-4095. 202/289-7442. **Fax:** 202/289-7097. **World Wide Web address:** http://www.siia.net. **Description:** The SIIA is the principal trade association for the software and digital content industry. SIIA provides services in government relations, business development, corporate education and intellectual property protection to leading companies.

USENIX ASSOCIATION
2560 Ninth Street, Suite 215, Berkeley CA, 94710. 510/528-8649. **Fax:** 510/548-5738. **E-mail address:** office@usenix.org. **World Wide Web address:** http://www.usenix.org. **Description:** Founded in 1975 the association fosters technical excellence and innovation, supports and disseminates practical research, provides a neutral forum for discussion of technical issues, and encourages computing outreach to the community. USENIX brings together engineers, system administrators, scientists, and technicians working on the cutting edge of the computing world.

EDUCATIONAL SERVICES

AMERICAN ASSOCIATION OF SCHOOL ADMINISTRATORS
801 North Quincy Street, Suite 700, Arlington VA 22203-1730. 703/528-0700. **Fax:** 703/841-1543. **E-mail address:** info@aasa.org. **World Wide Web address:** http://www.aasa.org. **Description:** The professional organization for more than 14,000 educational leaders in the U.S. and other countries. The association supports and develops effective school system leaders who are dedicated to the highest quality public education for all children.

AMERICAN ASSOCIATION FOR HIGHER EDUCATION
One Dupont Circle, Suite 360, Washington DC 20036-1143. 202/293-6440. **Fax:** 202/293-0073. **E-mail address:** info@aahe.org. **World Wide Web address:** http://www.aahe.org. **Description:** An independent, membership-based, nonprofit organization dedicated to building human capital for higher education.

AMERICAN FEDERATION OF TEACHERS
555 New Jersey Avenue, NW, Washington DC 20001. 202/879-4400. **E-mail address:** online@aft.org. **World Wide Web address:** http://www.aft.org. **Description:** Improves the lives of its members and their families, gives voice to their professional, economic and social aspirations, brings together members to assist and support one another and to promote democracy, human rights and freedom.

COLLEGE AND UNIVERSITY PROFESSIONAL ASSOCIATION FOR HUMAN RESOURCES
Tyson Place, 2607 Kingston Pike, Suite 250, Knoxville TN 37919. 865/637-7673. **Fax:** 865/637-7674. **World Wide Web address:** http://www.cupa.org. **Description:** Promotes the effective management and development of human resources in higher education and offers many professional development opportunities.

NATIONAL ASSOCIATION FOR COLLEGE ADMISSION COUNSELING
1631 Prince Street, Alexandria VA 22314-2818. 703/836-2222. **Fax:** 703/836-8015. **World Wide Web address:** http://www.nacac.com. **Description:** Founded in 1937, NACAC is an organization of 8,000 professionals dedicated to serving students as they make choices about pursuing postsecondary education. NACAC supports and advances the work of college admission counseling professionals.

NATIONAL ASSOCIATION OF COLLEGE AND UNIVERSITY BUSINESS OFFICERS
2501 M Street, NW, Suite 400, Washington DC 20037. 202/861-2500. **Fax:** 202/861-2583. **World Wide Web address:** http://www.nacubo.org. **Description:** A nonprofit professional organization representing chief

administrative and financial officers at more than 2,100 colleges and universities across the country.

NATIONAL SCIENCE TEACHERS ASSOCIATION
1840 Wilson Boulevard, Arlington VA 22201-3000. 703/243-7100. **World Wide Web address:** http://www.nsta.org. **Description:** Promotes excellence and innovation in science teaching and learning.

ELECTRONIC/INDUSTRIAL ELECTRICAL EQUIPMENT AND COMPONENTS

AMERICAN CERAMIC SOCIETY
P.O. Box 6136, Westerville OH 43086-6136. 614/890-4700. **Fax:** 614/899-6109. **E-mail address:** info@ceramics.org. **World Wide Web address:** http://www.acers.org. **Description:** Provides technical, scientific and educational information to its members and others in the ceramics and related materials field, structures its services, staff and capabilities to meet the needs of the ceramics community, related fields, and the general public.

ELECTRONIC INDUSTRIES ALLIANCE
2500 Wilson Boulevard, Arlington VA 22201. 703/907-7500. **World Wide Web address:** http://www.eia.org. **Description:** A national trade organization including 2,500 U.S. manufacturers. The Alliance is a partnership of electronic and high-tech associations and companies whose mission is promoting the market development and competitiveness of the U.S. high-tech industry through domestic and international policy efforts.

ELECTRONICS TECHNICIANS ASSOCIATION, INTERNATIONAL
5 Depot Street, Greencastle IN 46135. **Fax:** 765/653-4287. **Toll-free phone:** 800/288-3824. **E-mail address:** eta@tds.net. **World Wide Web address:** http://www.eta-sda.org. **Description:** A not-for-profit, worldwide professional association founded by electronics technicians and servicing dealers in 1978. Provides professional credentials based on an individual's skills and knowledge in a particular area of study.

FABLESS SEMICONDUCTOR ASSOCIATION
Three Lincoln Center, 5430 LBJ Freeway, Suite 280, Dallas TX 75240. 972/866-7579. **Fax:** 972/239-2292. **World Wide Web address:** http://www.fsa.org. **Description:** An industry organization aimed at achieving an optimal balance between wafer supply and demand.

INSTITUTE OF ELECTRICAL AND ELECTRONICS ENGINEER (IEEE)
3 Park Avenue, 17th Floor, New York NY 10016-5997. 212/419-7900. **Fax:** 212/752-4929. **E-mail address:** ieeeusa@ieee.org. **World Wide Web address:** http://www.ieee.org. **Description:** Advances the theory and application of electrotechnology and allied sciences, serves as a catalyst for technological innovation and supports the needs of its members through a wide variety of programs and services.

INTERNATIONAL SOCIETY OF CERTIFIED ELECTRONICS TECHNICIANS
3608 Pershing Avenue, Fort Worth TX 76107-4527. 817/921-9101. **Fax:** 817/921-3741 **Toll-free phone:** 800/946-0201 **E-mail address:** info@iscet.org **World Wide Web address:** http://www.iscet.org. **Description:** Prepares and tests technicians in the electronics and

appliance service industry. Designed to measure the degree of theoretical knowledge and technical proficiency of practicing technicians.

NATIONAL ELECTRONICS SERVICE DEALERS ASSOCIATION
3608 Pershing Avenue, Fort Worth TX 76107-4527. 817/921-9061. **Fax:** 817/921-3741. **World Wide Web address:** http://www.nesda.com. **Description:** A trade organization for professionals in the business of repairing consumer electronic equipment, appliances, or computers

ENVIRONMENTAL & WASTE MANAGEMENT SERVICES

AIR & WASTE MANAGEMENT ASSOCIATION
One Gateway Center, 3rd Floor, 420 Fort Duquesne Boulevard, Pittsburgh PA 15222-1435. 412/232-3444. **Fax:** 412/232-3450. **E-mail address:** info@awma.org. **World Wide Web address:** http://www.awma.org. **Description:** A nonprofit, nonpartisan professional organization providing training, information, and networking opportunities to thousands of environmental professionals in 65 countries.

AMERICAN ACADEMY OF ENVIRONMENTAL ENGINEERS
130 Holiday Court, Suite 100, Annapolis MD 21401. 410/266-3311. **Fax:** 410/266-7653. **World Wide Web address:** http://www.aaee.net. **Description:** AAEE was founded in 1955 for the principal purpose of serving the public by improving the practice, elevating the standards, and advancing public recognition of environmental engineering through a program of specialty certification of qualified engineers.

NATIONAL SOLID WASTES MANAGEMENT ASSOCIATION
4301 Connecticut Avenue, NW, Suite 300, Washington DC 20008-2304. 202/244-4700. **Fax:** 202/364-3792. **Toll-free phone:** 800/424-2869. **World Wide Web address:** http://www.nswma.org. **Description:** A non-profit, trade association that represents the interests of the North American waste services industry.

INSTITUTE OF CLEAN AIR COMPANIES
1660 L Street, NW, Suite 1100, Washington DC 20036. 202/457-0911. **Fax:** 202/331-1388. **World Wide Web address:** http://www.icac.com. **Description:** The nonprofit national association of companies that supply air pollution monitoring and control systems, equipment, and services for stationary sources.

WATER ENVIRONMENT FEDERATION
601 Wythe Street, Alexandria VA 22314-1994. 703/684-2452. **Fax:** 703/684-2492. **Toll-free phone:** 800/666-0206. **World Wide Web address:** http://www.wef.org. **Description:** A not-for-profit technical and educational organization, founded in 1928, with members from varied disciplines. The federation's mission is to preserve and enhance the global water environment. The WEF network includes water quality professionals from 79 Member Associations in over 30 countries.

FABRICATED METAL PRODUCTS AND PRIMARY METALS

ASM INTERNATIONAL: THE MATERIALS INFORMATION SOCIETY
9639 Kinsman Road, Materials Park OH 44073-0002. 440/338-5151. **Fax:** 440/338-4634. **Toll-free phone:** 800/336-5152. **E-mail address:** cust-srv@asminternational.org. **World Wide Web address:** http://www.asm-intl.org. **Description:** An organization for materials engineers and scientists, dedicated to advancing industry, technology and applications of metals and materials.

AMERICAN FOUNDRYMEN'S SOCIETY
505 State Street, Des Plaines IL 60016-8399. 847/824-0181. **Fax:** 847/824-7848. **Toll-free phone:** 800/537-4237. **World Wide Web address:** http://www.afsinc.org. **Description:** An international organization dedicated to provide and promote knowledge and services that strengthen the metalcasting industry. AFS was founded in 1896 and has approximately 10,000 members in 47 countries.

AMERICAN WELDING SOCIETY
550 NW LeJeune Road, Miami FL 33126. 305/443-9353. **Toll-free phone:** 800/443-9353. **E-mail address:** info@aws.org. **World Wide Web address:** http://www.aws.org. **Description:** Founded in 1919 as a multifaceted, nonprofit organization with a goal to advance the science, technology and application of welding and related joining disciplines.

FINANCIAL SERVICES

FINANCIAL EXECUTIVES INSTITUTE
200 Campus Drive, PO Box 674, Florham Park NJ 07932-0674. 973/765-1000. **Fax:** 973/765-1018. **E-mail address:** conf@fei.org. **World Wide Web address:** http://www.fei.org. **Description:** An association for financial executives working to alert members to emerging issues, develop the professional and management skills of members, provide forums for peer networking, advocate the views of financial executives, and promote ethical conduct.

WOMEN'S INSTITUTE OF FINANCIAL EDUCATION
PO Box 910014, San Diego CA 92191. 760/736-1660. **E-mail address:** info@wife.org. **World Wide Web address:** http://www.wife.org. **Description:** A non-profit organization dedicated to providing financial education to women in their quest for financial independence.

NATIONAL ASSOCIATION FOR BUSINESS ECONOMICS
1233 20th Street, NW, #505, Washington DC 20036. 202/463-6223. **Fax:** 202/463-6239. **E-mail address:** nabe@nabe.com. **World Wide Web address:** http://www.nabe.com. **Description:** An association of professionals who have an interest in business economics and who want to use the latest economic data and trends to enhance their ability to make sound business decisions. Founded in 1959.

NATIONAL ASSOCIATION OF CREDIT MANAGEMENT
8840 Columbia 100 Parkway, Columbia MD 21045. 410/740-5560. **Fax:** 410/740-5574. **E-mail address:** nacm_info@nacm.org. **World Wide Web address:** http://www.nacm.org. **Description:** Founded in 1896 to promote good laws for sound credit, protect businesses against fraudulent debtors, improve the interchange of credit information, develop better credit practices and methods, and establish a code of ethics.

NATIONAL ASSOCIATION OF REAL ESTATE INVESTMENT TRUSTS
1875 Eye Street, NW, Washington DC 20006. 202/739-9400. **Fax:** 202/739-9401. **E-mail address:** info@nareit.org. **World Wide Web address:** http://www.nareit.com. **Description:** NAREIT is the national trade association for REITs and publicly traded real estate companies. Members are real estate investment trusts (REITs) and other businesses that own, operate and finance income-producing real estate, as well as those firms and individuals who advise, study and service these businesses.

THE BOND MARKET ASSOCIATION
360 Madison Avenue, New York NY 10017-7111. 646/637-9200. **Fax:** 646/637-9126. **World Wide Web address:** http://www.bondmarkets.com. **Description:** The trade association representing the largest securities markets in the world. The Association

speaks for the bond industry, advocating its positions and representing its interests in New York; Washington, D.C.; London; Frankfurt; Brussels and Tokyo; and with issuer and investor groups worldwide. The Association represents a diverse mix of securities firms and banks, whether they are large, multi-product firms or companies with special market niches.

SECURITIES INDUSTRY ASSOCIATION
120 Broadway, 35th Floor, New York NY 10271-0080. 212/608-1500. **Fax:** 212/968-0703. **E-mail address:** info@sia.com. **World Wide Web address:** http://www.sia.com. **Description:** The Securities Industry Association (SIA) was established in 1972 through the merger of the Association of Stock Exchange Firms (1913) and the Investment Banker's Association (1912). The Securities Industry Association brings together the shared interests of more than 600 securities firms to accomplish common goals. SIA member-firms (including investment banks, broker-dealers, and mutual fund companies) are active in all U.S. and foreign markets and in all phases of corporate and public finance.

FOOD AND BEVERAGES/AGRICULTURE

AMERICAN ASSOCIATION OF CEREAL CHEMISTS (AACC)
3340 Pilot Knob Road, St. Paul MN 55121-2097. 651/454-7250. **Fax:** 651/454-0766. **World Wide Web address:** http://www.aaccnet.org. **Description:** A non-profit international organization of nearly 4,000 members who are specialists in the use of cereal grains in foods. The association gathers and disseminates scientific and technical information to professionals in the grain-based foods industry worldwide for over 85 years.

CROPLIFE AMERICA
1156 15th Street, NW, Suite 400, Washington DC 20005. 202/296-1585. **Fax:** 202/463-0474. **World Wide Web address:** http://www.croplifeamerica.org. **Description:** Fosters the interests of the general public and member companies by promoting innovation and the environmentally sound manufacture, distribution, and use of crop protection and production technologies for safe, high-quality, affordable and abundant food, fiber and other crops.

AMERICAN FROZEN FOOD INSTITUTE
2000 Corporate Ridge, Suite 1000, McLean VA 22102. 703/821-0770. **Fax:** 703/821-1350. **E-mail address:** info@affi.com. **World Wide Web address:** http://www.affi.com. **Description:** A national trade association representing all aspects of the frozen food industry supply chain, from manufacturers to distributors to suppliers to packagers; the Institute is industry's voice on issues crucial to future growth and progress.

AMERICAN SOCIETY OF AGRICULTURAL ENGINEERS
2950 Niles Road, St. Joseph MI 49085. 269/429-0300. **Fax:** 269/429-3852. **World Wide Web address:** http://www.asae.org. **Description:** An educational and scientific organization dedicated to the advancement of engineering applicable to agricultural, food, and biological systems.

AMERICAN SOCIETY OF BREWING CHEMISTS
3340 Pilot Knob Road, St. Paul MN 55121-2097. 651/454-7250. **Fax:** 651/454-0766. **World Wide Web address:** http://www.asbcnet.org. **Description:** Founded in 1934 to improve and bring uniformity to the brewing industry on a technical level.

CIES – THE FOOD BUSINESS FORUM
8455 Colesville Road, Suite 705, Silver Spring MD 20910. 301/563-3383. **Fax:** 301/563-3386. **E-mail address:** us.office@ciesnet.com. **World Wide Web address:** http://www.ciesnet.com. **Description:** An independent global food business network. Membership in CIES is on a company basis and includes more than two thirds of the world's largest food retailers and their suppliers.

INTERNATIONAL DAIRY FOODS ASSOCIATION
1250 H Street, NW, Suite 900, Washington DC 20005. 202/737-4332. **Fax:** 202/331-7820. **Description:** IDFA represents more than 500 dairy food manufacturers, marketers, distributors and industry suppliers in the U.S. and 20 other countries, and encourages the formation of favorable domestic and international dairy policies.

NATIONAL BEER WHOLESALERS' ASSOCIATION
1101 King Street, Suite 600, Alexandria VA 22314-2944. 703/683-4300. **Fax:** 703/683-8965. **E-mail address:** info@nbwa.org. **World Wide Web address:** http://www.nbwa.org. **Description:** Founded in 1938 as a trade association for the nations' beer wholesalers. NBWA provides leadership which enhances the independent malt beverage wholesale industry; advocates before government and the public on behalf of its members; encourages the responsible consumption of beer; and provides programs and services that will enhance members' efficiency and effectiveness.

NATIONAL FOOD PROCESSORS ASSOCIATION
1350 I Street, NW, Suite 300, Washington DC 20005. 202/639.5900. **E-mail address:** nfpa@nfpa-food.org. **World Wide Web address:** http://www.nfpa-food.org. **Description:** NFPA is the voice of the $500 billion food processing industry on scientific and public policy issues involving food safety, nutrition, technical and regulatory matters and consumer affairs.

NATIONAL SOFT DRINK ASSOCIATION
1101 16th Street, NW, Washington DC 20036. 202/463-6732. **Fax:** 202/463-8277. **World Wide Web address:** http://www.nsda.org. **Description:** An association for America's non-alcoholic beverage industry, serving the public and its members for more than 75 years.

HEALTH CARE SERVICES, EQUIPMENT, AND PRODUCTS

ACCREDITING COMMISSION ON EDUCATION FOR HEALTH SERVICES ADMINISTRATION
2000 14th Street North, Arlington VA 22201. 703/894-0960. **Fax:** 703/894-0941. **World Wide Web address:** http://www.acehsa.org. **Description:** An association of educational, professional, clinical, and commercial organizations devoted to accountability and quality improvement in the education of health care management and administration professionals.

AMERICAN ACADEMY OF ALLERGY, ASTHMA, AND IMMUNOLOGY
611 East Wells Street, Milwaukee WI 53202-3823. 414/272-6071. **E-mail address:** info@aaaai.org. **World Wide Web address:** http://www.aaaai.org. **Description:** A professional medical specialty organization representing allergists, asthma specialists, clinical immunologists, allied health professionals, and other physicians with a special interest in allergy. Established in 1943.

AMERICAN ACADEMY OF FAMILY PHYSICIANS
11400 Tomahawk Creek Parkway, Leawood KS 66211-2672. 913/906-6000. **Toll-free phone:** 800/274-2237. **E-mail address:** fp@aafp.org. **World Wide Web address:** http://www.aafp.org. **Description:** Founded in 1947, the Academy represents family physicians, family practice residents and medical students nationwide. AAFP's mission is to preserve and promote the science and art of family medicine and to ensure high quality, cost-effective health care for patients of all ages.

AMERICAN ACADEMY OF PEDIATRIC DENTISTRY
211 East Chicago Avenue, Suite 700, Chicago IL 60611-2663. 312/337-2169. **Fax:** 312/337-6329. **World Wide Web address:** http://www.aapd.org. **Description:** A membership organization representing the specialty of pediatric dentistry.

AMERICAN ACADEMY OF PERIODONTOLOGY
737 North Michigan Avenue, Suite 800, Chicago IL 60611-2690. 312/787-5518. **Fax:** 312/787-3670. **World Wide Web address:** http://www.perio.org. **Description: A** 7,900-member association of dental professionals specializing in the prevention, diagnosis and treatment of diseases affecting the gums and supporting structures of the teeth and in the placement and maintenance of dental implants. The Academy's purpose is to advocate, educate, and set standards for advancing the periodontal and general health of the public and promoting excellence in the practice of periodontics.

AMERICAN ACADEMY OF PHYSICIANS ASSISTANTS
950 North Washington Street, Alexandria VA 22314-1552. 703/836-2272. **Fax:** 703/684-1924. **E-mail address:** aapa@aapa.org. **World**

Wide Web address: http://www.aapa.org. **Description:** Promotes quality, cost-effective, accessible health care, and the professional and personal development of physician assistants.

AMERICAN ASSOCIATION FOR CLINICAL CHEMISTRY
2101 L Street, NW, Suite 202, Washington DC 20037-1558. 202/857-0717. **Fax:** 202/887-5093. **Toll-free phone:** 800/892-1400. **World Wide Web address:** http://www.aacc.org. **Description:** Founded in 1948 as an international scientific/medical society of clinical laboratory professionals, physicians, research scientists and other individuals involved with clinical chemistry and other clinical laboratory science-related disciplines. The society has 10,000 members.

AMERICAN ASSOCIATION FOR ORAL AND MAXILLOFACIAL SURGEONS
9700 West Bryn Mawr Avenue, Rosemont IL 60018-5701. 847/678-6200. **E-mail address:** inquiries@aaoms.org. **World Wide Web address:** http://www.aaoms.org. **Description:** The American Association of Oral and Maxillofacial Surgeons (AAOMS), is a not-for-profit professional association serving the professional and public needs of the specialty of oral and maxillofacial surgery.

AMERICAN ASSOCIATION FOR RESPIRATORY CARE
9425 North MacArthur Boulevard, Suite 100, Irving TX 75063-4706. 972/243-2272. **Fax:** 972/484-2720. **E-mail address:** info@aarc.org. **World Wide Web address:** http://www.aarc.org. **Description:** Advances the science, technology, ethics, and art of respiratory care through research and education for its members and teaches the general public about pulmonary health and disease prevention.

AMERICAN ASSOCIATION OF COLLEGES OF OSTEOPATHIC MEDICINE
5550 Friendship Boulevard, Suite 310, Chevy Chase MD 20815-7231. 301/968-4100. **Fax:** 301/968-4101. **World Wide Web address:** http://www.aacom.org. **Description:** Promotes excellence in osteopathic medical education throughout the educational continuum, in research and in service; to enhance the strength and quality of the member colleges; and to improve the health of the American public.

AMERICAN ASSOCIATION OF COLLEGES OF PODIATRIC MEDICINE
15850 Crabbs Branch Way, Suite 320, Rockville MD 20855. **Fax:** 301/948-1928. **Toll-free phone:** 800/922-9266. **E-mail address:** aacpmas@aacpm.org. **World Wide Web address:** http://www.aacpm.org. **Description:** An organization advancing podiatric medicine and its education system.

AMERICAN DENTAL EDUCATION ASSOCIATION
1625 Massachusetts Avenue, NW, Suite 600, Washington DC 20036-2212. 202/667-9433. **Fax:** 202/667-0642. **World Wide Web address:** http://www.adea.org. **Description:** A national organization for dental

education. Members include all U.S. and Canadian dental schools, advanced dental education programs, hospital dental education programs, allied dental education programs, corporations, faculty, and students.

AMERICAN ASSOCIATION OF HEALTHCARE CONSULTANTS
5938 North Drake Avenue, Chicago IL 60659. **Fax:** 773/463-3552. **Toll-free phone:** 888/350-2242. **E-mail address:** info@aahc.net. **World Wide Web address:** http://www.aahc.net. **Description:** Founded in 1949 as the professional membership society for leading healthcare consultants and consulting firms.

AMERICAN ASSOCIATION OF HOMES AND SERVICES FOR THE AGING
2519 Connecticut Avenue, NW, Washington DC 20008. 202/783.2242. **Fax:** 202/783-2255. **World Wide Web address:** http://www.aahsa.org. **Description:** The American Association of Homes and Services for the Aging (AAHSA) is committed to advancing the vision of healthy, affordable, ethical aging services for America. The association represents 5,600 not-for-profit nursing homes, continuing care retirement communities, assisted living and senior housing facilities, and home and community-based service providers.

AMERICAN ASSOCIATION OF MEDICAL ASSISTANTS
20 North Wacker Drive, Suite 1575, Chicago IL 60606. 312/899-1500. **World Wide Web address:** http://www.aama-ntl.org. **Description:** The mission of the American Association of Medical Assistants is to enable medical assisting professionals to enhance and demonstrate the knowledge, skills and professionalism required by employers and patients; protect medical assistants' right to practice; and promote effective, efficient health care delivery through optimal use of multiskilled Certified Medical Assistants (CMAs).

AMERICAN ASSOCIATION OF NURSE ANESTHETISTS
222 South Prospect Avenue, Park Ridge IL 60068. 847/692-7050. **World Wide Web address:** http://www.aana.com. **Description:** Founded in 1931 as the professional association representing more than 30,000 Certified Registered Nurse Anesthetists (CRNAs) nationwide. The AANA promulgates education, and practice standards and guidelines, and affords consultation to both private and governmental entities regarding nurse anesthetists and their practice.

AMERICAN CHIROPRACTIC ASSOCIATION
1701 Clarendon Boulevard, Arlington VA 22209. **Fax:** 703/243-2593. **Toll-free phone:** 800/986-4636. **E-mail address:** memberinfo@amerchiro.org. **World Wide Web address:** http://www.americhiro.org. **Description:** A professional association representing doctors of chiropractic that provides lobbying, public relations, professional and educational opportunities for doctors of chiropractic, funds research regarding chiropractic and health issues, and offers leadership for the advancement of the profession.

AMERICAN COLLEGE OF HEALTH CARE ADMINISTRATORS
300 North Lee Street, Suite 301, Alexandria VA 22314. 703/739-7900. **Fax:** 703/739-7901. **Toll-free phone:** 888/882-2422. **E-mail address:** membership@achca.org. **World Wide Web address:** http://www.achca.org. **Description:** A non-profit membership organization that provides educational programming, certification in a variety of positions, and career development for its members. Founded in 1962.

AMERICAN COLLEGE OF HEALTHCARE EXECUTIVES
One North Franklin Street, Suite 1700, Chicago IL 60606-4425. 312/424-2800. **Fax:** 312/424-0023. **World Wide Web address:** http://www.ache.org. **Description:** An international professional society of nearly 30,000 healthcare executives who lead our nation's hospitals, healthcare systems, and other healthcare organizations.

AMERICAN COLLEGE OF MEDICAL PRACTICE EXECUTIVES
104 Inverness Terrace East, Englewood CO 80112-5306. 303/799-1111. **Fax:** 303/643-4439. **Toll-free phone:** 877/275-6462. **E-mail address:** acmpe@mgma.com. **World Wide Web address:** http://www.mgma.com/acmpe. **Description:** Established in 1956, the ACMPE offers board certification, self-assessment and leadership development for medical practice executives.

AMERICAN COLLEGE OF OBSTETRICIANS AND GYNECOLOGISTS
409 12th Street, SW, PO Box 96920, Washington DC 20090-6920. **World Wide Web address:** http://www.acog.org. **Description:** Founded in 1951, the 46,000-member organization is the nation's leading group of professionals providing health care for women.

AMERICAN COLLEGE OF PHYSICIAN EXECUTIVES
4890 West Kennedy Boulevard, Suite 200, Tampa FL 33609. 813/287-2000. **Fax:** 813/287-8993. **Toll-free phone:** 800/562-8088. **E-mail address:** acpe@acpe.org. **World Wide Web address:** http://www.acpe.org. **Description:** A specialty society representing physicians in health care leadership. Provides educational and career development programs.

AMERICAN DENTAL ASSOCIATION
211 East Chicago Avenue, Chicago IL 60611-2678. 312/440-2500. **World Wide Web address:** http://www.ada.org. **Description:** A dental association serving both public and private physicians. Founded in 1859.

AMERICAN DENTAL HYGIENISTS ASSOCIATION
444 North Michigan Avenue, Suite 3400, Chicago IL 60611. 312/440-8900. **E-mail address:** mail@adha.net. **World Wide Web address:** http://www.adha.org. **Description:** Founded in 1923, the association develops communication and mutual cooperation among dental hygienists and represents the professional interests of the more than 120,000 registered dental hygienists (RDHs) in the United States.

AMERICAN HEALTH INFORMATION MANAGEMENT ASSOCIATION
233 North Michigan Avenue, Suite 2150, Chicago IL 60601-5800.
312/233-1100. **Fax:** 312/233-1090. **E-mail address:** info@ahima.org.
World Wide Web address: http://www.ahima.org. **Description:**
Represents more than 46,000 specially educated health information
management professionals who work throughout the healthcare industry.
Health information management professionals serve the healthcare
industry and the public by managing, analyzing, and utilizing data vital for
patient care -- and making it accessible to healthcare providers when it is
needed most.

AMERICAN HOSPITAL ASSOCIATION
One North Franklin, Chicago IL 60606-3421. 312/422-3000. **Fax:**
312/422-4796. **World Wide Web address:** http://www.aha.org.
Description: A national organization that represents and serves all types
of hospitals, health care networks, and their patients and communities.
Approximately 5,000 institutional, 600 associate, and 27,000 personal
members belong to the AHA.

AMERICAN MEDICAL ASSOCIATION
515 North State Street, Chicago IL 60610. **Toll-free phone:** 800/621-
8335. **World Wide Web address:** http://www.ama-assn.org.
Description: American Medical Association speaks out on issues
important to patients and the nation's health. AMA policy on such issues
is decided through its democratic policy-making process, in the AMA
House of Delegates, which meets twice a year.

AMERICAN MEDICAL INFORMATICS ASSOCIATION
4915 St. Elmo Avenue, Suite 401, Bethesda MD 20814. 301/657-1291.
Fax: 301/657-1296. **World Wide Web address:** http://www.amia.org.
Description: The American Medical Informatics Association is a
nonprofit membership organization of individuals, institutions, and
corporations dedicated to developing and using information technologies
to improve health care. Founded in 1990.

AMERICAN MEDICAL TECHNOLOGISTS
710 Higgins Road, Park Ridge IL 60068. 847/823-5169. **Fax:** 847/823-
0458. **Toll-free phone:** 800/275-1268. **World Wide Web address:**
http://www.amt1.com. **Description:** A nonprofit certification agency and
professional membership association representing nearly 27,000
individuals in allied health care. Provides allied health professionals with
professional certification services and membership programs to enhance
their professional and personal growth.

AMERICAN MEDICAL WOMEN'S ASSOCIATION
801 North Fairfax Street, Suite 400, Alexandria VA 22314. 703/838-
0500. **Fax:** 703/549-3864. **E-mail address:** info@amwa-doc.org. **World
Wide Web address:** http://www.amwa-doc.org. **Description:** An
organization of 10,000 women physicians and medical students

dedicated to serving as the unique voice for women's health and the advancement of women in medicine.

AMERICAN NURSES ASSOCIATION
600 Maryland Avenue, SW, Suite 100 West, Washington DC 20024. 202/651-7000. **Fax:** 202/651-7001. **Toll-free phone:** 800/274-4ANA. **World Wide Web address:** http://www.nursingworld.org. **Description:** A professional organization representing the nation's 2.6 million Registered Nurses through its 54 constituent state associations and 13 organizational affiliate members. Fosters high standards of nursing practice, promotes the economic and general welfare of nurses in the workplace, projects a positive and realistic view of nursing, and by lobbies Congress and regulatory agencies on health care issues affecting nurses and the public.

AMERICAN OCCUPATIONAL THERAPY ASSOCIATION
4720 Montgomery Lane, PO Box 31220, Bethesda MD 20824-1220. 301/652-2682. **Fax:** 301/652-7711. **Toll-free phone:** 800/377- 8555. **World Wide Web address:** http://www.aota.org. **Description:** A professional association of approximately 40,000 occupational therapists, occupational therapy assistants, and students of occupational therapy.

AMERICAN OPTOMETRIC ASSOCIATION
243 North Lindbergh Boulevard, St. Louis MO 63141. 314/991-4100. **Fax:** 314/991-4101. **World Wide Web address:** http://www.aoanet.org. **Description:** The American Optometric Association is the acknowledged leader and recognized authority for primary eye and vision care in the world.

AMERICAN ORGANIZATION OF NURSE EXECUTIVES
325 Seventh Street, NW, Washington DC 20004. 202/626-2240. **Fax:** 202/638-5499. **E-mail address:** aone@aha.org. **World Wide Web address:** http://www.aone.org. **Description:** Founded in 1967, the American Organization of Nurse Executives (AONE), a subsidiary of the American Hospital Association, is a national organization of nearly 4,000 nurses who design, facilitate, and manage care. Its mission is to represent nurse leaders who improve healthcare.

AMERICAN ORTHOPEDIC ASSOCIATION
6300 North River Road, Suite 505, Rosemont IL 60018-4263. 847/318-7330. **Fax:** 847/318-7339. **E-mail address:** info@aoassn.org **World Wide Web address:** http://www.aoassn.org. **Description:** Founded in 1887, The American Orthopaedic Association is the oldest orthopaedic association in the world.

AMERICAN PHYSICAL THERAPY ASSOCIATION
1111 North Fairfax Street, Alexandria VA 22314-1488. 703/684-2782. **Fax:** 703/684-7343. **Toll-free phone:** 800/999-2782. **World Wide Web address:** http://www.apta.org. **Description:** The American Physical Therapy Association (APTA) is a national professional organization

representing more than 63,000 members. Its goal is to foster advancements in physical therapy practice, research, and education.

AMERICAN PODIATRIC MEDICAL ASSOCIATION
9312 Old Georgetown Road, Bethesda MD 20814. 301/571-9200. **Fax:** 301/530-2752. **Toll-free phone:** 800/ASK-APMA. **World Wide Web address:** http://www.apma.org. **Description:** The American Podiatric Medical Association is the premier professional organization representing the nation's Doctors of Podiatric Medicine (podiatrists). The APMA represents approximately 80 percent of the podiatrists in the country. APMA includes 53 component societies in states and other jurisdictions, as well as 22 affiliated and related societies.

AMERICAN PSYCHIATRIC ASSOCIATION
1000 Wilson Boulevard, Suite 1825, Arlington VA.22209-3901. 703/907-7300. **E-mail address:** apa@psych.org **World Wide Web address:** http://www.psych.org. **Description:** With 35,000 members, the American Psychiatric Association is a medical specialty society recognized worldwide.

AMERICAN PUBLIC HEALTH ASSOCIATION
800 I Street, NW, Washington DC 20001. 202/777-2742. **Fax:** 202/777-2534. **E-mail address:** comments@apha.org. **World Wide Web address:** http://www.apha.org. **Description:** The American Public Health Association (APHA) is the oldest and largest organization of public health professionals in the world, representing more than 50,000 members from over 50 occupations of public health.

AMERICAN SOCIETY OF ANESTHESIOLOGISTS
520 N. Northwest Highway, Park Ridge IL 60068-2573. 847/825-5586. **Fax:** 847/825-1692. **E-mail address:** mail@asahq.org. **World Wide Web address:** http://www.asahq.org. **Description:** An educational, research and scientific association of physicians organized to raise and maintain the standards of the medical practice of anesthesiology and improve the care of the patient. Founded in 1905.

AMERICAN SPEECH-LANGUAGE-HEARING ASSOCIATION
10801 Rockville Pike, Rockville MD 20852-3226. **Toll-free phone:** 800/638-8255. **E-mail address:** actioncenter@asha.org. **World Wide Web address:** http://www.asha.org. **Description:** The professional, scientific, and credentialing association for more than 110,000 audiologists, speech-language pathologists, and speech, language, and hearing scientists with a mission to ensure that all people with speech, language, and hearing disorders have access to quality services to help them communicate more effectively.

AMERICAN VETERINARY MEDICAL ASSOCIATION
1931 North Meacham Road, Suite 100, Schaumburg IL 60173. 847/925-8070. **Fax:** 847/925-1329. **E-mail address:** avmainfo@avma.org. **World Wide Web address:** http://www.avma.org. **Description:** A not-for-profit association founded in 1863 representing more than 69,000

veterinarians working in private and corporate practice, government, industry, academia, and uniformed services.

ASSOCIATION OF AMERICAN MEDICAL COLLEGES
2450 North Street, NW, Washington DC 20037-1126. 202/828-0400. **Fax:** 202/828-1125. **World Wide Web address:** http://www.aamc.org. **Description:** A non-profit association founded in 1876 to work for reform in medical education. The association represents the nation's 126 accredited medical schools, nearly 400 major teaching hospitals, more than 105,000 faculty in 96 academic and scientific societies, and the nation's 66,000 medical students and 97,000 residents.

ASSOCIATION OF UNIVERSITY PROGRAMS IN HEALTH ADMINISTRATION
2000 North 14th Street, Suite 780, Arlington VA 22201. 703/894-0940. **Fax:** 703/894-0941. **E-mail address:** aupha@aupha.org. **World Wide Web address:** http://www.aupha.org. **Description:** A not-for-profit association of university-based educational programs, faculty, practitioners, and provider organizations. Its members are dedicated to continuously improving the field of health management and practice. It is the only non-profit entity of its kind that works to improve the delivery of health services throughout the world - and thus the health of citizens - by educating professional managers.

HEALTH INFORMATION AND MANAGEMENT SYSTEMS SOCIETY
230 East Ohio Street, Suite 500, Chicago IL 60611-3269. 312/664-4467. **Fax:** 312/664-6143. **World Wide Web address:** http://www.himss.org. **Description:** Founded in 1961 and provides leadership for the optimal use of healthcare information technology and management systems for the betterment of human health.

HEALTHCARE FINANCIAL MANAGEMENT ASSOCIATION
2 Westbrook Corporate Center, Suite 700, Westchester IL 60154-5700. 708/531-9600. **Fax:** 708/531-0032. **Toll-free phone:** 800/252-4362. **World Wide Web address:** http://www.hfma.org. **Description:** A membership organization for healthcare financial management professionals with 32,000 members.

NATIONAL ASSOCIATION FOR CHIROPRACTIC MEDICINE
15427 Baybrook Drive, Houston TX 77062. 281/280-8262. **Fax:** 281/280-8262. **World Wide Web address:** http://www.chiromed.org. **Description:** A consumer advocacy association of chiropractors striving to make legitimate the utilization of professional manipulative procedures in mainstream health care delivery.

NATIONAL MEDICAL ASSOCIATION
1012 Tenth Street, NW, Washington DC 20001. 202/347-1895. **Fax:** 202/898-2510. **World Wide Web address:** http://www.nmanet.org. **Description:** Promotes the collective interests of physicians and patients of African descent with a mission to serve as the collective voice of

physicians of African descent and a leading force for parity in medicine, elimination of health disparities and promotion of optimal health.

HOTELS AND RESTAURANTS

AMERICAN HOTEL AND LODGING ASSOCIATION
1201 New York Avenue, NW, #600, Washington DC 20005-3931. 202/289-3100. **Fax:** 202/289-3199. **World Wide Web address:** http://www.ahla.org. **Description:** Provides its members with assistance in operations, education, and communications, and lobbies on Capitol Hill to provide a business climate in which the industry can continue to prosper. Individual state associations provide representation at the state level and offer many additional cost-saving benefits.

THE EDUCATIONAL FOUNDATION OF THE NATIONAL RESTAURANT ASSOCIATION
175 West Jackson Boulevard, Suite 1500, Chicago IL 60604-2702. 312/715-1010. **Toll-free phone:** 800/765-2122. **E-mail address:** info@nraef.org. **World Wide Web address:** http://www.nraef.org. **Description:** A not-for-profit organization dedicated to fulfilling the educational mission of the National Restaurant Association. Focusing on three key strategies of risk management, recruitment, and retention, the NRAEF is the premier provider of educational resources, materials, and programs, which address attracting, developing and retaining the industry's workforce.

NATIONAL RESTAURANT ASSOCIATION
1200 17th Street, NW, Washington DC 20036. 202/331-5900. 202/331-5900. **Fax:** 202/331-2429. **Toll-free phone:** 800/424-5156. **World Wide Web address:** http://www.restaurant.org. **Description:** Founded in 1919 as a business association for the restaurant industry with a mission to represent, educate and promote a rapidly growing industry that is comprised of 878,000 restaurant and foodservice outlets employing 12 million people.

INSURANCE

AMERICA'S HEALTH INSURANCE PLANS
601 Pennsylvania Avenue, NW, S0uth Building, Suite 500, Washington DC 20004. 202/778-3200. **Fax:** 202/331-7487. **World Wide Web address:** http://www.ahip.org. **Description:** A national association representing nearly 1,300 member companies providing health insurance coverage to more than 200 million Americans.

INSURANCE INFORMATION INSTITUTE
110 William Street, New York NY 10038. 212/346-5500. **World Wide Web address:** http://www.iii.org. **Description:** Provides definitive insurance information. Recognized by the media, governments, regulatory organizations, universities and the public as a primary source of information, analysis and referral concerning insurance.

NATIONAL ASSOCIATION OF PROFESSIONAL INSURANCE AGENTS
400 North Washington Street, Alexandria VA 22314. 703/836-9340. **Fax:** 703/836-1279. **E-mail address:** piaweb@pianet.org. **World Wide Web address:** http://www.pianet.com. **Description:** Represents independent agents in all 50 states, Puerto Rico and the District of Columbia. Founded in 1931.

PROPERTY CASUALTY INSURERS ASSOCIATION OF AMERICA
3025 Highland Parkway, Suite 800, Downers Grove IL 60515-1289. 630/724-2100. **Fax:** 630/724-2190. **World Wide Web address:** http://www.allianceai.org. **Description:** A property/casualty trade association representing more than 1,000 member companies, PCI advocates its members' public policy positions at the federal and state levels and to the public.

LEGAL SERVICES

AMERICAN BAR ASSOCIATION
750 North Clark Street, Chicago IL 60610. 312/988-5000. **E-mail address:** askaba@abanet.org. **World Wide Web address:** http://www.abanet.org. **Description:** A voluntary professional association with more than 400,000 members, the ABA provides law school accreditation, continuing legal education, information about the law, programs to assist lawyers and judges in their work, and initiatives to improve the legal system for the public.

FEDERAL BAR ASSOCIATION
2215 M Street, NW, Washington DC 20037. 202/785-1614. **Fax:** 202/785-1568. **E-mail address:** fba@fedbar.org. **World Wide Web address:** http://www.fedbar.org. **Description:** The professional organization for private and government lawyers and judges involved in federal practice.

NATIONAL ASSOCIATION OF LEGAL ASSISTANTS
1516 South Boston, #200, Tulsa OK 74119. 918/587-6828. **World Wide Web address:** http://www.nala.org. **Description:** A professional association for legal assistants and paralegals, providing continuing education and professional development programs. Founded in 1975.

NATIONAL FEDERATION OF PARALEGAL ASSOCIATIONS
2517 Eastlake Avenue East, Suite 200, Seattle WA 98102. 206/652-4120. **Fax:** 206/652-4122. **E-mail address:** info@paralegals.org. **World Wide Web address:** http://www.paralegals.org. **Description:** A non-profit professional organization representing more than 15,000 paralegals in the United States and Canada. NFPA is the national voice and the standard for excellence for the paralegal profession through its work on the issues of regulation, ethics and education.

MANUFACTURING: MISCELLANEOUS CONSUMER

ASSOCIATION FOR MANUFACTURING EXCELLENCE
380 Palantine Road West, Wheeling IL 60090-5863. 847/520-3282. **Fax:**
847/520-0163. **World Wide Web address:** http://www.ame.org.
Description: A not-for-profit organization founded in 1985 consisting of
6000 executives, senior and middle managers who wish to improve the
competitiveness of their organizations.

ASSOCIATION FOR MANUFACTURING TECHNOLOGY
7901 Westpark Drive, McLean VA 22102-4206. 703/893-2900. **Fax:**
703/893-1151. **Toll-free phone:** 703/893-2900. **World Wide Web
address:** http://www.amtonline.org. **Description:** Supports and
promotes American manufacturers of machine tools and manufacturing
technology. Provides members with industry expertise and assistance on
critical industry concerns.

ASSOCIATION OF HOME APPLIANCE MANUFACTURERS
1111 19th Street, NW, Suite 402, Washington DC 20036. 202/872-5955.
Fax: 202/872-9354. **World Wide Web address:** http://www.aham.org.
Description: Represents the manufacturers of household appliances
and products/services associated with household appliances.

SOCIETY OF MANUFACTURING ENGINEERS
One SME Drive, Dearborn MI 48121. 313/271-1500. **Fax:** 313/425-3401.
Toll-free phone: 800/733-4763. **World Wide Web address:**
http://www.sme.org. **Description:** Promotes an increased awareness of
manufacturing engineering and helps keep manufacturing professionals
up to date on leading trends and technologies. Founded in 1932.

MANUFACTURING: MISCELLANEOUS INDUSTRIAL

ASSOCIATION FOR MANUFACTURING EXCELLENCE
380 Palantine Road West, Wheeling IL 60090-5863. 847/520-3282. **Fax:** 847/520-0163. **World Wide Web address:** http://www.ame.org. **Description:** A not-for-profit organization founded in 1985 consisting of 6000 executives, senior and middle managers who wish to improve the competitiveness of their organizations.

INSTITUTE OF INDUSTRIAL ENGINEERS
3577 Parkway Lane, Suite 200, Norcross GA 30092. 770/449-0460. **Fax:** 770/441-3295. **Toll-free phone:** 800/494-0460. **World Wide Web address:** http://www.iienet.org. **Description:** A non-profit professional society dedicated to the support of the industrial engineering profession and individuals involved with improving quality and productivity. Founded in 1948.

NATIONAL ASSOCIATION OF MANUFACTURERS
1331 Pennsylvania Avenue, NW, Washington DC 20004-1790. 202/637-3000. **Fax:** 202/637-3182. **E-mail address:** manufacturing@nam.org. **World Wide Web address:** http://www.nam.org. **Description:** With 14,000 members, NAM's mission is to enhance the competitiveness of manufacturers and to improve American living standards by shaping a legislative and regulatory environment conducive to U.S. economic growth, and to increase understanding among policymakers, the media and the public about the importance of manufacturing to America's economic strength.

NATIONAL TOOLING AND MACHINING ASSOCIATION
9300 Livingston Road, Fort Washington MD 20744-4998. 800/248-6862. **Fax:** 301/248-7104. **World Wide Web address:** http://www.ntma.org. **Description:** A trade organization representing the precision custom manufacturing industry throughout the United States.

SOCIETY OF MANUFACTURING ENGINEERS
One SME Drive, Dearborn MI 48121. 313/271-1500. **Fax:** 313/425-3401. **Toll-free phone:** 800/733-4763. **World Wide Web address:** http://www.sme.org. **Description:** Promotes an increased awareness of manufacturing engineering and helps keep manufacturing professionals up to date on leading trends and technologies. Founded in 1932.

MINING, GAS, PETROLEUM, ENERGY RELATED

AMERICAN ASSOCIATION OF PETROLEUM GEOLOGISTS
P.). Box 979, Tulsa OK 74101-0979. 918/584-2555. **Physical address:** 1444 South Boulder, Tulsa OK 74119. **Fax:** 918/560-2665. **Toll-free phone:** 800/364-2274. **E-mail address:** postmaster@aapg.org. **World Wide Web address:** http://www.aapg.org. **Description:** Founded in 1917, the AAPG's purpose is to foster scientific research, advance the science of geology, promote technology, and inspire high professional conduct. The AAPG has over 30,000 members.

AMERICAN GEOLOGICAL INSTITUTE
4220 King Street, Alexandria VA 22302-1502. 703/379-2480. **Fax:** 703/379-7563. **World Wide Web address:** http://www.agiweb.org. **Description:** A nonprofit federation of 42 geoscientific and professional associations that represents more than 100,000 geologists, geophysicists, and other earth scientists. Provides information services to geoscientists, serves as a voice of shared interests in the profession, plays a major role in strengthening geoscience education, and strives to increase public awareness of the vital role the geosciences play in society's use of resources and interaction with the environment.

AMERICAN NUCLEAR SOCIETY
555 North Kensington Avenue, La Grange Park IL 60526. 708/352-6611. **Fax:** 708/352-0499. **World Wide Web address:** http://www.ans.org. **Description:** A not-for-profit, international, scientific and educational organization with a membership of 10,500 engineers, scientists, administrators, and educators representing 1,600 corporations, educational institutions, and government agencies.

AMERICAN PETROLEUM INSTITUTE
1220 L Street, NW, Washington DC 20005-4070. 202/682-8000. **World Wide Web address:** http://www.api.org. **Description:** Functions to insure a strong, viable U.S. oil and natural gas industry capable of meeting the energy needs of our Nation in an efficient and environmentally responsible manner.

GEOLOGICAL SOCIETY OF AMERICA
3300 Penrose Place, P.O. Bos 9140, Boulder CO 80301. 303/447-2020. **Fax:** 303/357-1070. **Toll-free phone:** 888/443-4472. **E-mail address:** gsaservice@geosociety.org. **World Wide Web address:** http://www.geosociety.org. **Description:** The mission of GSA is to advance the geosciences, to enhance the professional growth of its members, and to promote the geosciences in the service of humankind.

SOCIETY FOR MINING, METALLURGY, AND EXPLORATION
8307 Shaffer Parkway, Littleton CO 80127-4102. 303/973-9550. **Fax:** 303/973-3845. **Toll-free phone:** 800/763-3132. **E-mail address:** sme@smenet.org. **World Wide Web address:** http://www.smenet.org.

Description: An international society of professionals in the mining and minerals industry.

SOCIETY OF PETROLEUM ENGINEERS
P.O. Box 833836, Richardson TX 75083-3836. 972/952-9393. **Physical address:** 222 palisades Creek Drive, Richardson TX 75080. **Fax:** 972/952-9435. **E-mail address:** spedal@spe.org. **World Wide Web address:** http://www.spe.org. **Description:** SPE is a professional association whose 60,000-plus members worldwide are engaged in energy resources development and production. SPE is a key resource for technical information related to oil and gas exploration and production and provides services through its publications, meetings, and online.

PAPER AND WOOD PRODUCTS

AMERICAN FOREST AND PAPER ASSOCIATION
1111 Nineteenth Street, NW, Suite 800, Washington DC 20036. **Toll-free phone:** 800/878-8878. **E-mail address:** info@afandpa.org. **World Wide Web address:** http://www.afandpa.org. **Description:** The national trade association of the forest, pulp, paper, paperboard and wood products industry.

FOREST PRODUCTS SOCIETY
2801 Marshall Court, Madison WI 53705-2295. 608/231-1361. **Fax:** 608/231-2152. **E-mail address:** info@forestprod.org. **World Wide Web address:** http://www.forestprod.org. **Description:** An international not-for-profit technical association founded in 1947 to provide an information network for all segments of the forest products industry.

NPTA ALLIANCE
500 Bi-County Boulevard, Suite 200E, Farmingdale NY 11735. 631/777-2223. **Fax:** 631/777-2224. **Toll-free phone:** 800/355-NPTA. **World Wide Web address:** http://www.gonpta.com. **Description:** An association for the $60 billion paper, packaging, and supplies distribution industry.

PAPERBOARD PACKAGING COUNCIL
201 North Union Street, Suite 220, Alexandria VA 22314. 703/836-3300. **Fax:** 703/836-3290. **E-mail address:** http://www.ppcnet.org. **World Wide Web address:** http://www.ppcnet.org. **Description:** A trade association representing the manufacturers of paperboard packaging in the United States.

TECHNICAL ASSOCIATION OF THE PULP AND PAPER INDUSTRY
15 Technology Parkway South, Norcross GA 30092. 770/446-1400. **Fax:** 770/446-6947. **Toll-free phone:** 800/332-8686. **World Wide Web address:** http://www.tappi.org. **Description:** The leading technical association for the worldwide pulp, paper, and converting industry.

PRINTING AND PUBLISHING

AMERICAN BOOKSELLERS ASSOCIATION
828 South Broadway, Tarrytown NY 10591. 914/591-2665. **Fax:**
914/591-2720. **Toll-free phone:** 800/637-0037. **E-mail address:**
info@bookweb.org. **World Wide Web address:**
http://www.bookweb.org. **Description:** A not-for-profit organization
founded in 1900 devoted to meeting the needs of its core members of
independently owned bookstores with retail storefront locations through
advocacy, education, research, and information dissemination.

AMERICAN INSTITUTE OF GRAPHIC ARTS
164 Fifth Avenue, New York NY 10010. 212/807-1990. **Fax:** 212/807-
1799. **E-mail address:** comments@aiga.org. **World Wide Web
address:** http://www.aiga.org. **Description:** Furthers excellence in
communication design as a broadly defined discipline, strategic tool for
business and cultural force. AIGA is the place design professionals turn
to first to exchange ideas and information, participate in critical analysis
and research and advance education and ethical practice. Founded in
1914.

AMERICAN SOCIETY OF NEWSPAPER EDITORS
11690B Sunrise Valley Drive, Reston VA 20191-1409. 703/453-1122.
Fax: 703/453-1133. **E-mail address:** asne@asne.org. **World Wide Web
address:** http://www.asne.org. **Description:** A membership organization
for daily newspaper editors, people who serve the editorial needs of daily
newspapers and certain distinguished individuals who have worked on
behalf of editors through the years.

ASSOCIATION OF AMERICAN PUBLISHERS, INC.
71 Fifth Avenue, 2nd Floor, New York NY 10003. 212/255-0200. **Fax:**
212/255-7007. **World Wide Web address:** http://www.publishers.org.
Description: Representing publishers of all sizes and types located
throughout the U.S., the AAP is the principal trade association of the
book publishing industry.

ASSOCIATION OF GRAPHIC COMMUNICATIONS
320 Seventh Avenue, 9th Floor, New York NY 10001-5010. 212/279-
2100. **Fax:** 212/279-5381. **E-mail address:** info@agcomm.org. **World
Wide Web address:** http://www.agcomm.org. **Description:** The AGC
serves as a network for industry information and idea exchange,
provides graphic arts education and training, promotes and markets the
industry, and advocates legislative and environmental issues.

BINDING INDUSTRIES OF AMERICA
100 Daingerfield Road, Alexandria VA 22314. 703/519-8137. **Fax:**
703/548-3227. **World Wide Web address:**
http://www.bindingindustries.org. **Description:** A trade association
representing Graphic Finishers, Loose-Leaf Manufacturers, and

suppliers to these industries throughout the United States, Canada, and Europe.

THE DOW JONES NEWSPAPER FUND
P.O.Box 300, Princeton NJ 08543-0300. 609/452-2820. **Fax:** 609/520-5804. **E-mail address:** newsfund@wsj.dowjones.com. **World Wide Web address:** http://djnewspaperfund.dowjones.com. **Description:** Founded in 1958 by editors of The Wall Street Journal to improve the quality of journalism education and the pool of applicants for jobs in the newspaper business. It provides internships and scholarships to college students, career literature, fellowships for high school journalism teachers and publications' advisers and training for college journalism instructors. The Fund is a nonprofit foundation supported by the Dow Jones Foundation, Dow Jones & Company, Inc. and other newspaper companies.

GRAPHIC ARTISTS GUILD
90 John Street, Suite 403, New York NY 10038-3202. 212/791-3400. **World Wide Web address:** http://www.gag.org. **Description:** A national union of illustrators, designers, web creators, production artists, surface designers and other creatives who have come together to pursue common goals, share their experience, raise industry standards, and improve the ability of visual creators to achieve satisfying and rewarding careers.

INTERNATIONAL GRAPHIC ARTS EDUCATION ASSOCIATION
1899 Preston White Drive, Reston VA 20191-4367. 703/758-0595. **World Wide Web address:** http://www.igaea.org. **Description:** An association of educators in partnership with industry, dedicated to sharing theories, principles, techniques and processes relating to graphic communications and imaging technology.

MAGAZINE PUBLISHERS OF AMERICA
810 Seventh Avenue, 24th Floor, New York NY 10019. 212/872-3746. **E-mail address:** infocenter@magazine.org. **World Wide Web address:** http://www.magazine.org. **Description:** An industry association for consumer magazines representing more than 240 domestic publishing companies with approximately 1,400 titles, more than 80 international companies and more than 100 associate members.

NATIONAL ASSOCIATION FOR PRINTING LEADERSHIP
75 West Century Road, Paramus NJ 07652-1408. 201/634-9600. **Fax:** 201/986-2976. **E-mail address:** information@napl.org. **World Wide Web address:** http://www.napl.org. **Description:** A not-for-profit trade association founded in 1933 for commercial printers and related members of the Graphic Arts Industry.

NATIONAL NEWSPAPER ASSOCIATION
P.O. Box 7540,, Columbia MO 65205-7540. 573/882-5800. **Fax:** 573/884-5490. **Toll-free phone:** 800/829-4662. **World Wide Web address:** http://www.nna.org. **Description:** A non-profit association promoting the common interests of newspapers.

NATIONAL PRESS CLUB
529 14th Street, NW, Washington DC 20045. 202/662-7500. **Fax:** 202/662-7512. **World Wide Web address:** http://npc.press.org. **Description:** Provides people who gather and disseminate news a center for the advancement of their professional standards and skills, the promotion of free expression, mutual support and social fellowship. Founded in 1908.

NEWSPAPER ASSOCIATION OF AMERICA
1921 Gallows Road, Suite 600, Vienna VA 22182-3900. 703/902-1600. **Fax:** 703/917-0636. **World Wide Web address:** http://www.naa.org. **Description:** A nonprofit organization representing the $55 billion newspaper industry.

THE NEWSPAPER GUILD
501 Third Street, NW, Suite 250, Washington DC 20001. 202/434-7177. **Fax:** 202/434-1472. **E-mail address:** guild@cwa-union.org. **World Wide Web address:** http://www.newsguild.org. **Description:** Founded as a print journalists' union, the Guild today is primarily a media union whose members are diverse in their occupations, but who share the view that the best working conditions are achieved by people who have a say in their workplace.

TECHNICAL ASSOCIATION OF THE GRAPHIC ARTS
68 Lomb Memorial Drive, Rochester NY 14623-5604. 585/475-7470. **Fax:** 585/475-2250. **E-mail address:** tagaofc@aol.com. **World Wide Web address:** http://www.taga.org. **Description:** A professional technical association founded in 1948 for the graphic arts industries.

WRITERS GUILD OF AMERICA WEST
7000 West Third Street, Los Angeles CA 90048. 323/951-4000. **Fax:** 323/782-4800. **Toll-free phone:** 800/548-4532. **E-mail address: World Wide Web address:** http://www.wga.org. **Description:** Represents writers in the motion picture, broadcast, cable and new technologies industries.

REAL ESTATE

INSTITUTE OF REAL ESTATE MANAGEMENT
430 North Michigan Avenue, Chicago IL 60611-4090. 312/329-6000. **Fax:** 800/338-4736. **Toll-free phone:** 800/837-0706. **E-mail address:** custserv@irem.org. **World Wide Web address:** http://www.irem.org. **Description:** IREM, an affiliate of the National Association of Realtors, is an association of professional property and asset managers who have met strict criteria in the areas of education, experience, and a commitment to a code of ethics.

INTERNATIONAL REAL ESTATE INSTITUTE
1224 North Nokomis, NE, Alexandria MN 56308. 320/763-4648. **Fax:** 320/763-9290. **E-mail address:** irei@iami.org. **World Wide Web address:** http://www.iami.org/irei. **Description:** A real estate association with members in more than 100 countries, providing media to communicate on an international basis.

NATIONAL ASSOCIATION OF REALTORS
30700 Russell Ranch Road, Westlake Village CA 91362. 805/557-2300. **Fax:** 805/557-2680. **World Wide Web address:** http://www.realtor.com. **Description:** An industry advocate of the right to own, use, and transfer real property; the acknowledged leader in developing standards for efficient, effective, and ethical real estate business practices; and valued by highly skilled real estate professionals and viewed by them as crucial to their success.

RETAIL

NATIONAL ASSOCIATION OF CHAIN DRUG STORES
413 North Lee Street, PO Box 1417-D49, Alexandria VA 22313-1480. 703/549-3001. **Fax:** 703/836-4869. **World Wide Web address:** http://www.nacds.org. **Description:** Represents the views and policy positions of member chain drug companies accomplished through the programs and services provided by the association.

INTERNATIONAL COUNCIL OF SHOPPING CENTERS
1221 Avenue of the Americas, 41st floor, New York NY 10020-1099. 646/728-3800. **Fax:** 212/589-5555. **E-mail address:** icsc@icsc.org. **World Wide Web address:** http://www.icsc.org. **Description:** A trade association of the shopping center industry founded in 1957.

NATIONAL RETAIL FEDERATION
325 7th Street, NW, Suite 1100, Washington DC 20004. 202/783-7971. **Fax:** 202/737-2849. **Toll-free phone:** 800/NRF-HOW2. **World Wide Web address:** http://www.nrf.com. **Description:** A retail trade association, with membership that comprises all retail formats and channels of distribution including department, specialty, discount, catalog, Internet and independent stores as well as the industry's key trading partners of retail goods and services. NRF represents an industry with more than 1.4 million U.S. retail establishments, more than 20 million employees - about one in five American workers - and 2003 sales of $3.8 trillion.

STONE, CLAY, GLASS, AND CONCRETE PRODUCTS

THE AMERICAN CERAMIC SOCIETY
PO Box 6136, Westerville OH 43086-6136. 614/890-4700. **Fax:** 614/899-6109. **E-mail address:** info@ceramics.org. **World Wide Web address:** http://www.acers.org. **Description:** An organization dedicated to the advancement of ceramics.

NATIONAL GLASS ASSOCIATION
8200 Greensboro Drive, Suite 302, McLean VA 22102-3881. 866/342-5642. **Fax:** 703/442-0630. **World Wide Web address:** http://www.glass.org. **Description:** A trade association founded in 1948 representing the flat (architectural and automotive) glass industry. The association represents nearly 5,000 member companies and locations, and produces the industry events and publications.

TRANSPORTATION AND TRAVEL

AIR TRANSPORT ASSOCIATION OF AMERICA
1301 Pennsylvania Avenue, NW, Suite 1100, Washington DC 20004-1707. 202/626-4000. **Fax:** 301/206-9789. **Toll-free phone:** 800/497-3326. **E-mail address:** ata@airlines.org. **World Wide Web address:** http://www.air-transport.org. **Description:** A trade organization for the principal U.S. airlines.

AMERICAN SOCIETY OF TRAVEL AGENTS
1101 King Street, Suite 200, Alexandria VA 22314. 703/739-2782. **Fax:** 703/684-8319. **World Wide Web address:** http://www.astanet.com. **Description:** An association of travel professionals whose members include travel agents and the companies whose products they sell such as tours, cruises, hotels, car rentals, etc.

AMERICAN TRUCKING ASSOCIATIONS
2200 Mill Road, Alexandria VA 22314. 703/838-1700. **Toll-free phone:** 888/333-1759. **World Wide Web address:** http://www.trucking.org. **Description:** Serves and represents the interests of the trucking industry with one united voice; positively influences Federal and State governmental actions; advances the trucking industry's image, efficiency, competitiveness, and profitability; provides educational programs and industry research; promotes highway and driver safety; and strives for a healthy business environment.

ASSOCIATION OF AMERICAN RAILROADS
50 F Street, NW, Washington DC 20001-1564. 202/639-2100. **World Wide Web address:** http://www.aar.org. **Description:** A trade associations representing the major freight railroads of the United States, Canada and Mexico.

INSTITUTE OF TRANSPORTATION ENGINEERS
1099 14th Street, NW, Suite 300 West, Washington DC 20005-3438. 202/289-0222. **Fax:** 202/289-7722. **E-mail address:** ite_staff@ite.org. **World Wide Web address:** http://www.ite.org. **Description:** An international individual member educational and scientific association whose members are traffic engineers, transportation planners and other professionals who are responsible for meeting society's needs for safe and efficient surface transportation through planning, designing, implementing, operating and maintaining surface transportation systems worldwide.

MARINE TECHNOLOGY SOCIETY
5565 Sterrett Place, Suite 108, Columbia MD 21044. 410/884-5330. **Fax:** 410/884-9060. **E-mail address:** mtsmbrship@erols.com. **World Wide Web address:** http://www.mtsociety.org. **Description:** A member-based society supporting all the components of the ocean community: marine sciences, engineering, academia, industry and government. The society

is dedicated to the development, sharing and education of information and ideas.

NATIONAL TANK TRUCK CARRIERS
2200 Mill Road, Alexandria VA 22314. 703/838-1960. **Fax:** 703/684-5753. **E-mail address:** inquiries@tanktruck.org. **World Wide Web address:** http://www.tanktruck.net. **Description:** A trade association founded in 1945 and composed of approximately 180 trucking companies, which specialize in the nationwide distribution of bulk liquids, industrial gases and dry products in cargo tank motor vehicles.

UTILITIES: ELECTRIC, GAS, AND WATER

AMERICAN PUBLIC GAS ASSOCIATION
11094-D Lee Highway, Suite 102, Fairfax VA 22030-5014. 703/352-3890. **Fax:** 703/352-1271. **E-mail address:** website@apga.org. **World Wide Web address:** http://www.apga.org. **Description:** A nonprofit trade organization representing publicly owned natural gas local distribution companies (LDCs). APGA represents the interests of public gas before Congress, federal agencies and other energy-related stakeholders by developing regulatory and legislative policies that further the goals of our members. In addition, APGA organizes meetings, seminars, and workshops with a specific goal to improve the reliability, operational efficiency, and regulatory environment in which public gas systems operate.

AMERICAN PUBLIC POWER ASSOCIATION (APPA)
2301 M Street, NW, Washington DC 20037-1484. 202/467-2900. **Fax:** 202/467-2910. **World Wide Web address:** http://www.appanet.org. **Description:** The service organization for the nation's more than 2,000 community-owned electric utilities that serve more than 40 million Americans. Its purpose is to advance the public policy interests of its members and their consumers, and provide member services to ensure adequate, reliable electricity at a reasonable price with the proper protection of the environment.

AMERICAN WATER WORKS ASSOCIATION
6666 West Quincy Avenue, Denver CO 80235. 303/794-7711. **Fax:** 303/347-0804. **Toll-free phone:** 800/926-7337. **World Wide Web address:** http://www.awwa.org. **Description:** A resource for knowledge, information, and advocacy to improve the quality and supply of drinking water in North America. The association advances public health, safety and welfare by uniting the efforts of the full spectrum of the drinking water community.

NATIONAL RURAL ELECTRIC COOPERATIVE ASSOCIATION
4301 Wilson Boulevard, Arlington VA 22203. 703/907-5500. **E-mail address:** nreca@nreca.coop. **World Wide Web address:** http://www.nreca.org. **Description:** A national organization representing the national interests of cooperative electric utilities and the consumers they serve. Founded in 1942.

MISCELLANEOUS WHOLESALING

NATIONAL ASSOCIATION OF WHOLESALER-DISTRIBUTORS (NAW)
1725 K Street, NW, Washington DC 20006-1419. 202/872-0885. **Fax:** 202/785-0586. **World Wide Web address:** http://www.naw.org. **Description:** A trade association that represents the wholesale distribution industry active in government relations and political action; research and education; and group purchasing.

INDEX OF PRIMARY EMPLOYERS

A

ADT Security Services/70
AMC Industries/154
AT&T Business Solutions/79
Abbott Laboratories/110
Abilene Aero Inc./150
Abilene Christian University/85
J.D. Abrams International Inc./58
Abraxas Petroleum Corporation/135
Accenture/79
Advanced Micro Devices, Inc.
    (AMD)/92
Aeriform Corporation/135
AIDS Services of Austin/73
Alamo Café/125
Alamo Group, Inc./132
Alamo Iron Works, Inc./98
ALCOA (Aluminum Company of
    America)/98
Allied Security Inc./70
Amarillo College/85
Amarillo Globe-News/140
Amarillo National Bank/64
American Bank/64
American Express Financial
    Advisors/100
American Flat Glass Distributors,
    Inc. (AFGD)/148
American Physicians Service
    Group, Inc. (APS)/100
American Red Cross/73
Amfels, Inc./98
Analysts International Corporation
    (AiC)/79
Ancira Enterprises Inc./145
Angelo State University/85
Anthony Nak Fine Jewelry/146
Apple Computer, Inc./80
Aquent/80
Armbrust & Brown LLP/130
Asarco Inc./99
Austin American-Statesman/140
Austin Community College/86
Austin Diagnostic Center/110
Austin Independent School
    District/86
Austin Museum of Art/61
Austin Nature Center/61
Austin Regional Clinic/110
Austin State Hospital/111

Austin, City of/Employment
    Division/106
Avnet, Inc/80.

B

BAE Systems/92
BRSG (Black Rogers Sullivan
    Goodnight)/52
Baldwin Distribution Services/150
Bank of America/64
Baptist Medical Center/111
Baptist St. Anthony Health
    System/111
Bay, Ltd./58
Beldon Roofing Company/58
Benchmark Company/71
Bernard Johnson Young, Inc./58
Best Value Inn & Suites/125
Betty Hardwick Center/73
Big Spring State Hospital/112
Blood and Tissue Center of Central
    Texas/112
Blue Whale Moving Company/150
Bobbit, Halter & Watson/130
Boeing Company/54
Border Apparel Laundry Ltd./56
Bradfield Properties Inc./143
Bridgestone Americas Holding
    Inc./145
Bruce Foods Corporation/102

C

CFAN Company/54
Cactus Feeders Inc./102
Capital City Container Corp./139
Capital Metro/150
Caprock Manufacturing, Inc./75
Capstone Real Estate Services/143
Carbomedics, Inc./112
Cardinal Health/112
Celanese AG/75
Cerutti Productions/61
Charles Schwab/100
CHRISTUS Santa Rosa
    Hospital/113
CHRISTUS Spohn Hospital
    Shoreline/113
Cirrus Logic, Inc./81
Cisco Junior College/86
Citgo/Corpus Christi Refinery/135
Citicorp USSC/64

Citizens Medical Center/113
Citizens, Inc./128
City Machine & Welding, Inc./151
Clark, Thomas & Winters/130
Clarke American Checks, Inc./140
Clear Channel Communications/77
Coca-Cola Bottling Company of the
   Southwest/103
Coca-Cola Bottling Company/102
Coldwell Banker/143
Commemorative Brands/131
Computer Sciences Corporation
   (CSC)/81
Construction Data Corporation/141
Corpus Christi Caller-Times/140
Corpus Christi, City of/106
Corrections Products Company/132
Cox Media/52
Cyberbasin Internet Services/81
Cypress Semiconductor Texas
   Incorporated/93

D
DPT Laboratories Inc./68
Dankworth Packaging/103
Del Monte Foods/103
Dell Inc. /81
Derco Aerospace/54
Doubletree Guest Suites Hotel/125
E.I. DuPont de Nemours &
   Company/75

E
ETS Lindgren/93
Eckert, Ingrum, Tinkler, Oliphant, &
   Featherston, L.L.P./51
Edinburg Regional Medical
   Center/114
El Paso Association for the
   Performing Arts/61
El Paso Electric Company/152
El Paso Natural Gas Company/152
El Paso Times Inc./141
El Paso Water Utilities/152
El Paso, City of/106
Embassy Suites Hotel/125
Emerson Process Management/93
Energy Transfer/136
Engine Components Inc./54
Epsiia Corporation/82
Ethicon, Inc./114

J.C. Evans Construction Co./59
Exploration Company/136

F
FIC Insurance Group/128
Family Christian Stores/145
Farm Credit Bank of Texas/64
Farmers Insurance Group/128
Farsight Computer/82
Ferguson Enterprises, Inc./145
Finsa Industrial Parks/59
First American Flood Data
   Services/71
First National Bank of Abilene/65
Flint Hills Resources LP/76
Food Basket IGA/145
Fordyce Company/148
Frontier Enterprises/125
Frost National Bank/
   Cullen/Frost Bankers, Inc./65

G
GSD&M Advertising/52
Galactic Technologies, Inc./82
Gandy's Dairies Inc./104
Golfsmith International Inc./131
Goodrich Aerospace Aerostructures
   Group/54
W.W. Grainger/154
Great Western Directories/141
Greater Tuna Corporation/61
C.H. Guenther & Son, Inc./104
Gulf Marine Fabricators/136

H
HEB Grocery Company/146
Harbor View Care Center/114
Harcourt Assessment, Inc./86
Hardin-Simmons University/87
Harmony Family Services/73
Harrington Cancer Center/114
Harris Corporation/93
Hart & Cooley/132
Harte-Hanks, Inc./52
Helen of Troy Ltd./131
Hendrick Health System/114
Hill County Memorial Hospital/115
Holland Photo Imaging/141
Holly Sugar Corporation/104
Hoover's, Inc./71
Hyatt Regency Hill Country Resort/126

I

IBM Corporation/82
IKON Office Solutions/154
Industrial Molding Corporation/76
Initial Security/71
Institutional Sales Associates/104
International Bank of Commerce/65
International Biomedical, Inc./115
International SEMATECH/93

J

Jobe Concrete Products Inc./149

K

KCI (Kinectic Concepts, Inc.)/115
KFDA-TV/News Channel 10/77
KLBK-TV/77
KVII-TV/77
Kasper Wire Works Inc./132
Kerrville State Hospital/115
Kewaunee Scientific
  Corporation/132
Kimberly-Clark Tecnol Inc./115
Kohler Company/131
Kuper Realty Corporation/143

L

La Quinta Inns, Inc./126
LDB Corporation/126
Labatt Food Service/126
Laboratory Corporation of America
  (LabCorp)/68
Lady Bird Johnson Wildflower
  Center/62
Lancer Corporation/133
Laredo Community College/87
Laredo National Bank/65
Lauren Engineers &
  Constructors/59
Lead Dogs/52
Lepco/94
Liant Software Corporation/83
Linco-Electromatics, Inc./133
Loomis, Fargo & Company/71
Lower Colorado River Authority
Lubbock Avalanche-Journal/141
Lubbock Christian University/87
Luby's Cafeterias/126
Lucchese Boot Company/56
Luminex Corporation/116
Lyda Company/59

M

MKS Instruments/94
M7 Aerospace/55
Mann & Mann Media Services,
  Inc./72
Martin Luther Homes of Texas
  Inc./73
Martin Marietta Materials/149
McAllen Medical Center/116
McKenna Memorial Hospital/116
McMurry University/87
McNeil Consumer and Specialty
  Pharmaceuticals/68
Medical Center
  Hospital/Odessa/116
Mensor Corporation/133
Merrill Lynch/101
Mesa Hills Specialty Hospital/116
Mesquite Software, Inc./83
Methodist Specialty and Transplant
  Hospital/117
Metropolitan Methodist Hospital/117
Metrowerks Inc./83
Midland Memorial Hospital/117
Mission Hospital, Inc./117
Mur-Tex Fiberglass/149

N

National Alliance for Insurance
  Education & Research/88
National Electric Coil/94
National Instrument Corporation/94
NetQoS/83
New Systems/55
Newtek Inc./83
Nix Health Care System/117
Noble Construction Equipment,
  Inc./133
Northeast Baptist MRI Center/118
Northwest Texas Healthcare
  System/118
Norwood Promotional Products,
  Inc./142

O

O&M Sales, Inc./94
Oaks Treatment Center/74
Odessa Regional Hospital/118
Office Depot, Inc./146
Office of the Secretary of the State
  of Texas/107

O'Hair Shutters/59

P
PPD Development/68
Pabst Brewing Company/104
Pak-Mor Ltd./63
Panhandle Community Services/74
Parkview Metal Products Inc./99
Passage Supply Company/154
Patterson-UTI Energy, Inc./136
Paychex, Inc./51
Sid Peterson Memorial Hospital/118
Pervasive Software Inc./83
PharMerica/69
Plunkett & Gibson, Inc./130
Pool Company/136
Price's Creameries/104
Prime Medical Services, Inc./118
Principal Financial Group/128
Progressive County Mutual
   Insurance Company/129

Q
QVC/77
Quantum Research International/72

R
RailAmerica, Inc/151
Raymond James & Associates/101
Reynolds International Inc./133
Rio Vista Rehabilitation
   Hospital/119
Rock-Tenn Company/139
Round Rock Medical Center/119

S
SBC Communications Inc./
   Southwestern Bell/78
Safety Steel Service Inc./99
Samsung Austin Semiconductor/94
San Antonio Aerospace LP/55
San Antonio Express News/142
San Antonio Independent School
   District/88
San Antonio, City of/107
San Marcos Treatment Center/119
Savane International
   Corporation/56
Sea World of Texas/62
Securitas/72
Seed Resource, Inc./105

SEMCO Dot Metal Products/99
SETON Healthcare Network/120
Severn Trent Laboratories, Inc./96
Shannon Clinic/120
Shannon Medical Center/120
Siemens Intelligent Transportation
   Systems/95
Sierra Providence Health
   Network/120
Silicon Hills Design, Inc./95
Six Flags Fiesta Texas/62
South Austin Hospital/121
South Plains College/89
Southern Clay Products Inc./136
Southern Union Company/152
Southwest Collegiate Institute for
   the Deaf/89
Southwest General Hospital/121
Southwest Research Institute/69
Southwest Royalties, Inc./137
Southwest Texas Methodist
   Hospital/Methodist Women's &
   Children's Hospital/121
Specialty Hospital of San
   Antonio/121
St. David's Medical Center/119
St. Edward's University/88
St. Mary's University/88
Starlite Recovery Center/122
Sterling Foods Inc./105
Stitches Inc./56
Straus-Frank Company/Car
   Quest/146
Super S Foods/147

T
Taco Cabana, Inc./127
Tanknology-NDE International,
   Inc./96
Techworks, Inc./84
Temple-Inland, Inc./139
Tesoro Petroleum Corporation/137
Tex Tan Western Leather
   Company/56
Texace Corporation/57
Texas Center for Infectious
   Disease/122
Texas Department of Criminal
   Defense/107
Texas Department of Health/108

Texas Department of Human
Services/108
Texas Department of Mental Health
and Retardation/108
Texas Department of Public
Safety/108
Texas Department of
Transporation/109
Texas Higher Education
Coordinating Board/109
Texas Monthly/142
Texas Parks & Wildlife/109
Texas State Auditor's Office/109
Texas State University/San
Marcos/89
Texas Tech University/90
Texas Veterinary Medical
Diagnostic Laboratory/69
Thermon Manufacturing
Company/133
3M/134
TL Marketing Inc./53
Tony Lama Company/56
Toro Irrigation/76
Trans Healthcare, Inc./122
TransWestern Publishing/142
Trico Technologies/63
Trilogy Development Group/84
Trinity University/90
Tyson Fresh Meats/105

U
U.S. Department of Veterans
Affairs/Amarillo VA Health Care
System/123
U.S. Department of Veterans
Affairs/El Paso VA Health Care
System/123
U.S. Department of Veterans
Affairs/South Texas Veterans
Health Care System/123
U.S. Department of Veterans
Affairs/West Texas Veterans
Health Care System/123
UMC Health System/122
United Supermarkets/147

University of Texas at Austin/90
University of Texas at
Brownsville/90
University of Texas at El Paso/91
University of the Incarnate Word/91
URS Corporation/96
USAA Real Estate Company/144
UTI Drilling, LP/137

V
VTEL Corporation/78
Valero Energy Corporation/137
Valero Energy Corporation/Credit
Card Center/101
Valley Baptist Medical Center/123
Valley Regional Medical Center/124
Verizon Communications/78
Via Metropolitan Transit/151
Vignette Corporation/84
Vulcan Materials/149

W
Waid and Associates/97
Walls Industries, Inc./57
Webb, Stokes & Sparks, L.L.P./130
Wells Fargo Bank/66
West Teleservices/72
Western Playland Inc./62
Whataburger, Inc./127
Whole Foods Market Inc./147
Wildwood Management Group/144
Williamson-Dickie Manufacturing
Company/57
World Financial Group/101
Wukasch Company/101

X
Xcel Energy/153
Xerox Corporation/134
Xerox Omnifax/78

Z
H.B. Zachry Company/59
Zilker Botanical Garden/62
Zimmer, Inc./124